THE LITERATURE OF
CONTEMPORARY SIERRA LEONE

THE LITERATURE OF CONTEMPORARY SIERRA LEONE

TRAUMA, RESILIENCE, AND CREATIVITY

Edited by
Ernest Cole and Mohamed Kamara

JAMES CURREY

© Contributors 2025

All Rights Reserved. Except as permitted under current legislation no part of this work may be photocopied, stored in a retrieval system, published, performed in public, adapted, broadcast, transmitted, recorded or reproduced in any form or by any means, without the prior permission of the copyright owner

First published 2025
James Currey

ISBN 978 1 84701 417 7

James Currey is an imprint of Boydell & Brewer Ltd
PO Box 9, Woodbridge, Suffolk IP12 3DF (GB)
www.jamescurrey.com
and of Boydell & Brewer Inc.
668 Mt Hope Avenue, Rochester, NY 14620–2731 (US)
www.boydellandbrewer.com

A CIP catalogue record for this book is available from the British Library

The publisher has no responsibility for the continued existence or accuracy of URLs for external or third-party internet websites referred to in this book, and does not guarantee that any content on such websites is, or will remain, accurate or appropriate

CONTENTS

Notes on Contributors   vii

Acknowledgements   xi

Introduction
ERNEST COLE AND MOHAMED KAMARA   1

SECTION I: THE CREATIVE IMAGINATION: LANGUAGE, HISTORY, AND CULTURE

1. Unacknowledged Creative Loops: Orature, Literature and Society in Sierra Leone's Contemporary History
MOHAMED GIBRIL SESAY   15

2. The Past Flows: Water as a Metaphor for Nostalgia in Ahmed Koroma's *The Moon Rises Over Isale Eko*
OUMAR FAROUK SESAY   32

3. English Language Learning and Intelligibility: Idiomaticity, Sierra Leonean English and Sierra Leonean Fiction
MOMODU TURAY   50

4. The Female Condition in the Novels of Aminatta Forna
SAIDU BANGURA   59

SECTION II: LEGACIES OF WAR AND PANDEMIC: LITERATURE AS WITNESS TO VIOLENCE, TRAUMA, AND RESILIENCE

5. Syl Cheney-Coker's *Stone Child and Other Poems:* A Graphic Exploration of War Trauma
EUSTACE PALMER   77

6. Space, Trauma, and Healing in Delia Jarrett-Macauley's *Moses, Citizen and Me*
OUMAR CHÉRIF DIOP   91

7. Learning How to Smile Again: Ebola, Resilience, and Sierra Leonean Fiction
   JOYA URAIZEE   101

8. War and Social Degradation in Oumar Farouk Sesay's *Landscape of Memories*
   ELIZABETH L.A. KAMARA   120

SECTION III: VISIONS OF THE FUTURE: NEW GENRES, AESTHETICS, AND EPISTEMOLOGIES

9. "A Window to Society": The Human Condition in the Context of Interspecies Relations in J.M. Coetzee's *Disgrace* and Aminatta Forna's *The Window Seat*
   ERNEST COLE   133

10. Namina Forna's *The Gilded Ones:* An Afrocentric Vision of the Beloved Community
    MOHAMED KAMARA   153

11. Smartphone Literature in Today's Sierra Leone: Assessing Claims of Continuity with Traditional Fireside Folktales
    STEPHEN NEY   172

12. The Intersection of Life and History in Eldred Jones' *The Freetown Bond: A Life under Two Flags*
    SAMUEL KAMARA   185

13. Relatability, Spaces, Symbols and Legends: Fiction as a Mirror Image for Social Transformation in Abdulai Walon-Jalloh's "Dharmendra Died"
    GIBRILLA KARGBO   196

Index   203

NOTES ON CONTRIBUTORS

Saidu Bangura holds a PhD in Translation, Communication and Culture with a specialty in Sociolinguistics from the University of Las Palmas, Spain. He is an Assistant Professor of English, University of Cape Verde, where he has directed the MA in English Studies, a program he helped build. He is presently the Vice President/Vice Dean of the Faculty of Social Sciences, Humanities and Arts, University of Cape Verde. He has co-authored book chapters and articles around the Cape Verdean and Sierra Leonean linguistic situations, and African Regional Integration. He has authored chapters on African and Sierra Leonean literature. He has published several poems in poetry anthologies, books, and newspapers. He has won academic awards in Portugal, University of Coimbra (2011); Brazil, State University of Campinas (2014), and Spain, University of Las Palmas (2015).

Ernest Cole, PhD, is the John Dirk Werkman Endowed Professor of English at Hope College, Michigan, where he teaches Postcolonial literatures of Sub-Saharan Anglophone Africa, India, and the Caribbean. He has published two monographs, *Theorizing the Disfigured Body* (2014) and *Space and Trauma in the Writing of Aminatta Forna* (2017); and three collected volumes, *Emerging Perspectives on Syl Cheney-Coker* (2014, with Eustace Palmer), and *Ousmane Sembene, Writer, Filmmaker, & Revolutionary Artist* (2016, with Oumar Chérif Diop), and *Critical Masters on Eustace Palmer* (2021). His current monograph is tentatively titled *Black Bodies in White Spaces: The Politics of Migration, the African Diaspora, and Return*.

Oumar Chérif Diop, PhD, is Professor at the English department at Kennesaw State University in Georgia, USA. His research deals with violence, trauma, and silence in postcolonial literature. His recent publications include "Lost & Found Memories: Letters to Dr. P. from his Senegalese Students" (2021); "Voices from the Margins: Female Protagonists Navigating Power-geometries" (2020); "Happiness, The Wound and the Word: Aminatta Forna Joins the Conversation on Trauma" (2019); and, a monograph, *Violence and Trauma in Selected African literature* (2018).

Elizabeth L.A. Kamara is a lecturer of Literature in English in the Department of Language Studies at Fourah Bay College, University of Sierra Leone, where she was Head of the English Unit. She has published three anthologies of poetry and is currently working on her fourth. *Stolen Laughter* (2022) is her most recent publication. The West African Examinations Council adopted her poem "New Tongue" for inclusion in the West African Senior Secondary Certificate Exam (WASSCE) for the years 2026–2030.

Mohamed Kamara, PhD, is Professor of French and Africana Studies and Chair of the Romance Languages department at Washington and Lee University. Mohamed's teaching and research interests include French and Francophone literatures and cultures. He is the author of *When Mosquitoes Come Marching In: A Play in Spectacles* (2021, on the Sierra Leone Civil War of 1991–2002) and *Colonial Legacies in Francophone African Literature: The School and the Invention of the Bourgeoisie* (Rowman & Littlefield, 2023). Mohamed has also published short stories as well as articles on human rights, the African child soldier, and other areas of African and Francophone literatures. He is a co-editor of *Children and Violence: Agency, Experience and Representation in and Beyond Armed Conflict*, a volume under contract with Routledge. From 2020 to 2023, Mohamed served as vice president, president, and past president of the African Literature Association, after previously serving as treasurer and executive council member of the same.

Samuel Kamara, PhD, is Associate Graduate Faculty at Minnesota State University, Mankato. He is a native of Sierra Leone, where he has taught English and literature as well as in The Gambia, Jamaica, and the United States of America. He is a recipient of numerous awards, has published articles in several peer-reviewed journals, and has book chapters in many collections. His research interests are in postcolonial feminism, violence in African and Caribbean literature, African life writing, and diaspora literature. He is currently working on a monograph about breaking the cycle of violence in Caribbean female novels.

Rev. Gibrilla Kargbo holds two Master of Arts degrees in the Teaching of English to Speakers of Other Languages (TESOL) and Educational Administration from Teachers College Columbia University (TCCU), New York, and the Institute of Public Administration and Management (IPAM), University of Sierra Leone, Freetown, Sierra Leone, respectively. He is a clergyman, a lecturer, and a public servant. He teaches Foundation English at Fourah Bay College (FBC), University of Sierra Leone (USL) as a remedial measure to address the challenges faced by university students in the Use of English for Special Purposes.

Stephen Ney, PhD, lives in Freetown and lectures in the graduate program at the University of Makeni. He also works for the IFES Logos and Cosmos Initiative, which allows him to train scholars across Africa in science and theology dialogue. A graduate of UBC Vancouver, his research interests are in postcolonial and West African literatures. He has published research articles on African poets and novelists from the contemporary and colonial periods.

Eustace Palmer, PhD, a native Sierra Leonean, is Distinguished Professor Emeritus of English and Africana Studies at Georgia College & State University. He taught for several years at the University of Sierra Leone, where he was Professor and Chair of English, Dean of the Faculty (School) of Arts, and Dean of Graduate Studies. One of the pioneer critics of African literature, he has published five books on the subject, one on the English novel, a general textbook on Africa (*Africa: An Introduction*), over seventy articles on English and African literatures, four novels, and a memoir, *My Epic Journey: The Making of a Cosmopolitan*. He was for several years Associate Editor of *African Literature Today* (James Currey) and President of the African Literature Association.

Mohamed Gibril Sesay grew up in Crojimmy, Eastern Freetown. He was educated at Fourah Bay College, University of Sierra Leone, where he now teaches Sociology. His recent creative writings include *Falang and Other Short Stories* (ed., 2023), and *Destiny Drive and Other Stories* (2021). Sesay has also published several non-fiction works, including *Excess Sociology: An African Journeying* (2022). He has also authored several book chapters; worked with civil society organizations, as a newspaper columnist, a senior public official, and a consultant for several national and international organizations.

Oumar Farouk Sesay is a poet, playwright, and novelist. He has been published in many anthologies; *Lice in the Lion's Mane*, *Songs that Pour the Heart*, *Kalashnikov in the Sun*, and *Afrika Im Gedicht*. His first volume of poems, *Salute to the Remains of a Peasant*, was published in 2007 in the USA, followed by five more collections of poetry; *The Edge of a Cry*, *Broken Metaphor*, *Before the Twisted Rib*, *400 Years of Servitude*, and *There was Eden*. Farouk's Novel, *Landscape of Memories*, was first published in 2015 and republished in 2018 by Sierra Leonean Writers Series.

Momodu Turay, PhD, is a Congressian and a Wellingtonian who has taught English in various tertiary institutions in Sierra Leone, including Fourah Bay College where he teaches in the Language Studies Department. He served as Chief Examiner for the National Council for Technical, National and Academic Awards between 2004 and 2015. His research interests center on the nativization of the English Language in non-native contexts and what the teacher of English should teach and how it should be taught.

Joya Uraizee, PhD, is Professor of English at Saint Louis University in St. Louis, Missouri, where she teaches postcolonial literature and film. She is the author of *This is No Place for a Woman: Nadine Gordimer, Nayantara Sahgal, Buchi Emecheta and the Politics of Gender* (2000), *In the Jaws of the Leviathan: Genocide Fiction and Film* (2010), and *Writing That Breaks Stones: African Child Soldier Narratives* (2020). She is working on a monograph analyzing African child refugee narratives. She has published articles on same sex desire in East African cinema, migrant African children, and religious fanaticism in Bollywood movies, among others.

ACKNOWLEDGEMENTS

As editors, we thank all contributors to the present volume for their commitment to this communal effort in the name of Sierra Leone. We also thank those who, though not contributors to this volume, have helped make Sierra Leone literature visible, from its inception in the colonial period to now, through their writings, research, teaching, and conference presentations. We thank the African Literature Association for offering us a platform over the last several years to have at least one panel dedicated to Sierra Leonean literature at its annual conference.

We would like to thank Henri Oripeloye and Gilbert Ndi Shang for their thorough review of the manuscript. Special thanks to Megan Milan, Commissioning Editor at James Currey, for her faith in and steadfast support and guidance of this project from the start.

Ernest Cole would like to register his deepest appreciation to his wife and two daughters for their invaluable support throughout the process. He also acknowledges Hope College's John Dirk Werkman Endowment Fund that facilitated research through conferences and workshops on Sierra Leonean literature.

For his part, Mohamed Kamara would like to thank his wife and children for their love and understanding as well as Washington and Lee University whose support, especially through the Summer Lenfest Grant, has helped make research for this project possible.

INTRODUCTION

In the Introduction to *A Critical Introduction to Sierra Leonean Literature* (2008), Eustace Palmer and Abioseh Porter (eds.) explore Sierra Leonean literature in the context of its historical and literary growth and development. In this volume, they present a literary landscape of Sierra Leonean writing from Gladys Casely-Hayford and Crispin George, among others, to post-independence writers like Lemuel Johnson, Yulisa Amadu Maddy, and Syl Cheney-Coker. The breadth of literature and literary productions depicted in the collection is indicative of the "literary development that led to the works of authors discussed in the [volume] and upon which they built" (Palmer and Porter 2). They concluded that the volume "attempted to make a comprehensive critical survey of Sierra Leonean Literature in order to demonstrate its importance and its value and to make it more accessible both to a Sierra Leonean and world audience, and thus place it within the mainstream of African literature" (31). Palmer and Porter also did well to present a precis of Sierra Leonean history from precolonial to colonial times. The value of this is to show how much the literary texts and traditions as well as the issues they engage emerge organically from the country's history of trauma and resilience.

The publication of that seminal volume created the awareness in several literary circles that Sierra Leonean fiction was to be contended with. Since its publication, a lot of new works, by both known and budding writers, have appeared on the scene and have been making meaningful contributions to what is clearly emerging as a bona fide national literature. These include novels such as Nabie Yayah Swarray's *The Rape of Fatimah* (2008); Eustace Palmer's *Canfira's Travels* (2010), *A Hanging is Announced* (2011), and *A Tale of Three Women* (2011); Pede Hollist's *So the Path Does Not Die* (2012); Aminatta Forna's *The Memory of Love* (2011); Eldred Durosimi Jones' life narrative *The Freetown Bond* (2012); J. Sorie Conteh's *Journey to Dreamland* (2012); Yema Lucilda Hunter's *Joy Came in the Morning* (2013); Ishmael Beah's *The Radiance of Tomorrow* (2014); Gloria Allen's *Smoke in the Kitchen: A Novel About Second Chances* (2014); Yema Lucilda Hunter's *Seeking Freedom* (2016); Aminatta Forna's *Happiness* (2018); and Hassan Baraka's *Pains of a Mother* (2020). More recently, at this start of the third decade of the twenty-first century, new works have been published, including Aminatta Forna's *The Window Seat* (2021); M'Bha Kamara's play *When Mosquitoes Come*

Marching In (2021); Namina Forna's fantastic young-adult novels *The Gilded Ones* (2021), *The Merciless Ones* (2022), and *The Eternal Ones* (2024); and Eustace Palmer's memoir, *My Epic Journey: The Making of a Cosmopolitan* (2023). These texts complete the picture of a vibrant literary landscape of Sierra Leonean writing, suggesting in the process that Sierra Leonean literature has come of age.

As a complement to the 2008 *A Critical Introduction to Sierra Leonean Literature,* the current collection, *The Literature of Contemporary Sierra Leone: Trauma, Resilience, and Creativity*, interrogates a number of prominent themes and critical perspectives on contemporary Sierra Leonean literature while acknowledging the country's literary and creative heritage that it seeks to keep alive and relevant. How much has Sierra Leonean writing changed in the decade and a half since the publication of the aforementioned seminal volume? How do those changes illustrate the diversity of genres and themes in Sierra Leonean creative output today? In what ways do the new intellectual traditions reflect the changes that have taken place in the country since 2008? To what extent does contemporary Sierra Leonean writing serve as a barometer for future directions in the growth and development of Sierra Leonean literature both in terms of form and content? The present project brings together established and emerging scholars deploying the latest theoretical and empirical research methods in critical and innovative ways to explore these and other questions germane to the historical trajectory and contemporary Sierra Leonean zeitgeist. Drawing from body studies, postcolonial theory, spatial theory, trauma theory, eco-criticism, history, and cultural studies, contributors tease out the beginnings, ecology, and dynamism of an identifiable national literature. They do this through a careful examination of themes such as: social oppression and class distinction, dystopia, ethnocentricity, homophobia, misogyny and gender disparities, anthropocentrism, self-discovery, social transformation, identity, social degradation, genocide, and trauma, while also theorizing constructs such as home, community, migration, displacement, and return. *The Literature of Contemporary Sierra Leone: Trauma, Resilience, and Creativity* contains thirteen submissions by writers both native to and affiliated with Sierra Leonean history, culture, and literature.

The contributions cover writing in several genres: from Eustace Palmer's exploration of Syl Cheney-Coker's latest anthology; Oumar Farouk Sesay's exegesis of Ahmed Koroma's third poetry collection; Samuel Kamara's review of Eldred Jones' autobiography; Mohamed Gibril Sesay's foray into orature, history, and the creative impulse in Sierra Leonean literature; and Stephen Ney's examination of the connections and continuities between literature and digital technology; to Momodu Turay's critique of idiomaticity and its significance in literary expressions in Sierra Leonean literature; and a socio-critique by Gibrilla Kargbo of Walon-Jalloh's short story.

Section I of the collection is titled "The Creative Imagination: Language, History, and Culture," and it features the contributions of Mohamed Gibril Sesay, Oumar Farouk Sesay, Momodu Turay, and Saidu Bangura.

Mohamed Gibril Sesay's "Unacknowledged Creative Loops: Orature, Literature and Society in Sierra Leone's Contemporary History" is a capacious acknowledgement of what he characterizes as "the loops of understandings" of creative output – from the novel to the short story, poetry, and drama – by Sierra Leoneans. His ambitious project of dis-alienating the country's "organic imaginary" is essentially a history of creativity and performance in Sierra Leone. He also pays homage to the creative artists and others working to make more visible, and perhaps more memorable, the creative heritage of the country. In his effort to make the connections and distinctions among the creative sound, the spoken word, the written word, and the read word, Mohamed Gibril Sesay's perspective of cultural and historical hybridities, or at least the potentials for their emergence, offers a new breath to the complexity of creativity and performance in and beyond Sierra Leone over the *longue durée*.

Sesay's piece is remarkable for its scope of historical analysis, depth of literary criticism, and cogency of literary and creative expressions. As he contends, "Sierra Leonean creativity, its performativity, orature or literature may be more entrained to this intentional '*cut ya put ya*' about happenings, or imaginations about happenings, in the territories that come to be known as Sierra Leone." Clearly, then, as he notes,

> Sierra Leonean literature, orature, and other performance arts and acts may thus be seen as imaginative transcriptions and communications of how these migrations and encounters got concentrated in the places that come to form part of Sierra Leone; and of dispersions from these territories of our fallopian migrations, uterine experiences and birth-lands to other places.

Sesay sets out to unveil the distinctions between

> the written word of the imaginative type [and] the read word as but the visible tip of some underlying creative narrative rhizomes [noting that] these distinctions are useful – those between the creative sound, the spoken word, the written word and the read-word. Else the story of Sierra Leone and its literature may miss out on some of their rhizomes and underpinnings, the musical sounds, the oral narrative forms, folklore, proverbs, and dramatic renditions.

He concludes by stating that "these underpinnings are largely communal, sometimes instant and oftentimes performative means of getting all to imbibe the wisdom and norms of the land through storytelling and songs."

Oumar Farouk Sesay's "The Past Flows: Water as a Metaphor for Nostalgia in Ahmed Koroma's *The Moon Rises Over Isale Eko*" is a critical commentary on the thematic preoccupation of Ahmed Koroma in his third collection of poems. Sesay notes that *The Moon Rises Over Isale Eko* "delves into the soul of a small yet culturally significant community in Freetown, Sierra Leone. This enclave, Isale Eko, is adjacent to the Fullah Tong and Fourah Bay neighborhoods," localities that emerged out of a blend of Islamic and traditional African cultures like Ojeh and hunting fraternities. He points out that "Isale Eko" is a Yoruba expression meaning "down under", a toponym influenced by the land's topography. The term refers to Lagos Island, and the appropriation of the name Isale Eko in nineteenth-century Sierra Leone is consistent with "the settlers' practice of adopting names from their places of origin."

He analyzes Ahmed Koroma's use of the predominant imagery of water in his poetry to treat various themes of spirituality, nostalgia, history, and rituals within his community at Isale Eko in the Eastend of Freetown. Through his discussion of setting and such linguistic and rhetorical devices as irony, imagery, and symbolism in Koroma's poems, Sesay makes and demonstrates the claim that the poet's mission is to capture and preserve the essence of his community's cultural integrity amid threats to it from both within and without. On the theme of nostalgia as it relates to other themes in the collection, he states: "Ahmed Koroma's unique choice of water as a thematic metaphor in his collection to express nostalgia, spirituality, and decadence is a testament to the depth and complexity of his work and the power of poetry to heal even those in exile seeking refugee from the carnage in their country" Ultimately, Sesay argues that the merit of Koroma's collection lies not only in the sociocultural landscape it evokes, but also in the poet's ability to sieve through the sights and sounds of his community to capture the essence of his people and the spaces and times they live in.

Momodu Turay's chapter, "English Language Learning and Intelligibility: Idiomaticity, Sierra Leonean English and Sierra Leonean Fiction" foregrounds the role of language in the conceptualization and articulation of thematic constructs of contemporary Sierra Leonean writers. While acknowledging that Sierra Leonean writers have given little attention to local idioms in creative and literary productions, Turay investigates idioms from selected Sierra Leonean texts that highlight their contributions in shaping themes and critical perspectives on contemporary and emerging fiction.

Examining such texts as Hollist's *So the Path Does Not Die* (2012) and Koso-Thomas's *The Dream* (2018), Turay emphasizes that idioms are critical to the creative process and imagination of writers and argues that their focalization in these writings demonstrate the relationship between the evolving Sierra Leonean variety and the corresponding emerging national literature. Leaning on examples of local Sierra Leonean idioms, Turay critiques Loreto Todd's definition of idioms and her conception of their function in literature, arguing that the present trend of communication on both national and global levels allows for the use of new Englishes that Todd did not take into consideration in her work.

Saidu Bangura's "The Female Condition in the Novels of Aminatta Forna" focuses on the works of one of the most prominent and influential writers from Sierra Leone – Aminatta Forna. Using the "female condition" as aesthetics of exploration, Bangura focuses on two of Forna's novels — *Ancestor Stones* and *The Memory of Love* – to articulate the "nuance and ... intricacies of life" in Sierra Leonean society both during and after the Civil War. On this note, he engages themes like patriarchy, subalternity, violence, trauma, and healing. Additionally, in his reading of the lives of the female characters in Aminatta Forna's works, Bangura explores "Aminatta Forna's motivation as a writer based on how female writers are considered."

Finally, Bangura argues that interest in these two novels should transcend "the politics of literature [and] the literature of politics," even though both are important for an understanding of Forna's project. We should focus instead on Forna's representation of the female condition in her novels and situate this representation within the larger question of the visibility or invisibility of women in African literature from precolonial to contemporary times.

Section II of the collection, titled "Legacies of War and Pandemic: Literature as Witness to Violence, Trauma, and Resilience," showcases the contributions of Eustace Palmer, Oumar Chérif Diop, Joya Uraizee, and Elizabeth L.A. Kamara.

Eustace Palmer's exegesis of Syl Cheney-Coker's anthology *Stone Child and Other Poems* (2008) adds another layer of flavor, critical excellence and sophistication to the volume. Palmer analyzes the poet's engagement not only with the emotional, physical, or psychological suffering of the people of Sierra Leone during the country's Civil War of 1991–2002, but more importantly with the instigators of the war. In Palmer's analysis, historicity and literary criticism intersect to offer a context for interpreting the origins of the Civil War and the pain of a deeply traumatized nation. Exploring the relationships between political insurgency, military dictatorship, and diamonds, Palmer uses the symbol of the stone in its varied connotations of meaning to articulate a discourse of war-induced trauma specific to Sierra Leonean society.

Palmer's perspective of the war and the role of diamonds in the mayhem are crucial to understanding both the trauma and the resilience of survivors of the Civil War. Diamonds have become a force, like the attractive woman or the Madonna figure, that compels men to worship and adore her. In his analysis of the poem "Our Lady of Diamonds," for example, Palmer wonders how something "so beautiful and even desirable, could also be the cause of so much bestiality and suffering." In his careful analysis of Cheney-Coker's poems, Palmer points out that diamonds (a symbol of the resource curse as represented in such phrases as 'blood diamonds') is a malevolent force that attracts and then destroys its idolaters as well as innocent bystanders.

In "Space, Trauma, and Healing in Delia Jarrett-Macauley's *Moses, Citizen and Me*," Oumar Chérif Diop directs his focus on post-traumatic healing. He starts by underscoring the importance of public spaces like the Truth and Reconciliation Commission (TRC) which allow victims and perpetrators of violence to redirect their eyes toward themselves and to reconstitute themselves from where they are. However, he argues that because public truth-telling lacks deep roots in the local cultures of Sierra Leone, outlets like the TRC failed to adequately address and assuage the trauma of war in post-civil war Sierra Leone. Using Michel Foucault's analysis of the mirror in his article "Other Spaces" and Henri Lefebvre's concept of "spatial practice", Diop shows how Delia Jarrett-Macauley's *Moses, Citizen and Me* suggests alternative spaces where various activities emerge that allow the return of the gaze and subsequent healing. He notes, for example, that in many instances in Jarrett-Macauley's novel, "the virtual space behind the mirror ... helps child soldiers turn their gaze to themselves and reconfigure themselves."

Diop argues that the novel underscores the importance of designing post-war approaches to trauma that help community members re-member, re-organize, and re-assemble by taking due account of the social networks, power relations, and conflicts pertaining to each situation. Diop's analysis of trauma and healing, through his examination of spatial theory, demonstrates his understanding of the transformative potential and capacity for redemption in humans regardless of the past, if they are accorded the space and time for reflection, dialog, and community building.

In "Learning How to Smile Again: Ebola, Resilience, and Sierra Leonean Fiction," Joya Uraizee reflects on the representation of the trauma of Ebola on survivors in selected writings from Sierra Leone while, like Diop, focusing on healing. Utilizing the construct of resilience as a frame to read both the trauma of the disease and the resilience of survivors, she locates her exploration within psychological and historical contexts, while drawing from the trauma theorizations in the works of Ernest Cole, Stef Craps, and Boris Cyrulnik to advance her claim of resilience. Using the experience of an Ebola survivor as a launch point for her analysis, Uraizee writes about the resilience, humanity, and capacity of Sierra Leoneans in the face of multifarious adversity as portrayed in fiction written both before and after the epidemic: Véronique Tadjo's *En compagnie des hommes* (*In the Company of Men*, 2017), M'Bha Kamara's "Pregnancy in the Time of Ebola" (2018), Delia Jarrett-Macauley's *Moses, Citizen and Me* (2005), and Aminatta Forna's *The Memory of Love* (2010). Based on the experience of a survivor, Yusuf Kabba, Uraizee outlines "the obstacles that survivors like Kabba had to overcome in order to achieve resilience, namely, lack of knowledge about the virus, poor quarantine facilities, and the fragmentation of social support structures." In addition, she writes: "From the early years of the twenty-first century, Sierra Leonean writers have depicted unique, transformative forms of resilience against various forms of trauma ... Their transformative resilience, like that of Yusuf Kabba, is communal, embodied, and spiritual; thereby including the healing of minds and bodies on individual and social levels."

Uraizee concludes her chapter by noting that the transformative resilience of Sierra Leoneans in real life or in fiction is communal, embodied, and spiritual and also provides readers with insights about healing in general, while revealing the power of Sierra Leonean fiction to transform global theories about trauma.

Elizabeth L.A. Kamara's "War and Social Degradation in Oumar Farouk Sesay's *Landscape of Memories*" sheds light on the expectations of migrants; the dichotomy between their expectations and achievements; and the relationship between war and social degradation. Kamara explains that, in delineating the plot, Sesay focuses on the country's eleven-year Civil War, migration, social degradation, and the question of evil; and that the novel is written as both a reminder about the past and a tribute to the resilience of the human spirit. She postulates that it is a fitting example of the definition of the novel as a melting pot of ideas, cultures, and genres of literature.

In exploring migration as one of the dominant themes in the novel, Kamara traces the religious roots of migration and its manifestation in both the Bible and Quran. Drawing from migration theories postulated by Christian Dustmann and Yoram Weiss (2007), Kamara situates *Landscape of Memories* within this phenomenon of movement of the internally displaced. Through her discussion of the lives of characters in the novel, she highlights the significance of human choices and concludes that Sesay's novel "tells the unborn generation about the harrowing Sierra Leonean civil war, and all that is lost and found before, during, and after it."

Section III, titled "Visions of the Future: New Genres, Aesthetics, and Epistemologies," features the contributions of Ernest Cole, Mohamed Kamara, Stephen Ney, Samuel Kamara, and Gibrilla Kargbo.

Ernest Cole's "A Window to Society": The Human Condition in the Context of Interspecies Relations in J.M. Coetzee's *Disgrace* and Aminatta Forna's *The Window Seat*" makes the claim that *The Window Seat* offers a template for reading human behavior and society's aspirations and failings. Using J.M. Coetzee's *Disgrace* as a framework to analyze the three essays in which these animals are depicted – "The Last Vet," "Bruno," and "Wilder Things," Cole argues that the complexities of human-animal relations are largely informed by anthropocentrism and man's desire for control over nonhuman animals. The paper presents a historical and cultural context for understanding this relationship, and to offer a critical lens to read the three essays selected for study, beginning with a broad analysis of selected scenes in Coetzee's *Disgrace* that are both reflective of the treatment of animals in Sierra Leone and indicative of reciprocal acceptance in interspecies relationships.

Ernest Cole emphasizes that human-animal relationships must be configured on a basis of reciprocity and on an ethical consideration of the sufferings of animals, preservation of their lives, and humane treatment of them. In so doing, he supports Forna's assertion that humans' interactions with animals imply that the least humans can do is to ensure and preserve "an independent exchange of services" (149) between humans and animals. Cole further contends that human efforts in establishing a reciprocal relationship with animals are indicative of this manifestation of morality. He draws from theorizations on animal rights and African ethics to emphasize that ethical considerations of animals should constitute human relationship with the natural environment, and that moral relationship is established when they are capable of extending ethical rights to nonhuman animals. He concludes by making the case for the privileging of an ethical system of reciprocal relationships that can accommodate and validate animal-human coexistence on the basis of a humane and compassionate relationship.

In "Namina Forna's *The Gilded Ones*: An Afrocentric Vision of the Beloved Community," Mohamed Kamara notes that while Forna's story focuses on difference, it does so with a nod to an examination of its ambivalences and ambiguities in order to depict a broad canvas for engaging its gestures to unity, respect, solidarity, and community. It foregrounds love and a deep understanding and acceptance of individual and group differences as the basis of human existence and draws from Black feminist discourse as well as the poetics and praxis of the human as proposed by Martin Luther King, Jr., Léopold Sédar Senghor, and Sylvia Wynter to illustrate this in Forna's debut novel.

Kamara's analysis of social constructs as gender, sexuality, and identity are innovative and illuminating. His focus on the power of women as agents of positive transformation and reconfiguration of historical values underscores a new feminist vision and futuristic endeavor that he sees as foundational to society's reconstruction. From this theorization, he proposes "to read Forna's novel as representing and promoting an Afrocentric vision of the Beloved Community," noting that the Beloved Community as visualized by Martin Luther King, Jr. (like L.S. Senghor's Civilization of the Universal) "is not a melting pot where race, cultural, and personal differences are dissolved," but the perfect socio-political community characterized by dialogue and sharing where "hegemony of one over another is shunned" in favor of love and mutual respect as well as an "acceptance of the complementarity and interdependence of all telluric forces." He argues further that, unlike standard Western superhero narratives fascinated with one person as the hero, Forna's novel "promotes a community of heroines and heroes" guided by mutual respect and love as they work toward a common goal. Kamara concludes with the assurance that "the thematic thrust of *The Gilded Ones* is grounded in the long history of Black intellectualism and activism."

In chapter 11 of the volume, "Smartphone Literature in Today's Sierra Leone: Assessing Claims of Continuity with Traditional Fireside Folktales," Stephen Ney ventures into the worlds of literature and digital technology, exploring folklore tradition in Sierra Leone as context for examining historical and literary continuities through an analysis of two collections edited by Fatou Taqi and Philip Foday Yamba Thulla, *Contemporary Fireside Poems* and *Contemporary Fireside Stories*, composed in a WhatsApp group and published by the Sierra Leonean Writers Series in 2016 and 2017 respectively. Ney's chapter launches from a basic question: In what ways are indigenous traditions of storytelling kept alive through remediating technologies like WhatsApp? Drawing on classic research on Sierra Leonean storytelling by Ruth Finnegan (1970), among others, the author proposes interactivity, malleability, multimodality, immediacy, co-creativity, and social diversity as affordances of traditional fireside storytelling that also partially apply to WhatsApp literature.

To explore his claim of continuity, Ney uses work by Patrick Muana and Abioseh Porter as a starting point to argue that "folklore traditions are (1) thriving already; yet still (2) capable of evolution; and (3) their performance and appropriations are definitely worth studying." Ney blends Muana's work on oral texts and Porter's analysis of online poetry to engage what Porter saw as "a new beginning for highlighting literary creativity." In addition, Ney states continuity "gives attention in sequence to two implications of this claim for continuity: first, that the role played by technology in the interpretation of literary texts dependent on social media is far from decisive; and second, that there is more to be gained by looking at the social situation than at the technological medium of such texts." Ney then goes on to make some suggestions about how Sierra Leonean writers might in coming years find new ways to activate traditional knowledge and forms using digital media. He concludes with a caution against technological determinism in interpreting digital literature, proposing instead multiple axes of explanation – gender, class, generational, and geographical, in addition to technological – for contemporary evocations of traditional literary forms.

Samuel Kamara's "The Intersection of Life and History in Eldred Jones' *The Freetown Bond: A Life under Two Flags*" depicts a significant aspect of the growth and development of Sierra Leonean literature – emerging writings by Sierra Leonean writers that can be classified as life narratives such as autobiographies, memoirs, autoethnographies, and testimonios. Kamara suggests that these texts signal a "reversal of this trend of the critical dearth of critical essays on life writing in Sierra Leone," and he seeks to situate the significance of Eldred Jones' *The Freetown Bond: A Life under Two Flags* (2012) within the context of Sierra Leonean life narratives.

Kamara argues that "the publication of *The Freetown Bond* ushered a generic invention of life writing in Sierra Leone that intersects life and history." He uses Jaume Aurell's conception of the life-writing act as "intellectual autobiography" to engage the thematic and stylistic constructs in Jones' text and to emphasize in tandem with life-writing scholars/historians that "in attempting to recollect the past, our personal experiences can impinge and be impinged upon by collective cultural experiences." Even though *The Freetown Bond* cannot be called a historical treatise in the disciplinary sense of the word, Kamara argues, Jones certainly participates in "the historiographic project of understanding the past by contextualizing his public/private life within the milieu of the socio-political and cultural history of Sierra Leone." In concluding, Kamara makes the point that what we have ultimately in Jones' work is an academic autobiography that resists generic categorization; for it is at once an autobiography and a memoir, and a hybrid of both. Eustace Palmer's memoir, *My Epic Journey: The Making of a Cosmopolitan* (2023) is a recent contribution to this genre of writing in Sierra Leonean literature.

Gibrilla Kargbo's chapter on Abdulai Walon-Jalloh's short story "Dharmendra Died" is another contribution that attests to the variety of genres that illustrates contemporary writing in Sierra Leone and indicates the multiple directions in the growth and development of Sierra Leonean literature. Kargbo presents an evaluative perspective of Walon-Jalloh's short story in the context of the author's background, while also examining the roles of setting and characterization in elucidating meaning. He explores plot as an intricately woven network in the lives of the characters and seeks to address the question of familiarization, both in terms of names of characters and setting, and its contribution to meaning in the story.

Kargbo's contribution is "an exegesis of the didactic import of the work and its implications for national unity, reconciliation, and social cohesion." He examines the key themes discussed and implied in the story, in tandem with the mindset and creative thinking of the writer as far as it relates to the title of the story. He brings in other aspects of style, including the writer's use of dialogue and description to invoke atmosphere. In regards to plot, he contends that "the author invites reader participation and witnessing, as he takes us to the different places and introduces his characters one after the other with remarkable precision." Importantly, Kargbo notes that "Sierra Leonean writing has come of age, and that short-story writing, like that of Walon-Jalloh's, showcases the literary potential of the Sierra Leonean writer."

In his already referenced chapter in this volume, Mohamed Gibril Sesay laments that "Sierra Leone has not done very well acknowledging its rich oral traditions and wisdom in its printed forms, and it has also not done well in passing on its printed wisdom unto newer generations." It is the expectation of the editors of and contributors to the present volume, which acknowledges and builds on that seminal critical volume by Abioseh Porter and Eustace Palmer, that Sierra Leonean literature will not only continue to grow and flourish, that its new and emerging writers will continue to explore the tradition of excellence, intellectual inquiry, creativity and imaginative composition established by preceding generations of writers and for which they are beginning to secure a place in the corpus of literature that can be labeled Sierra Leonean. It is our fervent hope that the contributions in this volume will initiate conversations, nationally and globally, around the topic of a national Sierra Leonean literature and the paradigms that shape the contours of such a literature as well its place in and contribution to world literature.

Ernest Cole and Mohamed Kamara

Works Cited

Coetzee, J.M, *Disgrace* (London: Penguin Books, 2000).

Cheney-Coker, Syl, *Stone Child and Other Poems* (Ibadan: HEBN Publishers, 2008).

Forna, Aminatta, *Ancestor Stones* (New York: Grove Press, 2006).

Forna, Aminatta, *The Memory of Love* (London: Bloomsbury Publishers, 2010).

Forna, Aminatta, *The Window Seat: Notes From a Life in Motion* (New York: Grove Press, 2021).

Forna, Namina, *The Gilded Ones* (New York: Delacorte Press, 2021).

Forna, Namina, *The Merciless Ones* (New York: Delacorte Press, 2022).

Jarrett-Macauley, Delia, *Moses, Citizen and Me* (London: Granta Books, 2012).

Jones, Eldred, *The Freetown Bond: A Life Under Two Flags* (Woodbridge: James Currey, 2012).

Kamara, M'Bha, *When Mosquitoes Come Marching In* (South Gate, CA: NoPassport Press, 2021).

Koroma, Ahmed, *The Moon Rises Over Isale Eko* (Freetown: Sierra Leonean Writers Series, 2019).

Palmer, Eustace, *My Epic Journey: The Making of a Cosmopolitan* (Freetown: Sierra Leonean Writers Series, 2022).

Palmer, Eustace and Abioseh Michael Porter (eds.), *A Critical Introduction to Sierra Leonean Literature* (Trenton, NJ: Africa World Press, 2008).

Sesay, Oumar F., *Landscape of Memories* (Freetown: Sierra Leonean Writers Series, 2019).

Tadjo, Véronique, *In the Company of Men.* Trans. by the author in collaboration with John Cullen (New York: Other Press, 2021). Originally published as *En compagnie des hommes* (Paris: Don Quichotte éditions, 2017).

Taqi, Fatou and Philip Foday Yamba Thulla (eds.), *Contemporary Fireside Poems: An Anthology* (Freetown: Sierra Leonean Writers Series, 2016).

Taqi, Fatou and Philip Foday Yamba Thulla (eds.), *Contemporary Fireside Stories: An Anthology* (Freetown: Sierra Leonean Writers Series, 2017).

Walon-Jalloh, A, *Panbody Blues* (Freetown: Sierra Leonean Writers Series, 2017).

SECTION I

THE CREATIVE IMAGINATION: LANGUAGE, HISTORY, AND CULTURE

Chapter 1

Unacknowledged Creative Loops: Orature, Literature and Society in Sierra Leone's Contemporary History

MOHAMED GIBRIL SESAY

Orature is often seen as the voiced word, further tightened to mean the spoken word of the creative type, and again often tweaked to be perceived as the performative – folklore, music, proverbs, and perhaps more – that are transcribed or translated into becoming written words, i.e. literature. Literature is predominantly seen as referring to the orthographic, the written word, further tightened to mean written word of the creative type, and again tweaked to be perceived as the fictional creative type – novels, short stories, poetry, and drama. Our discussion of Sierra Leonean literature dances to these loops of understandings, and to the various tweaking of the chords, to render sounds that hearken to our varied experiences of the written and the read word, and perhaps the listened-to word. Both literature and orature are imaginative accounts. Orature tends to be group sourced; literature is mostly dominated by individual authorship of the imaginative.

The very name of the country – Sierra Leone – was the result of an imaginative account by a Portuguese sailor, Pedro da Cintra, of roaring lions in the flash-flooding peninsular of the place where the capital Freetown is located today. The establishment of what would become Freetown – in the first instance, as a Province of Freedom, in May 1787, for formerly enslaved Africans from Britain called the Black Poor – was originally premised on some almost fantastical narrative of the terrain sent by one Henry Smeathman who talked of rich soils, great vegetation, and game (Fyfe 1962). But Smeathman did not adequately admonish about the anopheles mosquitoes that would pump so much fatal plasmodium into Europeans that they called the place 'The White Man's Grave'. Three British Governors of Sierra Leone would die in a space of three years in 1826–1828. This prompted the colonialists, in 1830, to contemplate evacuation of European personnel from Sierra Leone, to be replaced by persons of African descent (Curtin 1961).

The British colonialists would, however, not implement this proposed evacuation. It seemed like the legion of the mosquito was not that successful in driving out the British and getting Africans to rule Africans. After the Black Poor, the return of a second group of formerly enslaved Africans in March 1792 – from Nova Scotia this time – had been made on that promise of self-rule. But that foundational promissory –like Smeathman's – faded into myth on contact with certain realities on the ground; the British broke the promise and imposed their rule. The returnees from Nova Scotia, in 1800, rebelled against this depreciation of the promissory; this transformation of the promise into myth. Their rebellion was defeated. Promise becoming myth was entrenching itself as one of the loops of the story of the land; some part and parcel of an original and spiraling imaginary in the mountainous peninsular, out of which the econym of the terrains of our modern existence – Sierra Leone – expanded, in 1896, to include all 27,915 square miles of the diamond shaped land mass that today bears this name.

This mountainous peninsular that lends Pedro da Cintra's description of thundering lions to the entire country is today blandly called the Western Area, and further unimaginatively divided into Western Area Urban and Western Area Rural. But the peninsula has had its fair share of imaginative econyms. It was called Romeron – the wailing places – by the Themne, from whom the land was acquired by the Sierra Leone Company for the formerly enslaved returnees. The first returnees – the Black Poor that is – originally named their new settlement Granville Town, in honor of the British abolitionist Granville Sharpe. A conflict would lead to the destruction of Granville Town by the people of Romeron in 1890 (Alie 1990: 54). The destruction was like an assertion of the earlier meaning of the place as one of tears, or wailing – either because of the noise the fast-flowing streams of the place made, like the lions that frightened Pedro da Cintra; or on account of the wailings of inhabitants as they drowned or cried as their relatives drowned in the fast-flowing streams; or wailed as they buried them in the slanted topographies of their forested necropolises. Freetown would be the econym of the second iteration of Granville Town, a little to its west, forming the nucleus of what would become the Colony of Sierra Leone in 1808. The Themne would change to calling the place Kiamp, which they say is their rendition of the English word 'camp', connoting a waiting place, transitory, wavering. And the Mende would render its name Sa-Law, one of the meanings of which is 'the place of strange strong laws' – that is the law of the colonizers. But could we not say that this law of the colonizers that imposed British rule in 1808 on what was supposed to be a free town, with inhabitants who were self-governing, was a contradiction in terms? Could we hazard that it was part of an attempt to resolve that contradiction that once led a colonial Governor, Thomas Thompson, to temporarily change the name of Freetown to Georgetown, in honor of a British Monarch? It was said that the Governor thought that Freetown brought all sorts of ideas about freedom to the inhabitants of the city (Alie 1990: 67). Perchance a change of name would break the gyves chaining them to the original promise.

But what is Sierra Leonean or Sierra Leone creativity, performance, orature or literature? Worthy, in this instance, may be a distinction between the consciously imaginative and the subconsciously so. We may say all retellings of happenings are imaginative ones – a sort of '*cut ya put ya*' as they say in Krio – cutting this piece here and adding it to that other one. But the creative person or group is more conscious of the '*cut ya put ya*' process at work. They intentionally employ this splicing and rejoining to construct stories. Sierra Leonean creativity, its performativity, orature or literature may be more entrained to this intentional '*cut ya put ya*' about happenings, or imaginations about happenings, in the territories that came to be known as Sierra Leone. Or of the people that came to live therein – the imaginative and mythical accounts of their migrations towards it and therein, of the obstacles they face(d), the joys they create(d), the tears they cause(d), or the ordinariness or extraordinariness they tease(d) out of their human condition, or of their encounters with others on the way and in the territories where they finally settle(d). Sierra Leonean literature, orature, and other performance arts and acts may thus be seen as imaginative transcriptions and communications of how these migrations and encounters got concentrated in the places that come to form Sierra Leone; and of dispersions from these territories of our fallopian migrations, uterine experiences and birth-lands to other places. But the accounts of happenings in the places to which people disperse – the Diaspora that is – have traces of their encounters in the place called Sierra Leone, or of dreams about its future. The gathering place now called Sierra Leone, the past and present encounters therein, exert some gravitational pull on the telling. Wherever the telling takes place, there is some sort of talking about, or orbiting of the fission and fusion of encounters, or of the density of experiences that took place, or that are taking place in, or which emit from, the territories now known as Sierra Leone. In another sense, the concentrate of experiences, the density of encounters and the gathering of people in the topographies now called Sierra Leone form a sort of what Muslims call *qibla* – the direction of prayers – but which in our case we would say the direction of the imaginary, or a primary source of its contours. Sierra Leonean creativity, orature or literature then draws from these histories, these encounters, or these dis-encounters or untangling, perhaps re-entangling, peradventure unraveling or reveling.

It may be wise to see the written word of the imaginative type or the read word as but the visible tip of some underlying creative narrative rhizomes. These distinctions are useful – those between the creative sound, the spoken word, the written word, and the read word. Else the story of Sierra Leone and its literature may miss out on some of their rhizomes and underpinnings, the musical sounds, the oral narrative forms, folklore, proverbs, and dramatic renditions. These underpinnings are largely communal, sometimes instant and oftentimes performative means of getting all to imbibe the wisdom and norms of the land through storytelling and songs. And many times, the songs are a means of easing the burden of work, or of grief, or even of existence. One is reminded of the work songs of work-gangs on farms, the funereal songs, and the dance-dirges of Baiti performers amongst the Themne, and the Mada amongst the Mende.

But throughout history, many of these narrative forms would face threats of extinction. Like even presently, new sects of puritanical Muslims often shout down the Baiti and Mada as *haram*. Why? Perhaps on account of the Baiti and Mada syncretism of indigenous African rhythms and choreographies with Bilal-like accents of the Arabic. Bilal ibn Rabah al Habashi, the first muezzin of Islam, he of the great voice, but who could not correctly pronounce some of the consonants of the Arabic, for which the fanatics of 'sound' sound cried him down, until the Prophet told them Bilal's accent ascends to God as most beautiful. But now we are seeing the latest fanatics of 'sound' sound, or the religionists for pure accents, taking down the Baiti and Mada. But many funereal and other art forms of yore would survive brute assaults and severances. Like rhizomes, the amputated stems would regrow, the DNA of their original narrativity embedded in the new experiences and retellings. Sometimes even across the oceans and through time, as Mende funeral songs passed on from generation to generation, they would be utilized by descendants of the enslaved in America – the Gullah – to trace their ancestral village to Sierra Leone. But the tension has always been there, the expansion of extinction up against the gravity of continuity embedded in human memory. Like the Receptives' remembrances of the dances and sacred songs of their Yoruba ancestry and rendering them through their sodalities marching in Freetown in the mid-nineteenth century, for which they would be attacked by fanatical Christian missionaries wanting to stamp out the guttural voices of the non-Christian belief systems. Because, well, after all, Freetown was founded as a beacon of Christianity in heathen Africa, as that other creative mythology, hagiography even, of its founding – Governor Clarkson's Prayer – reminds.

Some particular ways in which the peoples of the territories now known as Sierra Leone experienced the European contact created situations which inhibited translations of the oral, the spoken, and the performative into written forms. The language, Krio, a prime creation of that encounter with Europe, and the most widely spoken language in the country, would be disparaged, and seen as unworthy as a carrier of written renditions. In fact, it was even perceived as inhibiting the fuller utilization of English to convey the country's experience. While in primary and secondary school, Sierra Leoneans would even be severely punished for speaking Krio, which was condescendingly called patois, like it was some parasitic tick on the cognitive scalp.

Languages that predated the establishment of Sierra Leone – from mainly the Mel and the Mande language groupings – would fare worse. But Mel languages, which in Sierra Leone include Themne, Sherbro, Kissi, and the now extinct Dama and Krim, as well as the almost extinct Mani, are carriers of great memories of the inaugural encounters with Europe and of the early history of the lands stretching from Cape Coast in Modern Liberia to the lower Casamance in Senegal. And words in the languages bear the marks of these stories – '*potho*' in Themne, meaning 'white person', a reference to the Portuguese, since they were the first Europeans to come to their land.

The word '*tabanka*' as Filho (2016) reminds us, is etymologically a reference to fortifications during the violent eras of the slave trade in the Upper Guinea Coast, and now a cognate for words relating to house, shelter, and protection in several languages in these lands, from the Baga-Sitem in Guinea-Conakry to the Balanta people in Guinea Bissau, and the Themne in Sierra Leone. And it is a word that has further migrated – its semantics shifting a little here and there – to other places in the Atlantic world – or the Black Atlantic as Gilroy (1993) would say – as far as, for instance, Cape Verde, Trinidad, Guyana, and Grenada.

Speaking of migration, one is reminded of the languages of the Mande people. The marks of their history of migrations from the ancient empire of Mali are embedded in similar words in Mende, Mandingo, Kono, Vai, Loko, amongst others. And they are also lodged in the epics they narrate about that ancient Mali Empire centered in the Mande homelands in the upper reaches of the Niger River of West Africa. One is reminded of the narrations about the travails of the hunchback Sogolon and her son Sunjata, the founder of the empire. And about Sumanguru seizing the wife of his nephew and trusted general Fakoli, which forced the latter to side with Sunjata against him in the great battles for control of the Mande heartlands. And about the folktales the Mande tell, the proverbs they embellish speech with, their norms of joking and fictive relationships, and the musical instruments they play – from the Soso Balanji to the Mende Seigureh and the Mandingo Kora. But the disparaging in the formal education system of the languages to which these instruments are entrained, and of the wisdom the languages offer, and of the histories, folklores and proverbs, is like an alienating of Sierra Leonean literature from a key part of its organic imaginary, from a rich source of nutrients for the country's pregnancies of creativity.

Thus, literature as orthographic, as written words, as read words, would have some hard birthing in the country, extended gestational trimesters, long periods between birth of one creative book and another. And these births were often unheralded; or where heralded, unloved; or where loved, short lived and forgotten too soon in the country. This would be the fate of the plays and poetry of Gladys Caseley Hayford in the 1930s and '40s, and of Robert Wellesley Cole's *Kossoh Town Boy* published in 1960, a year before independence. And also, the fate of the immediate post-independence works of Abioseh Nicol, and Sarif Easmon, and then Yulisa Maddy's *No Past, No*

Present, No Future. And the fate too, of Farid Raymond Anthony's *Sawpit Boy* published in 1980, the year that Sierra Leone broke its bank to host the Organization of African Unity (OAU). And, though less so, but also the general fate of the poetry of Syl Cheney-Coker, and even his award-winning 1991 novel, *The Last Harmattan of Alusine Dunbar*, and of the novels of Lucilda Hunter, including *Road to Freedom* (1982) which conversations she creatively rendered in a sort of proto-Krio, or Krio as it would have been in the early Freetown era that she depicted.

Sierra Leone has had both famous and notorious renditions of its stories by Westerners. Perhaps Western Christendom's most popular hymn, 'Amazing Grace' was the result of the slaver John Newton's experience in Sierra Leone, where he would meet poetic justice in the hands of Queen Pyle of the Sherbro, who treated this slaver like he had treated his slaves, worse even, for as Newton wrote, he was made a servant of slaves by the African queen. But Newton would later find redemption and wrote 'Amazing Grace' in penitence. And then there was the British Second World War spy and renowned novelist Graham Greene who wrote his novel, *The Heart of the Matter* (1948) in the now burnt-down City Hotel in Freetown in the three years he spent in the country during what older Sierra Leoneans call the 'Hitler War' and sometimes the 'Burma War' on account of Sierra Leonean servicemen fighting the Japanese in Burma during the Arakan Campaign, and winning laurels at a place called Myohaung, celebrated for decades by the Sierra Leone Armed Forces. The Myohaung Day celebrations were later changed to the Armed Forces Day to reflect other actions of Sierra Leonean soldiers, especially in relation to the Civil War in the country. This is, so to speak, a commemoration of experiences within the country serving as radiating core for encounters in other places.

Narratives of the notorious about Sierra Leone are dominant themes in writings about the country. We see these accounts generally starting as early as the European narratives about man-eating Sumba battalions of Mane warriors of the 1550s and subsequent decades and running up to Paul Richard's *Fighting for the Rain Forest* (1998), Kaplan's *The Coming Anarchy* (1994), and the film *Blood Diamond* (2006) starring Leonardo DiCaprio. There would be pushbacks by Sierra Leoneans against these screaming stories. This was the mid-1990s, at the height of the Civil War that Sierra Leoneans call the Rebel War, when Yusuf Bangura, Ibrahim Abdullah, Ismail Rashid, Lans Gberie, and others would push forward multi-dimensional renditions of the Sierra Leone narrative. Theirs were not novels or poetry or drama, but historical and social science perspectives on the war and other traumas that convulsed the land in the ultimate decade of the twentieth century.

But there had been other pushbacks against certain one-sided or unsavory Eurocentric ways of looking at Sierra Leone stories in the pre-war period. This could be seen in the works of Arthur Abraham on Mende chieftaincies and Magbaily Fyle on the Sulima-Yalunka Kingdom. In doing this they were picking up some not-so-often-talked-about facts about Sierra Leoneans taking charge in the writing of their stories, as could be seen in E.W. Blyden's *Christianity, Islam and the Negro Race* (2016 [1888]).

However, even with Sierra Leoneans, especially when they put it in English printed forms, the notorious narrations about Sierra Leone have become integral to 'serious' telling about this land of mythical thundering lions. It is almost like the default clouds hanging over the land, like it is the recurring nativity of its narrativity, like only the notorious could be legitimate writing about the country. We witness this in the social science and journalistic accounts of the land, in its orthographic poems, short stories, and novels. Perhaps it is because the language – English – that they choose to write in is the language of formal power in the country, the language of seriousness and sternness in the nation, the lash-tongue of the disciplinary of the school, of the strictness of the bureaucracy, of the aggressions of the state.

But this fanatical equating of the serious with the notorious and with the worthy is itself some way off the often risible and comic and back-talk ways in which stories are told in the ordinary discourses of the land, even when it is about tragic events, as we see in the many funny ways the Rebel War and other events are often talked about. The teeth do not mourn, we say. We may be sad in a dead child's cortege from Cottage, the main pediatric hospital in the country. But we also laugh along the way to bury our dead killed too young by preventable diseases and curable illnesses. A Krio proverb says, however tight a place is, the fowl always finds a place to lay its eggs. We may creatively loop this to mean: however sad a situation is, there may be a place for laughter. There are always many things to laugh about. It is what it is.

One often hears that Sierra Leoneans 'don't write.' Or that Sierra Leone is like some 'Eliotic' wasteland as far as putting words to paper is concerned. But when I look into the history of the country I see a lot of writing by Sierra Leoneans, writings about how the literate felt the country felt, writings to protest certain trends. Newspapers were for long the carriers of these writings. The first newspapers were started almost as soon as Freetown was established. Since then, hundreds of newspapers have been founded. But hundreds have also floundered (Gordon 2004). Sierra Leone has for long been a graveyard of newspapers. But that graveyard has been like some badly kept one, with collapsed gravestones, flattened-out tombs, so much so that people do not even know that the cemeteries exist – like for instance many in Freetown do not know that what we now call the Sewa Grounds were the earliest burial grounds of the emerging Freetown. So? Well, newer generations felt not much had come before them, that there were no worthy ancestors in their line of writing, or what they know is so vague as to hardly have value in practice. Throughout Sierra Leone's history, newer writers, be they journalists, poets, short-story writers, or dramatists felt like they were starting anew – like there were no shoulders of giants for them to stand on. Or measure ourselves against. Or even fight. Or play some masculine fast-one on, like some adventurous teenagers do on their fathers, giving the fathers names of anti-heroes from films they have watched, a name like Garber Singh of Bollywood movies; or loop their father's name to that of a tough historical figure –like the irascible colonial Governor Cardew – and they see these labeled fathers as persons they, the heroic children, must battle against. Or the way girls also do, seeing their mothers as persons to play some feminine quick-ones on, outwitting them to meet friends and lovers, or to dance to loved genres, or just do girl things outside the supervision of stern parents. So it is then. There seem to be no fathers or mothers of Sierra Leone literature for newer writers to play these youthful creative games on; like the past is some authorial wasteland; like there is no past, or no history of creative orthography autographed by Sierra Leoneans that could provide some of the contextual backdrop for the writing life.

There have been some worthy efforts at writing down Sierra Leone's folklore by the People's Education Association (PEA) and the Sierra Leone Adult Education Association (SLADEA). Generally, however, Sierra Leone has not done very well acknowledging its rich oral traditions and wisdom in its printed forms, and it has also not done well in passing on its printed wisdom unto newer generations. There is little knowledge of Sierra Leone's creative or other archives. And the decade-long 1991–2002 Rebel War created big disruptions and discontinuities in whatever archival connections may have existed between generations. There is the discontinuity in the loss of the country's bureaucratic records on chieftaincy and other traditions when the Treasury Building where they were housed was burnt down when rebels entered Freetown in 1998. Or the arson of the sound archives of the Sierra Leone Broadcasting Service at New England Ville during those moments of temporary national insanity. Or the balding, dandruffy state of the once hirsute national archives at Kennedy Building, Mount Aureol; or the challenging circumstance of the once stolid Sierra Leone Collection at the Fourah Bay College Library housing graduate dissertations, articles and other scholarship on the Sierra Leone condition; or the bonfire of records and books at Njala University during the war. Or the fact that most of the papers of the Sierra Leonean pan Africanist, E.W. Blyden, a man buried at the Race Course cemetery in Freetown, and who spent the better part of his writing life in these territories – that this country does not have the originals of his writings.

It seems as if, post-independence, every decade has its own bobbling artistic genre. The 1970s was a decade of live band expression – Super Combo, Afro National, Sabanoh, Purple Haze. The 1980s was an era of drama and what Sierra Leoneans refer to as 'discorama' – a type of musical show of medley performances by singers, dancers, and other artists. The outstanding dramatists of the era included John Kolosa Kargbo, Raymond De Souza

George, Toni French, Akmid Bakarr Mansaray, Charlie Hafner, Julius Spencer, John Solo Fofana, Syl Johnson, Mohamed Bangura, Oumar Farouk Sesay, Dele Charley, Shefumi Garber, Kashor Woode, Fredrick Borbor James, and Mohamed Bobson Kamara. Notable plays included *Let Me Die Alone, Big Berrin, Yon Kon, Poyotong Wahala, The Blood of a Stranger, Indictment of a Nation, Tragedy of a Nation, Borbor Lehf, Cry of the Country Virgin, Got Sef Kin Swet*, and *Cry for Justice*. Quite a number of these plays discussed the tightening political situations in the country. But many, including *Titi Shayn Shayn, Sugar Daddy Na Case, Yu Hol Di Ring, Mami Sweh, Material Love, Victim of Love, Playboy Trobul, Abandoned Child*, and *Way di Cup Ful* were portrayals of the social scenes and sins of the era. Some were what we would call the interrogative plays posing questions in their very titles about emerging norms and moralities – *Moden law en fadenlaw oodat bad? Tiff man en witchman oose wan bad?* and such screaming titles as *Wara, The Life and Times of a Koro*. The challenge may be to reclaim these titles, to put them into books, turn them into written works as means of ensuring reflection, outside the performances, of what they contain, much like many now experience the insights of Shakespeare through written texts without ever watching the plays staged.

The aim is to build continuity; to tease out feedback loops that creatives and others could be very conscious of. Lack of continuity, that is a problem with Sierra Leone literature; and Orature; and Music. Perhaps even a problem with wider Sierra Leone society people thinking they are starting anew, a nation of starters or perhaps re-starters, too quick to forget earlier achievements, or just having some non-committal ephemeral knowledge of them, transforming into a precarity what was, what is, and what will be, almost akin to the screaming title of Pat Maddy's novel, *No Past, No Present, No Future* (1973). That is how it looks like, from the family business to public institutions, to music, to literature, to education even, never mind the vaulted talk of Fourah Bay College as some historical lodestar of education in Africa.

Fourah Bay College, the country's premier tertiary education institution founded in 1827, has itself, in a way, aided this hiatus between the land and its imaginary. The college had been seeking, so to speak, a metaphorical alliance with ancient Greece when it called itself the 'Athens of West Africa.' It prided itself for long in educating its students in classical occidental mythology, in Greek and Roman Civilization (GRECO), until, well, students got tired of it, laughing off the acronym GRECO as some strange thing to emphasize in an African University. GRECO is no longer taught at Fourah Bay College. But for long, the university's Sierra Leonean humanities graduates, tied to the mythical strings of the far-off times of the far-off places of Athens and Rome, would not be early starters in transcribing or transforming the country's story into orthographic creative forms. Unlike, say, Nigeria and Kenya, whose Soyinkas and Achebes and Ngugis would lead the orthographic transcriptions, translations, and transformations of the ancient myths and extant happenings of their lands.

Generations of writers, as already noted, and that we reiterate because of its importance, look cut off from, rather than cut out of other generations. Newer generations often think they are doing stuff that others had never done; it is secession, albeit unknowingly, rather than succession. Like rhizomes being cut off from parent corms without knowledge of the DNA they share, without conscious genetic memories of the strength and pitfalls. So! They are without the volitional knowhow to build on the strengths and avoid or inject better imaginaries into the genealogical pitfalls. There are little or no reflections on the works of earlier writers by later writers and artists. Gladys Casely-Hayford is hardly read by men and women dramatists and poets; Abioseh Nicol is hardly encountered by men and women poets; also there is non-availability of the works of Sarif Easmon, Yulisa Maddy, Syl Cheney-Coker, Kolosa Kargbo, and Yema Lucilda Hunter in discourses of the newer generations of Sierra Leonean writers. Generations of Sierra Leoneans are not experiencing Sierra Leonean modes of narrating through the written text as art, as literature, as unique creative forms.

The great Colombian novelist, Gabriel Marquez wrote that 'the end of all literature is the dustbin'. Agreed. But it looks like Sierra Leone has been consigning its own too soon to the dustbin. There have been some efforts to get some of the forgotten out of the amnesiac dump. The Languages department at FBC has, in the last decade, been including some Sierra Leone literature in the reading lists of its undergraduate honors classes.

Writers themselves have been making some worthy effort to transform the amnesiac dump to some biomass to feed into some of the grids of the country's artistic and other goals. In the 1990s, poets pushed themselves forward; a process crystallized by the founding of the Falui Poetry Society, under whose aegis poets would organize well-attended poetry evenings. Later many of the poems would be anthologized as *Songs that Pour the Heart* (2004) by M.G. Sesay and Moses Kainwo. The poems of that decade and subsequent years included Tatafway Tumoe's easy-to-read poems about loss, war, abortion, and love; Sydnella Shooter's trident renditions of tragedies; Bridgette James' poems about the everyday, Ambrose Massaquoi's reflections on the personal moral depravities of the times; Gbanabom Hallowell's labyrinthine metaphors of our convoluted circumstances, Musu Sandy's sage reflections in her short poems; Oumar Farouk's haunting alliterations of loss, and Abu Noah's forceful poems. And also, writing from the Diaspora, Ahmed Koroma's nostalgia about lost worlds.

The 1990s and 2000s were eras of gushing forth of Sierra Leonean writings from the faucets of different genres and subgenres, both within the country and in the Diaspora, and whatever spaces in between. The writings of Sierra Leoneans in the Diaspora included the poems of Ahmed Koroma; the reflections on the contours of the country's hopes and impediments by Kayode Robbin Coker; the sage insights of Lemuel Johnson on the listserv Leonenet; the memoirs and novels of Aminatta Forna; the novel *Moses, Citizen and Me* (2006) by Delia Jarrett-Macauley; the poetry of Sheikh Umarr Kamarah; the literary criticisms and novels of Eustace Palmer; the autobiographical reflection of life in the Diaspora in Germany by Osman Alimamy Sankoh, and that in China by Abdul B. Kamara; the memoirs and novels of Ishmael Beah and the novel and short fiction of Pede Hollist.

Within the country, Mohamed Sheriff of Pampana Communications and Charlie Haffner of Freetong Players would be at the fore of creating community plays to promote messages of peace, of reconciliation and of the emerging democracy. And there was also the creative journalism of Olu Gordon in his satirical portrayal of a country called Leonebanon, and his hymns and 'QEDs' in the 'Peep' column of *For Di People* newspaper and later the *Peep Magazine*. Also, within the boundaries of creative journalism, but less urgent than Olu Gordon's, and using colonial scenes and characters to reflect on emerging issues was the 'Last Word' column of *The New Citizen* newspaper by Ibrahim Ben Kargbo. And the country would also be treated to other satirical columns in such newspapers such as, amongst others, the *New Shaft* and the *Standard Times*. Performance poetry would create its own niche, often poetry evenings by the Falui Poetry Society, and the staging of one of the biggest poetry performances called 'Poets Live' at the British Council, the result of collaboration between Pampana Communications, the Falui Poetry Society, and the British Council. Sierra Leonean music would also stage a comeback in the mid-2000s, led by Jimmy Bangura, Emerson Bockarie, and others. Their music would develop new moral discourses and words for the situations in the country. The Ballanta Academy would inaugurate formal classes in Music, and the indefatigable efforts of Kitty Fadlu Deen would continue. Ballanta Academy was named for a famous Sierra Leonean music classicist and collector of indigenous African Music, Nicholas G.J. Ballanta. It was an attempt at reconnecting Sierra Leonean music to a past often forgotten by contemporary musicians. Or where the creativity of traditional musicians like Bassie Kondie, Salia and Amy Kallon were, are, little known to the newer generation of Sierra Leonean musicians; nor was there such cultural creativity in the 1940s and '50s Freetown as the Ambasgeda, the Alimania, the Tarasisi, and Yankadi, drawing new migrants from the hinterland into transitional cultural matrices in a Freetown that doubled its population during the Second World War years of frenetic activities in its port teeming with soldiers and temporary employment and hundreds of ships involved in the supply chain activities of the Hitler War.

Apart from the musical efforts of the Fadlu Deens and Jimmy Banguras, there would also be films. Amongst the inaugural attempts at feature films were the titles *The Betrayal of Africa* written by Akmid Bakarr and directed by Pat Maddy, and Premier Media's *Off to America* written by Esme James and directed by Julius Spencer. Another pivotal moment was the Scriptnet Film project that produced six film scripts that were made into six short films, which are still among the best films Sierra Leone has produced. They included *Scars*, written and directed by John Solo Fofana; *Toy Gun*, written and directed by Alfred Pangu; *A Hole in the Wall*, written by M.G. Sesay and directed by Sarah King; *Victims*, written and directed by Mohamed Sheriff, and *The Curse*, written by Brian James. Greater popularization of Sierra Leonean films would, however, be ensured by such notable persons as Desmond Finney and Jimmy Bangura.

A number of film companies and organizations have since been formed, producing feature films in Freetown, Bo, Kenema, and Makeni. A large number of the films look amateurish and sometimes feel like poor copies or palimpsests of foreign narrative arcs and aesthetics, just as is the case with sizable numbers of the plays, novels, poetry, and emerging songs. It is as if, lacking conversations with the history of their genres in the land, they pick up whatever flotsam comes in from foreign shores. But is the creative work not also about the debris and the amazing, about the good, the bad, and the ugly, both in terms of the themes it handles and also in respect of the very form and construction of the creative works themselves?

Many forums that would be catalysts for Sierra Leonean writings emerged in the last three decades. Falui Poetry Society, coordinated by its inaugural president Moses Kainwo and Secretary General Gbanabom Hallowell, was the leading forum for poetry discussions, workshops and readings in the 1990s. From the mid-1990s, the two Leonenet listserv forums would be meeting places for non-fictional (and some fictional) renditions of the Sierra Leonean situation. The Sierra Leonean Writers Forum commencing in the mid-2010s would become an online meeting place and catalyst for the publication of several anthologies, short stories, and novels by the Sierra Leonean Writers Series. And also, the Sierra Leone chapter of Pen International, whose revivification efforts were led by Mike Butscher and further sustained by Mohamed Sheriff and Nathaniel Pearce. Pen Sierra Leone would soon find a niche for promoting the writing of literature for children.

In all of these revivifications, Latinate orthography dominates. We must, however, note the existence of the Ajami scripts in which many Sierra Leoneans are literate; the script, for instance, is the orthographic base for writing in Fula. The Ajami orthography has its own long history, a carrier of the scholarship of African peoples including the Mande and others in the Sahel, many of whom, in the great eras of migrations southwards would come into the territories now called Sierra Leone, enriching its stories, its imaginary, its norms and values. Worthy of conscious looping into the narrativity of creativity in the country would be the Mende Kikakui script created by Quranic scholar Mohamed Turay and further developed and popularized by Kisimi Kamara, the Lavali or Speaker and second most important chief of Barri Chiefdom in southern Sierra Leone from 1932 to 1957 when he was deposed and exiled to Bo. The script would flourish in the 1920s, '30s and '40s, embraced by many for writing agreements and taking note of the transactions of their lives. But it would be given a deathblow by the counter promotion of the Latinate Westermann script for writing Mende. Kisimi Kamara died in 1961, leaving a trove of written Kikakui papers with his family in Bo. This archive was, however, destroyed by the family when they moved to another location in the city (Tuchscherer 1995: 179). Kikakui and the Ajami scripts are lost or getting lost for newer generations through these archival attritions and the aggressive promotion of Latinate orthographies as vehicles for conveying written remembrances. Being cut off from knowledge of what is contained in these scripts is akin to being cut off from certain foundational streams of the orthographic of the land.

The memoir, the autobiographical and the biographical have been favored genres by a number of Sierra Leonean writers. The autobiographical included *Kossoh Town Boy* by R.W. Cole in the 1960s; *Sawpit Boy* by F.A. Anthony at the end of the 1970s; and the country's long-term ruler Siaka Stevens would write *What Life has Taught Me* in the 1980s, as would also another President, Ahmad Tejan Kabbah, in the 2000s, the entrepreneur M.K. Suma's *In and Out of Millions*, the medical doctor Bailah Leigh's *Dilemma of Freedom*, and the politician Sama Banya's *Looking Back*. Other autobiographies included that of the literary critic Eldred Jones, *The Freetown Bond*, the former child soldier Ishmael Beah's *A Long Way Gone*, the novelist Aminatta Forna's *The Devil that Danced on the Water*, the journalist Sheka Tarawallie's *Pope Francis, Politics and the Mabanta Boy*, and the civil servant Umu Tejan Jalloh's *Telling it As it Was*. There is also the biography of prominent woman paramount chief Ella Koblo by Talabi Lucan; of the musician, playwright, poet, and teacher Gladys Casely-Hayford by her daughter-in-law, Yema Lucilda Hunter; of the churchman and teacher Modupe Taylor Pearce by Brian James and Esme James; and of the jurist Livesey Luke by the engineer, poet, and artist Kosonike Koso-Thomas.

There is growing interest amongst Sierra Leoneans in writing short stories. This could be seen in anthologies of short stories, *Leonanthology,* that Gbanabom Hallowell put together, and *Contemporary Fireside Stories* that Yamba Thulla and Fatou Taqi edited. These anthologies by Hallowell, Thulla, and Taqi – the subject of Stephen Ney's chapter in this volume – were collected through the Sierra Leonean Writers Forum, a WhatsApp group for Sierra Leonean writers that is alive with the emerging reconfiguring of the boundaries between individual and group creativity, between in-country and diaspora distinctions and those between the different literary genres. But long before these stories, the Sierra Leonean writing scene was enlivened by Abioseh Nicol's short stories, *Two African Tales*, and *The Truly Married*

Woman and Other Stories, and by the beautiful short stories in Sarif Easmon's *The Feud and Other Stories*. There would also be short stories by Brian James (*Simple Economics*), and M.G. Sesay (*Half-man and the Curse of the Ancient Buttocks*) which won the Caine Prize for African Writing in 2009, Pede Hollist's short story, 'Foreign Aid', Mohamed Sheriff's award-winning story, 'A Voice in Hell', M.G. Sesay's short story 'Monkey Teeth', and Mohamed Sheriff's 'Sori Clever' published by the *Focus on Africa* magazine. In 2012, Mohamed Combo Kamanda put together a collection of Sierra Leonean short stories, *The Price and Other Short Stories*, and, in 2015, Bakarr Mansaray published his short-story collection, *A Suitcase Full of Dried Fish*.

There has been remarkable flowering of children's literature in the last ten years. Published titles during the period included *Our Bird* by Rainy Ansumana, *Amidu's Day Off* by Foday Sawi, *Yammah and the Tumbeke Project* by Nathaniel Pearce, *Magic* by Allieu Kamara, and *Tibujang Must Not Come* by Mohamed Sheriff. But we must not forget the efforts in earlier decades by Talabi Lucan, Osman Pios Conteh, and Mohamed Sheriff.

Experiences of war and the trauma of such catastrophes as Ebola would be major themes in many Sierra Leoneans' writings in the new millennium. These themes are explored in the novels *Landscape of Memories* by O. Farouk Sesay, *This Side of Nothingness* by M.G. Sesay, *Redemption Song* by Yema Lucilda Hunter, *The Road to Kaibara* by Gbanabom Hallowell, *Youthful Yearning* by Jedidah Johnson, and many others; also in the poetry of Sydnella Shooter, Gbanabom Hallowell, and Frederick Borbor James. The Ebola epidemic would feature in the non-fiction works of Chernor Bah, Ismael Rashid, and Ibrahim Bangura, as well as in several poetry collections. But other themes are also emerging, of love, of desire, as can be seen in the writings of Samuella Conteh and Elizabeth L.A. Kamara, in Moses Kainwo's *Ayo, Ayo, Ayo and Other Love Poems* and in the offerings of emerging poets like Celia Thompson, Amara Sesay, and Kemurl Fofanah, and in the performance poetry of Fatou Wurie and Adeola, exploring themes of sexual abuse and women's liberation.

The English language monopolizes writings by Sierra Leoneans. And even where we have had attempts at writing in other Sierra Leonean languages – as in Sheikh Umarr Kamarah's and Marjorie Jones' *Beg Sɔl Nɔba Kuk Sup: An Anthology of Krio Poetry* – the Latinate dominates. There may be no escape from that, or from the colonial library, as Mudimbe would say (Wai 2015). But the colonial library, as Mudimbe again advises, has tools for moving forward our projects. We must, however, be aware of its limitations, of the possibilities that lie therein for orthographic forgetting, or genealogical amnesia, or false notions about the origins of civilization, creativity, and education – as is implied in the epithet of Fourah Bay College as the 'Athens of West Africa'.

There are now emerging, slowly but assuredly, writings in Krio. The fluttering can be seen on social media, where many write in Krio. This is welcome development, for as can be seen in the great reception that prominent

Krio-language poet, Daphne Pratt, receives when she reads her poem, writing in Sierra Leonean languages would bring forth fresher voices and newer ways of rendering experiences in the printed text. But it must not also be forgotten that English is also ours, like those wax cottons made in Holland that have become African attire, and so many other visible and invisible forms from other places that we made ours. The trick, then, is not to allow use of English to restrict us; or for its Latinate orthography to make the Sierra Leonean writer forget other orthographies like the Ajami and Kikakui scripts that had carried the stories of the land. But also, the Sierra Leonean writer may not want to jettison centuries of experiencing and experimenting with the English language, for that also would be limiting. Sierra Leone, after all, is a pivotal location in the Black Atlantic – that cultural mix of languages and arts and music and histories about which Gilroy (1993) theorized. A higher trick then, if we should build on Gordon's (2004) postulations, may be to have a creolizing imagination, a mixing of the semantic, syntactic, and orthographic heritages of Sierra Leone to render the creative arcs of the stories of the land.

We may be getting into the field of literary criticism with our assertions above. But literary criticism has renowned precursors in Sierra Leone. One of Africa's profoundest Shakespearean scholars, Soyinka expert and literary critic was Sierra Leonean professor Eldred Durosimi Jones. There are also Eustace Palmer's seminal books, *Introduction to the African Novel* and *Growth of the African Novel*, and the literary insights of Sheikh Umarr Kamarah and Lemuel Johnson; in 2019, Abdulai Walon-Jalloh wrote a book-length, veritable critique of several contemporary Sierra Leonean literary works.

Sierra Leonean fiction has come a long way, sometimes winning prizes and international accolades along the way – Syl Cheney-Coker's *The Last Harmattan of Alusine Dunbar* winning the Commonwealth Writers' Prize; Olufemi Terry's short story 'Stick Fighting Days' winning the Caine Prize in 2010; Pede Hollist's short story, 'Foreign Aid' making it to the short list of the Caine Prize in 2013; Mohamed Sheriff's novella *Secret Fear* was co-winner of the ECOWAS Prize for Excellence in Literature in 1999; Osman Pios Conteh's *Unanswered Cries* winning a Macmillan Prize for children's literature; Mohamed Sheriff winning BBC playwriting prizes for his radio plays *Just Me and Mama* and *Spots of the Leopard*; and Ishmail Beah, Aminata Forna, and others winning international accolades for their writings.

Despite this, for many Sierra Leonean writers, it feels like they are but toiling in the tailings of telling, sometimes hopeful, like miners in the gambling pits of the diamond fields, perchance they may be lucky to get the gems of being acknowledged. Perhaps the challenge in all this is the very nature of the paper text as media for engagement. Perhaps writing or reading is too personal and private for a very sociable people, too passive for our performance-centric cultures, too consciously individual for a society where creativity is communal and often spontaneous; perhaps it is because the creation of literature as written words is too one-sided, too monologue-like, indirect and distant for our culture of direct and instant conversations. Perhaps Sierra Leonean writers do not actually have in mind Sierra Leonean audiences when they write. The advisory, then, could be to make literary texts more dynamic, like through book fairs and art festivals, getting Sierra Leonean literature in college and school curricula, mobile libraries, audio books, and the dynamic screens of the new multi-media. Perhaps it could be communal creative projects and collaborations as we saw facilitated on the Sierra Leonean Writers Forum WhatsApp group; and/or such other emerging reconfigurations online or offline or a mix of the two. So that, like Gabriel Marquez would say, had he been Sierra Leonean, the literature of the land would not become, too very quickly, wrapping papers for sellers of groundnuts and *akara* (fritters of rice). The advisory is about getting the Sierra Leonean writer to also write with Sierra Leonean audiences in their mind. The suggestion is about ways to defeat the ephemerality of no past, no present, and no future that tends to etch itself, like a crab louse, on the nation's destiny. The hope, simply put, is about building conversations amongst and across the generations, texts, contexts, scripts, writers, audiences; to also bring onboard the risible ordinary discourses of whatever the topic is; the challenge would be to sustain these efforts, towards weaving, or unweaving, re-weaving or perhaps just having glimpses of the varied strands of its genres, eras, media, experimentation, and experiences.

Works Cited

Abraham, A. (ed.), *Topics in Sierra Leone History: A Counter Colonial Interpretation* (Freetown: Leone Publishers, 1975).

Alie, Joe A.D., *A New History of Sierra Leone* (Oxford: Macmillan Publishers, 1990).

Blyden, Edward W. *Christianity, Islam and the Negro Race* (Eastford, CT: Martino Fine Books, 2016 [1888]).

Curtin, P.D., 'The "White Man's Grave": Image and Reality, 1780–1850', *Journal of British Studies* 1.1 (1961), pp. 94–110.

Filho, Wilson Trajano, 'Travelling Terms: An Analysis of Semantic Fluctuations in the Atlantic World', in J. Knor & C. Kohl (eds.), *The Upper Guinea Coast in Global Perspectives* (New York and Oxford: Berghan Books, 2016), pp. 157–73.

Fyfe, Christopher, *History of Sierra Leone* (London: Oxford University Press, 1962).

Gilroy, Paul, *The Black Atlantic: Modernity and Double Consciousness* (Cambridge, MA: Harvard University Press, 1993).

Gordon, J., 'Creolizing Political Identity and Social Scientific Method', *Africa Development/ Afrique et Developpment* 39.1 (2014), pp. 66–80.

Gordon, Olu, 'Civil Society against the State: The Independent Press and the AFRC-RUF Junta', in Ibrahim Abdullah (ed.), *Between Democracy and Terror: The Sierra Leone Civil War* (Dakar: CODESRIA, 2004).

Magbailey-Fyle, C., *The History of Sierra Leone: A Concise Introduction* (London and Ibadan: Evans Brothers, 1981).

Newton, R.C., 'Of Dangerous Energy and Transformations: "Nyamakalaya" and the Sunjata Phenomena', *Research in African Literatures 37.2* (2006), pp. 15–33.

Tuchscherer, Konrad, 'African Script and Scripture: The History of the Kikakui (Mende) Writing System for Bible Translations', *African Languages and Cultures* 8.2 (1995), pp. 169–88.

Wai, Zubairu, 'On the Predicament of Africanist Knowledge: Mudimbe, Gnosis and the Challenge of the Colonial Library', *International Journal of Francophone Studies* 18.2–3 (2015), pp. 263–90.

Chapter 2

The Past Flows: Water as a Metaphor for Nostalgia in Ahmed Koroma's *The Moon Rises Over Isale Eko*

OUMAR FAROUK SESAY

In much of Africa, poetry derives its richness and beauty from the oral traditions that celebrate our connections to each other and our mystic world, reflecting a deeply rooted African sense of aesthetics. Historically, poetry has been our medium of expression as we contended with natural phenomena and external invasions. We celebrated our remarkable achievements in art and technology, such as ironwork and pottery, through the lyrical cadence of oral poetry, thereby asserting the importance of orality in literature. This resilience and unwavering refusal to let violence dictate our narrative underscore the transformative power of art and literature, inspiring us to shape our society and culture.

Poetry rebirths were notable when the brutal Civil War erupted in Sierra Leone (1991–2002). Poets like Ahmed Koroma wrote not only to chronicle the collective trauma but also to heal it and restore language's capacity to narrate the grotesque tale of a war that seemed to have maimed the very soul of language, rendering it deficient in recording the horror of the war. Hence, poetry must bolster language, reinforcing it with the vigor of verse to tell the tale of the deluge.

Poetic response to trauma echoes Kahlil Gibran's sentiment: "Poetry is not an opinion expressed. It is a song that rises from a bleeding wound or a smiling mouth" (*Sand and Foam*). In Koroma's *The Moon Rises Over Isale Eko*, the poet's nostalgia and pain are vividly expressed, conveyed through the evocative imagery of water. Ahmed Koroma's unique choice of water as a thematic metaphor in his collection to express nostalgia, spirituality, and decadence is a testament to the depth and complexity of his work and the power of poetry to heal even those in exile seeking refugee from the carnage in their country.

To fully appreciate Koroma's poetry, one must delve into the historical and contemporary contexts that shape his work and the landscapes and soundscapes that inspire his verse. Immersing ourselves in the world that forms the backbone of his poetry allows us to unravel the intricate interplay between the ebb and flow of his verse and the tidal wave of change, which elevates water as a central metaphor in his work.

It is worth noting that the literary responses to historical events, such as the First World War, have given us enduring works like Erich Maria Remarque's war classic, *All Quiet on the Western Front*, and Wilfred Owen's posthumously published war poems, like "Dulce et Decorum Est," which continue to resonate with us well over a century later. Similarly, Ahmed Koroma's poetry, particularly his use of water as a metaphor, stands as a testament to the enduring power of literature to reflect and shape our understanding of significant historical events.

Significant events within Africa have profoundly shaped literature as well. Works such as Chimamanda Ngozi Adichie's *Half of a Yellow Sun* and Elechi Amadi's *Sunset in Biafra* seek to wrest the last word from the Biafra war. These works invite us to reflect and understand and serve as a powerful testament to the enduring influence of historical events on literature, shaping the narratives and themes of the works.

In Sierra Leone, this phenomenon is also visible. Writers like Ishmael Beah, with his memoir *A Long Way Gone*, Delia Jarrett-Macauley's *Moses, Citizen and Me*, Syl Cheney-Coker's *Stone Child*, Mohamed Gibril Sesay's *At the Gathering of Roads*, Kosonike Koso-Thomas's *Peacekeeper Lover*, and the war poetry of Gbanabom Hallowell and the Falui Poetry Society, among many others, are all on a mission to have the final say, exposing the inherent insanity of war and reinforcing a "never again" attitude. This literary boom can be attributed to various factors, including the information technology revolution, increased local investment in the publishing industry, and the emergence of new writers forged in the crucible of war. Among these emerging voices, some have risen hesitantly, experimenting in various tongues and genres, bringing hope and anticipation to the Sierra Leonean literary scene. Ahmed Koroma is one of those voices amplified after the war, with a resonance now echoing throughout the country.

His third collection of poems, *The Moon Rises Over Isale Eko*, published by the Sierra Leonean Writers Series in 2019, delves into the soul of a small yet culturally significant community in Freetown, Sierra Leone. This enclave, Isale Eko, is adjacent to the Fullah Tong and Fourah Bay neighborhoods. Isale Eko, a spatial metaphor in the collection, refers to present-day Rocklin Street, Sackville Lane, and part of Fifth Street. Early settlers, consisting primarily of liberated Yorubas known as Aku/Oku, established this area in the nineteenth century around the period of the abolition of slavery by Britain. "Isale Eko" is a Yoruba expression meaning "down under," influenced by the land's topography. This term originally referred to Lagos Island, Nigeria, and its adoption in nineteenth-century Sierra Leone aligns with the settlers' practice of adopting names from their places of origin. Isale Eko, Fullah Tong, and Fourah Bay, interconnected by the Muslim religion and enriched by cultural aspects such as Ojeh and hunting secret fraternities, form a fertile ground for Koroma's nostalgically driven poems.

The waters of the Odokoko River, which streak across the community on its way to the ocean, provide a backdrop for the water metaphors that flow throughout the collection. Furthermore, the poet's unwavering connection to water may be rooted in his affinity for a place whose origins trace back to the waters of the Atlantic Ocean. This very ocean facilitated the return of his ancestors to a patch of land known as Isale Eko, beside a river named Odokoko, more than two centuries ago. It is present in "In Her Dream," "The Winding Road," evoking resilience; it appears in "Infuriation," though as dirty water, symbolizing decadence and rust; it emerges in "The Rebirth of Isale Eko," signifying purification. Water is present in "Forgiveness," "His Return," "Hurricane," "Desolation," "The Bridge," "Doorpost," "Full Moon Rise," "Antelope," and "The Message." Water permeates the collection, acting as a vessel for nostalgia, longing, purification, resistance, and resilience.

In the opening poem, "Dear Freetown," the poet introduces the theme of nostalgia and the recurring metaphor of water, which permeates the entire collection. He mentions holy water, the illuminated sea, the bridge, the waterfall, and the bursting bay, thus emphasizing water's significance as a life-sustaining substance, a means of purification and cleansing, and a vehicle to convey themes of all sorts. As indicative in the quote from the poem "Dear Freetown,"

> Let the priest sprinkle holy water
> at the doorstep of the Tabernacle
> across where statues once stood. (13)

Here, the poet doses the reader with a sprinkle of consecrated water before unleashing the deluge from the ocean, streams, and gutter, transforming the whole landscape of the poetry into a waterlogged swamp that yells to be drained in some cases. The poet pens a heartfelt letter to the city of his childhood, setting the nostalgic tone that runs through Koroma's work like the derelict relic of the Odokoko River. Each poem resonates with the poet's yearning to return to Isale Eko, his childhood community, providing metaphorical nourishment for his creative spirit. Over time, these communities have been collectively called East End Freetown or simply "Istehn" in local parlance. Many view it as a melting pot of memories. In this place, the return to freedom of the formerly enslaved, the influences of Islam and Christianity, and cultural elements from across West Africa converge.

The theme of nostalgia is explored deeply, revealing a profound emotional connection to a place and time imbued with beauty and hardship. The poet employs vivid imagery, specific sensory details, and tone to convey the complexities of his relationship with his hometown, Freetown. The opening lines of the very first poem in the collection, "Dear Freetown," establish a tone of resilience, describing "battle scars" on the city's "tired face," invoking a sense of history and endurance. With its triumphs and struggles, the past plays a central role in the poet's nostalgic quest. Koroma uses perceptive imagery to immerse the reader in the experience of returning to Freetown, evoking the scents of "hot pepper soup" and the "odor of decayed compost," "holy water," "puddles," "waterfall," and "Hamlet by the sea" to anchor the reader or baptize the reader in the many waters of the city. The rejection of superficial embellishments becomes a poignant expression of the poet's desire for an unfiltered connection to Freetown's essence:

> Dear Freetown
> When I return to you
> I do not expect a delirious mask
> nor the pretense of a blissful town
> rather, it is the authentic you
> the battle scars down your tired face
> reminding me of your stunning past. (11)

The refusal of "bunting flags on crisscross wires" and the emphasis on placing the poet's portrait alongside a woman who spits at passers-by highlight the importance of embracing the city's raw, unadorned reality. This juxtaposition of the unconventional with the cherished underscores a profound understanding of nostalgia as an intimate, unvarnished attachment to the true character of a place.

The poet also employs cultural and religious references to evoke a sense of familiarity and shared history; the mention of the imam reading "Suratul al Naas" (the last chapter in the Quran), the *azan* (Islamic call to prayer), and the imagery of herding sheep on a grassy knoll evoke a shared memory and deep connection to a specific place. In "Dear Freetown," water's leitmotif symbolizes renewal and purification. The juxtaposition of "sewage rats and roaming pigs" with the aroma of "hot pepper soup on concrete" and the scent of decayed compost creates a striking contrast. This duality reflects the essence of a bustling and nourishing city, much like water's ability to cleanse and rejuvenate pleasant and unpleasant memories.

Additionally, mentioning "the grassy hill where we used to herd sheep" connects water to the pastoral landscape of the poet's childhood, fostering a sense of rootedness and spiritual resonance. The recurring water imagery throughout the collection enriches and deepens the theme of nostalgia.

Isale Eko, though Yoruba in origin, exists as an enclave within the broader Fullah Tong community, often blending seamlessly with neighboring areas, each with its claim to the poet's affection for his hometown. This locale serves as the poet's nostalgic community, where people of Yoruba, Igbo, and other African backgrounds settled, bringing diverse cultural and religious practices. In his doctoral thesis, linguist Saidu Bangura (2015, 176) noted that about 400 of the over 1,000 African languages spoken in nineteenth-century Freetown had written forms. Isale Eko served as a melting pot for many of these languages and cultures, leaving a tangible mark on its identity. This cultural fusion is evident in linguistic artifacts and cultural practices, particularly those upheld by esoteric societies like hunting and Orjeh (esoteric society of Yoruba origin that was founded in the nineteenth century by Africans rescued from slave ships and settled in what is the present day Freetown Peninsular). This linguistic evidence is seen in words such as *Awojo, ekushe, kabor, orja, wahala, egberi, awo, diyehdiyeh, rikishi, odun, Agba*, and numerous loanwords from dominant languages and neighboring cultures within the vicinity of Isale Eko.

Unsurprisingly, many of Sierra Leone's creative writers and performers hail from Freetown's Istehn, an area enriched by its cultural diversity. Prominent figures among them include Syl Cheney-Coker, Mohamed Gibril Sesay, Mohamed Sheriff, Eldred Jones, Mohamed Bobson Kamara, Akmid Bakkar Mansaray, Elizabeth L.A. Kamara, Robert Wellesley Cole, and many more. What sets the Isale Eko community apart is its vibrancy and resilience in the face of cultural shifts. While other communities abandoned their traditions in the name of progress, Isale Eko embraced change while preserving its cultural essence. For instance, when some communities discontinued the tradition of celebrating the birthday of Prophet Muhammad with the recitation of Arabic poetry, like the Tunisian Poet Ahmed Farage's famous praise poetry, known amongst Sunni Muslims as Munbihib, Isale Eko continued this practice during the Prophet's birthday celebration. This practice aligns with Islam's emphasis on fostering a united community, transcending individual concerns. The central role of the Mosque in Isale Eko symbolizes this sense of community and change, transforming the *azan* into a commitment to the larger *Ummah* (community of believers). The poet repeatedly references the *azan* as a reminder of what transcends personal needs.

> When I return to you
> I want the imam to read *surat ul naas*
> to remind me of my battles with rats
> deep in the abyss of the odokoko.
> I want him to scream the *Azan*
> atop of that grassy hill
> where we used to herd sheep. (11)

The strong sense of community in Isale Eko draws strength from Islam's emphasis on the *Ummah*. The poet's allusions to Islam and the Quran are recurrent themes, underscoring the profound influence of Islam on the poet's consciousness and the community's way of life. This influence is evident in the observance of the Islamic calendar, which guides and defines everyday life within the community. Some poems, like "Mosque of Cordoba," are steeped in Islamic references and Quranic teachings:

> The naked moon is perched tonight
> away from the dimly lit stars
> Clusters of flycatcher birds
> migrate over a minaret
> erected on a hill
> where scholars chant
> while counting beads
> around a stainless white sheet. (56)

Some other poems, like "The Haunting Cry," summon deities like Ogun, the Yoruba god of iron, into the fray:

> The deserted junction
> awaits the haunting cry of an *orisha*
> The voice of *Ogun* resonates
> within the soul of the heartbroken
> for he who breathes life into *ile aiye*
> brings undying hope. (25)

This juxtaposition underscores the enduring legacy of cultural richness and diversity in Isale Eko, where tradition and change harmonize uniquely and resiliently.

In essence, Isale Eko becomes a microcosm where cultural transformations, threatened by the erasure of traditional values, are met with resistance. The remnants of Yoruba and other languages scattered through songs, rituals, and everyday conversations serve as maps used by the poet to navigate the community's past. In this place, a delicate equilibrium exists between religion and culture. The coexistence of the Imam and the *Agba* the leader of the Orjeh esoteric society illustrates a unique blend of culture and religion that dangerously teeters on the edge of what some might consider as heresy, attracting scrutiny from Wahabi scholars in present-day Sierra Leone. Poets like Ahmed Koroma delve into the depths of history, culture, and religion, using these remnants to preserve the complex cultural heritage of the Isale Eko community. The poet's imagination negotiates through the myriad belief systems to tell a holistic story of his community in profound verses.

The aftermath of the decade-long RUF-Sierra Leone war witnessed a surge in rural-to-urban migration, uprooting cultural heritage, demystifying myths, and blurring lines of demarcation and cultural signposts. This new development poses challenges for communities like Isale Eko, which had forged a distinct identity over centuries. The influx of rural-urban migrants strains the city's capacity to meet the population's needs. The toll is mainly felt in the Istehn (used in the local parlance to refer to the eastern sector of Freetown) and communities like Isale Eko. The population surge and changing dynamics blur the historical portrait of the community in the poet's mind. Consequently, a persistent longing for what once existed creates an elegiac mood in the book, akin to the metronome beat of the *akometa* drums of the Orjeh fraternities echoing through the hills and valleys of Isale Eko during funeral rites. It takes a collaboration of a poet, drummer, muezzin, *Agba*, and other creatives to restore the cultural contours of what was and what Isale Eko has become.

The poems within his three collections, *Of Flour and Tears*, *Along the Odokoko River*, and *The Moon Rises Over Isale Eko*, read like a poet's final endeavor to preserve the cultural integrity of his community. He curates the artistic curves of a people burdened by the history of slavery and migration. The merit of this collection transcends the socio-cultural landscape; it speaks to the poet's ability to shift through the sights and sounds of his community to capture the essence of his people amidst a fading era and against the tide of change sweeping through post-war Sierra Leone. The poet's yearning for the land he left behind, now oceans away, fuels the nostalgia that permeates his work.

In the poem "Silent Soliloquy," the poet skillfully explores themes of migration, nostalgia, and patriotism while employing water as a recurring symbol. This poem offers a poignant reflection on the intricate emotions and experiences of leaving one's homeland. Through evocative imagery, the poet captures the complex emotions of someone who has left their hometown but remains deeply connected to it, highlighting the enduring impact of one's roots and the transformative nature of the immigrant experience.

The theme of migration subtly weaves its way through the poems. The poet hints at a sense of displacement and yearning for a distant homeland. This is evident in lines like, "This is Freetown, my very own town, that I never left in my mind and in my soul" (69), suggesting that physically leaving the town has not erased the poet's emotional connection to it. The mention of "across the ocean, in a rickety boat" alludes to the migration journey, often fraught with danger and uncertainty. Nostalgia permeates the poem as the poet reminisces about his hometown. The line "I carry you around along the Guinea coast" reflects the enduring emotional attachment to the place of origin. The memories of sounds, sights, and smells evoke a deep longing and nostalgia. The poet's inability to forget his town underscores the lasting impact of his past. The poem conveys a profound sense of patriotism and love for the hometown despite the poet's physical absence from it. The repeated reference to "my town" and "my very own town" emphasizes Koroma's strong connection to this homeland. Personal possessive adjectives convey a sense of ownership and pride, further underscored by the poet's vivid descriptions of the town and its people.

Water is a recurring motif in the poems, carrying both literal and metaphorical significance. The "filthy water" that splashes the poet's face on the sidewalk on his return represents the challenges and discomforts faced after migration. Water symbolizes the physical and emotional distance between the poet and his homeland, as the poet mentions being "across the ocean, in a rickety boat." Furthermore, the mention of "bright lights paint my evening sky, a roaring thunder and a rabid dog shiver from underneath a trader's stall" creates a sharp contrast between the new environment and the hometown. The "bright lights" and "roaring thunder" suggest urban life and modernity, while the "rabid dog" shivering under a trader's stall represents the unfamiliar and sometimes threatening aspects of the new place.

In poem after poem, the poet employs simple language, lucid imagery, and poetic license to reconstruct his childhood community. His frustration with his people's corruption, decadence, and obedience is eloquently captured in the poem "Infuriation I." The poem opens with the powerful phrase, "It is the audacity and callousness," immediately setting a tone of accusation and condemnation. The combination of 'audacity' (brazen arrogance) and 'callousness' (lack of empathy) strongly resonates with the theme of societal injustice. The subsequent line, "Born out of a decomposed state of mind," introduces a metaphor of decay, hinting at a corrupted mindset underlying the societal issues being explored. The imagery of "Tearing apart a woven fabric of hope" reinforces the idea of societal disintegration. The phrase "tearing apart" intensifies this image, which conveys a sense of violence and irreversible damage. The poet's reference to "religiosity and feigned optimism" and "calculated rationale of the elites" paints a picture of a society of religious and intellectual facades masking insincerity and self-interest. "Feigned optimism" suggests a superficial positivity that conceals deeper problems, while "calculated rationale" implies a manipulative and strategic approach to maintaining power and privilege.

The poet's intense and unconventional imagery becomes particularly striking with the lines "noxious fumes suffocating the masses / Emitting from the flatulent exhaust of pigs." Here, the juxtaposition of "noxious fumes" and "flatulent exhaust of pigs" gaudily illustrates the oppressive and dehumanizing effects of the actions of those in power. The use of animal imagery emphasizes the degrading nature of their behavior. Koroma portrays a dystopian scene where the streets are filled with "zombies and robots." This metaphorical description of the masses reinforces the idea of a dehumanized and docile population controlled by the whims of the elites. The rampant use of a synthetic drug in the poet's beloved city, leading to the mass zombification of the youth, underscores the poet's metaphor of zombies and robots.

The poem's closing lines convey a crescendo of frustration and disillusionment. Koroma evokes a sense of helplessness and betrayal with "futility of hope" and "courage betrayed." The refusal to "speak truth to power" further highlights the complacency that perpetuates the status quo. The final stanza, "denial of the ominous signs and lessons / From yesterday's war, of the litany in history," evokes a sense of historical amnesia and repetition. The poet suggests that the failure to learn from history and the refusal to acknowledge warning signs contribute to the cycle of infuriation and despair.

Indeed, the poem "Infuriation I," along with several others in the collection, employs evocative language and powerful imagery to convey the theme of societal disillusionment and frustration. Using decay, manipulation, and dehumanization metaphors, the poet sheds light on the stark divide between the privileged few and the suffering masses. The poem's language choices and rich imagery effectively contribute to a poignant exploration of the darker aspects of society and human nature in present-day Sierra Leone. Even the rot and frustration expressed in the poem come from deep love and longing for a change in the country of his birth, and the disappointment is anchored deep in his soul, even from afar:

> It is the futility of hope, of courage betrayed
> Of the refusal to speak truth to power
> It is the denial of the ominous signs and lessons
> From yesterday's war, of the litany in history
> That infuriates the crap out of me. (47)

In his 2022 lecture titled "Poetry and the Human Voice," delivered at the annual forum of the Nigerian National Order of Merit (NNOM), Niyi Osundare argued that: "Poetry has its own way of harking back to its primal origins, of insisting on a reunion of the Mouth and Ear, of reclaiming its primordial kingship with music. For no good poetry can do without music any more felicitously than honey can do without its sweetness" (16). Osundare's assertion is exemplified in Koroma's poetry, with its rhythm, music, and aspiration to transcend the confines of the printed page and come alive on the lips and in the ears.

The musical quality evident in these collections of poems is a persistent nostalgic melody that resonates throughout the verses. At times, it crescendos; at others, it softly serenades readers, guiding them along the Odokoko through tears and sacrificial flour from dawn to sunrise at Isale Eko. This lends credence to the notion that every language possesses unique music, and every poet interprets it differently. For Koroma, there is a persistent melancholy of longing for the homeland, which is evident in his work.

The collection's celestial images, water motifs, spiritual incantations, and everyday vignettes make it compelling. Whereas Koroma's first two collections prepare the reader for a journey of socio-cultural discovery, his latest work, *The Moon Rises Over Isale Eko*, transports the reader on a boat ride through a diverse range of waters to wharves, riverbanks, and places within the poet's imagination. His use of water to convey his thoughts becomes particularly compelling when one considers a metaphor within the context of an implicit comparison used to give meaning vividly. I.A. Richards' highly accepted work on metaphor distinguishes between the "tenor" and the "vehicle" of a metaphor. The "tenor" is the idea being expressed or the subject of the comparison, while the "vehicle" is the image by which the idea is conveyed.

In the poem "Road to Jange," the poet skillfully employs "tenor" and "vehicle" to create a rich, evocative piece that engages readers on multiple levels. The poem deepens our understanding of the emotional complexities and intense imagery associated with the described journey through these metaphorical elements. The "tenor" in this poem is the central theme or subject: the journey to Jange. The journey symbolizes more than just a physical passage; it carries emotional and symbolic weight. It is a journey of recollections, memories, and emotions, as suggested by the phrase "down this road of recollections." This "tenor" invites readers to consider the layered meanings of the journey beyond its literal aspect.

The "vehicle," on the other hand, is the set of metaphors and images used to convey and enhance the understanding of the "tenor." The poet masterfully weaves a series of glowing metaphors to evoke a sensory and emotional experience for the readers. First, there are the boulders and potholes, an assemblage of rocks. These images conjure a rough and challenging road, symbolizing the obstacles and hardships that life's journey presents. The "vehicle" paints a picture of a difficult path, mirroring the challenges one might face in navigating personal and emotional terrains. Second, "the crimson lorry moves at bicycle speed": Here, the metaphor of the "crimson lorry" moving at "bicycle speed" captures a sense of slowness, perhaps indicating the sluggish pace of progress. This image contrasts with the swifter movement normally associated with a lorry, highlighting the tension between anticipation and the slow passage of time. Third, "Tonight, the moon will come out early, and the smell of piassava and palm kernel will blend well with the aroma from the Jange River" (17). These scents evoke a multi-sensory experience, inviting readers to imagine the sensory richness of the landscape. The merging of scents suggests a harmonious blending of natural elements, potentially reflecting a sense of unity or connection. Fourth, "the ragged old truck blows dust into my eyes.... the unbearable sun melts my melanin pigment away" (16). These metaphors employ tactile and visual imagery to convey the physical discomfort and challenges of the journey. The "unbearable sun" that "melts my melanin pigment away" speaks to the intensity of the experience, perhaps hinting at a metaphorical exposure or vulnerability. Fifth, Tinkonko, Bumpeh, Sembehun, Serabu… Motuo, Bauya, Semabu, Luawa: These place names serve as "vehicles" that anchor the poem's journey in specific locations. They evoke a sense of geographic progression, enhancing the poem's sense of movement and journey.

Through the intricate layering of "tenor" and "vehicle," the poet creates a multi-dimensional reading experience. Readers are prompted to engage with the journey's emotional nuances, sensory details, and symbolic resonances. The metaphors facilitate a deeper appreciation of the poem's themes, such as the interplay between hope and despair, the passage of time, and the exploration of personal history. The poem's rich imagery and metaphorical language invite readers to reflect not only on the physical journey but also on the deeper emotional and psychological aspects of the human experience.

The poem "After the Rain" offers a rich and contemplative exploration of nature's transformations following a storm. The theory of "tenor" and "vehicle" of metaphor posits that metaphors work by associating one entity (the "tenor") with another (the "vehicle"), drawing parallels to illuminate aspects of the "tenor" that might not be immediately apparent. In this poem, the "tenor" could be interpreted as the emotional and physical aftermath of the storm, while the "vehicle" is the natural world and its various elements. The opening lines of "After the Rain," "Last night the sky split open / and the grey running clouds collide / into a mighty thunderstorm," establish the setting and the imminent change. Here, the "sky split open" could be seen as a symbolic representation of emotional intensity, while the "grey running clouds" colliding might symbolize the convergence of conflicting emotions or experiences. The line "A melancholic breeze blew past my house as we huddled tightly underneath a wooden bed" blends the "tenor" and "vehicle," intertwining the emotional state with the physical shelter. The "melancholic breeze" serves as a vehicle to represent the lingering emotions after the storm, and seeking refuge beneath the "wooden bed" symbolizes protection and vulnerability. Moving forward, "After the rain, we witness an egret perched atop a grazing cow, feeding on crickets, butterflies, and moths" creates an interesting metaphorical juxtaposition. The egret atop the grazing cow symbolizes how unexpected beauty can emerge from the mundane or chaotic. The "feeding on crickets, butterflies, and moths" emphasizes the natural order of life and implies the interconnectedness of all living things, echoing the theme of renewal after adversity and the concept of "interbeing" or interconnectedness. Similarly, "After the rain, we watch a fluffy ball float through the pungent air from the huge cotton tree at the bottom of the creek" captures the sense of enchantment and wonderment after the storm. The "fluffy ball" floating represents lightness and playfulness, contrasting with the heaviness of the storm. The "cotton tree" symbolizes resilience, as it remains rooted despite the storms. The closing lines, "But now the rushing clouds have departed the naked sky, and the overflowing dam no longer threatens the town," conclude the metaphorical journey. The "rushing clouds" departing and the "overflowing dam" no longer posing a threat signify a return to calmness and balance. The "naked sky" suggests a sense of exposure, vulnerability, and clarity after the storm's turmoil.

Aristotle views metaphor "as the greatest thing by far" (Holman and Hormon, 298) and Ezra Pound agrees by calling apt metaphor "the hallmark of genius" (ibid.). Both recognize the deeper insight of poets to see similarities in seemingly dissimilar things. When a metaphor is inclined to have dynamic and referential characteristics and becomes a direct means by itself, it is what Cleanth Brooks refers to as a metaphor behaving as a symbol (ibid., 299). In this collection, the metaphor morphs into symbols. Water meanders from lakes, rivers, ravines, and drainages to become a controlling image as dominant and compelling as the ocean separating the poet from his beloved homeland. The collection would not exist without water, just as life would not exist without water. Koroma uses the liquid of life to convey the idea of nostalgia, cleansing, purification, and sustenance.

The Moon Rises Over Isaleko is drenched in waters of all sorts with the compelling force to dial the nostalgic channel within the reader's soul. In "Hopscotch," where the poet recollects a childhood game, children play in the river with paper boats: "I wish you were here, / To throw pebbles into the air, / To dip a crumpled paper / Into water flowing down the gutter" (26). And in the last stanza of the poem, a longing for past innocence and joy looms: "Let us return to where we belong, / Underneath the breadfruit tree, / Where we found solace after a game / Of hopscotch, / At the corner where everything grows" (17).

The following poem, "The Morning Cobweb," features the diamondiferous Sewa River, which flows from the east to the south before depositing its water into the ocean. The poet perpetuates the dominant imagery of water as the ultimate vehicle for carrying his message from the Odokoko and Jange rivers to the sea. "My desire to dance along the riverbank, To the jaunty music of the Sewa, Overtakes my uneasiness, And my wish for a safer ground" (16). The poet employs the collective pronoun, inviting everyone to roll with him playfully on the sand: "Let us roll on the sand, / Among conch shells / Like unknown urchins, / Though I must admit, / The water around me Has grown against my stunted self" (16). The poem's pervasive river imagery culminates in a powerful waterfall in "Dance," where the poet immerses us in its shallow depths. This act cleanses our unforgiving souls and inspires a dance toward progress. The consistent use of water imagery and the quest for purification throughout the poems underscore the thematic significance of water as a vital, life-sustaining element in the poet's imagination.

"The Mystic Road" may remind the reader of Robert Frost's "The Road Not Taken." Both poems explore the theme of choices and the consequences of those choices in life's journey. While Frost's poem is a classic in American literature, Koroma's "Mystic Road" offers a fresh perspective on a similar theme. Robert Frost's "The Road Not Taken" is written in the first person, with a clear narrative structure. It presents a moment where the speaker must choose between two divergent paths in the woods. The poem employs a regular rhyme scheme and meter, creating a sense of order and control in the narration. In contrast, Ahmed Koroma's "Mystic Road" utilizes a more fragmented and free-form structure. The poem lacks a straightforward narrative and is presented in disjointed images and vignettes. It adopts a more modernist and experimental style, reflecting the chaotic nature of the journey it portrays. Frost's poem carries a tone of reflection and regret. The speaker contemplates their life choices and the roads not taken, suggesting a sense of longing and ambiguity about the path chosen. The imagery of the two diverging roads in the woods is a powerful metaphor for choices in life. On the other hand, Koroma's "Mystic Road" conveys a more immediate and visceral tone. The poem presents rich and often disturbing imagery, such as the "red guillotine blade" branded on the boy's arm or the "ragtag militias" that ransack the village square. These images evoke a sense of chaos, struggle, and resilience in the face of adversity.

Both poems explore the consequences of choices thematically, but they do so in distinct ways. Frost's "The Road Not Taken" focuses on individual agency and the impact of personal preferences on one's life. It suggests that even seemingly small decisions can have significant and lasting effects. "Mystic Road" by Koroma offers a broader perspective focused on collective and societal themes. It portrays a community grappling with hardship and loss, emphasizing that choices are not made in isolation but within the context of a larger, often tumultuous world. The poem's message centers on resilience and the enduring human spirit, even in adversity.

It is safe to say that the crossroads are a familiar home for poets, especially for a poet like Koroma who left a war-torn country to sojourn in America, while his soul readies itself to join him. The crossroads serve as a home for a poet who conceptualizes in his mother tongue and writes in an acquired language. Above all, the constant battle between the author's conscious and subconscious is a tour de force in his poetry, evident in every line, even when he agonizes on the Mystic Road before embarking on a path with no apparent return. The poem captures the eleven-year war and the trail of pain it left behind in the poet's native land. Yet it ends with hope anchored in celestial imagery. "But the sun will rise again another day, And the lives lost will be celebrated once more" (20).

We return once more to the image of water prevalent throughout the collection. In poem after poem, water flows through nearly every verse; in some, it is a river, a stream, and in others, a mere sprinkle; hence, water is the life-sustaining metaphor of the collection. It runs, washes, cleanses, drowns, and soaks everything in its path. The feeling of drowning or washing is evident in most lines. The poet subconsciously offers a canoe to the reader, but lo and behold, it is a broken canoe, abandoned and infested with termites. The canoe is not only broken but held back by storms. Despite this, the longing to embark, to venture forth, permeates, or is it to return to a fabled past with the aid of a flying mat, akin to the tale of Aladdin?

The flight of imagination soars deep into mysticism, spirituality, superstition, and rituals that shape Koroma's imaginary landscape. In "The Haunting Cry," the poet takes us to the shrine of the fraternities, otherwise known as *ile aiye*, to reveal the *orisha*s (deities) of Yoruba mythology. Our memories retrace the cultural footprints of the abolition of slavery and the return of free Africans to Fullah Tong and Bambara Tong: "The deserted junction awaits the haunting cry of an *orisha*. The voice of Ogun resonates within the soul of the heartbroken, for he who breathes life into *ile aiye* brings undying hope" (25). Juxtaposing this poem with "Dawn" gives readers a glimpse of the tensions wracking the poet. "Dawn" speaks of the Muezzin's call to prayer and the *kalimatu Shahadat*, Muslims' proclamation of belief in a monolithic God and in Mohamed as his Prophet – both pathways to Allah as taught by Mohammad, the messenger of Allah. Conversely, "The Haunting Cry" tells of Ogun, the Yoruba *orisha* of iron. The *ile aiye* (shrine) and the minaret both reside in our poet's mind and reflect in the multi-layered imagery of his work and the crossroads of his consciousness:

> The muezzin walks away from the tower
> his voice rumbling through the morning air.
> He pauses, not in a state of hurriedness
> to bear the burden of others and himself.
> He then mutters the shahada
> and returns to make the final call,
> his rasping voice piercing the masjid wall. ("Dawn," 25)

The recurring water imagery surfaces again in "Green Hill" surfaces again, with a destructive force mitigated only by the pastor's intervention: "Last night, the water came gushing out, and my brother and his paper boat drifted away. But he was rescued from the liquid spirit by the pastor of the church with the stained glass, the one who taught us to scream hallelujah and then traded our effigy for a tiny cross" (32). The significance of water in Koroma's poetry evokes the symbolism found in Herman Melville's *Moby Dick*, where water provides both the setting and the anchor for the narrative. In "Bondage," Koroma's fixation on the water as both a healing element and a destructive force reaches its zenith with an allusion to the waters of Noah's ark. He employs the imagery of a dove returning to a colorful nest, an ark that saves us from the flood of bondage, and a rainbow of our creation to signal the end of our captivity. Through this, the poet suggests that our destiny lies in our own hands:

> Son of Ham, in perpetual bondage,
> enslaved for his dark skin.
> So, we built the ark
> That saved us from the flood
> along the Odokoko River.

> We created the rainbow,
> then let the dove fly north
> and the crow you held in captivity.
> Heavy rock against my heaving heart,
> pain for rejecting to honour your gods.
> A crow will sing in the dead of night,
> A dove will return to its colourful nest,
> and the chains that held us in bondage
> shall be broken and made soft;
> freedom once again shall be free. ("Bondage" 34)

Even from the banks of the Rio Grande, which provides the backdrop for the poem "Lost in Juarez," the centrality of water as a vehicle to convey the tenor of nostalgia is effectively exploited:

> She revels in the drizzling rain
> against her window pane
> reminding her of those misty nights
> in Paso del Norte
> many moons ago
> alongside the Rio Grande
> She slept underneath palm fronds
> and bamboo sheets
> moonlit sky, fireflies
> and wet croaking frogs
> far from the country
> she called her home
> a beautiful land
> she named Sierra Leone. (35)

Even the burial ritual for Alagba in the poem titled "Elegy for Alagba" takes place by the stream, perpetuating the centrality of water in the purification of the departed soul for a life beyond: "Dust settles over an open field near the stream in Isale Eko, where we form a circle by a fireside and play a mournful tune, a farewell melody for a departing soul" (37). Similarly, the significance of water as a vessel for conveying meaning in offerings to God and deities is depicted in the poem "Hodge-Podge" (42). The poet longs for the purity of the water to be preserved before human neglect contaminates it for both humanity and the divine: "Let it sail down the Odokoko before we cast filth beneath the wooden bridge into the vibrant freshwater that meanders through the houses on rickety stilts. Can the tears we collect after the ritual dance suffice to cleanse our impure souls after we prostrate for Elegbara?" (37 – Elegbara is one of many Yoruba deities).

The thematic imagery of water takes center stage in the poem "Forgiveness," where the poet invokes Ogun, the god of iron, and Yemeja, the ocean goddess.

"As Ogun springs from the body of Yemeja": this line establishes a connection between Ogun, often associated with war and conflict, and Yemeja, the ocean goddess. Water, personified by Yemeja, serves as the source from which Ogun emerges, highlighting that even in conflict, water plays a central role in the cycle of life and transformation: "We wash our faces with tears of joy, the tears that roll after the mighty storm, the celebration following the thunderous roar" (53). Here, water is explicitly linked to emotions of joy and celebration. These tears of joy, akin to water, cleanse and heal the soul after a period of turmoil, symbolized by the mighty storm and thunderous roar. This imagery underscores how water, in the form of tears, fosters inner peace and emotional release.

"Ha! Not too long ago, Ogun wept; the path we tread was dark and muddy; the moon appeared red, depriving us of the radiance of chiefs and the departed" (53). The reference to a dark and muddy path and the red moon implies a period of strife and obscurity. Water, in this context, represents a return to clarity and purity. The memory of Ogun weeping and the muddy path serve as nostalgic reminders of past conflict, amplifying the significance of water in restoring peace and cleansing the soul. "The fire burns the shrub that cures the path to manhood." In this line, water is indirectly alluded to through its absence. Fire and burning symbolize destruction, while the shrub that cures represents healing. On the other hand, water can extinguish the fire and facilitate the curing process. This underscores water's role in restoring peace and balance.

"As the rain pours at the doorstep of the healer / Isale Eko is reborn / Peace resonates around the hills" (54). The rain, a potent representation of water, pours at the healer's doorstep, signifying healing and rejuvenation. Isale Eko's rebirth is intrinsically linked to the presence of rain, emphasizing water's central role in fostering peace and renewal. The mention of peace echoing around the hills reinforces the idea of water as a transformative force promoting tranquility and nostalgia. In this poem, water is both a physical element and a symbol of emotional cleansing, healing, and the restoration of peace. It is a powerful force connecting the past (nostalgia) with the present (peace) within the poem's narrative.

Water imagery has long been prevalent in literature, conveying various meanings based on context. For instance, in Shakespeare's *Macbeth*, water symbolizes purification following the heinous murder of King Duncan. Macbeth's quest for water to cleanse his hands enhances the image of water as a metaphor for purification in literature, even though he questions water's ability to wash away the sin he has committed: "Will all great Neptune's Ocean wash this blood clean from my hand?" (*Macbeth*, Act 2 Scene 2). Unlike Macbeth, who doubts the effectiveness of water in cleansing his hands or absolving his sins, our poet firmly believes in water's power as an agent of purification, renewal, and change. Koroma assigns equal relevance to water in this collection. His work effectively utilizes water as a symbol of rebirth, cleansing, renewal, fluidity, patience, freedom, and resilience.

The abundant presence of water in these evocative poems raises intriguing ideas about the deeper meanings the poet passionately intends to convey. In some poems, he vividly projects the unwavering resilience of water to his compatriots, gently teaching them the profound value of patience in persistently finding a way even when it seems impossible. Water is an enchanting metaphor for rebirth after death or renewed hope. It serves as a soulful ablution for the spirit of the nation, reflecting the poets background in chemistry, and a heartfelt offering to the revered ancestors, much like his compatriots' sacred offerings of *furrah* (rice flour) with water to invoke the spiritual. Water elegantly functions as a mode of transportation for the poet's perpetual, intricate physical and psychological journeys.

Koroma excels in expressing his yearning to return to his homeland, earning recognition as a poet of nostalgia among his colleagues. The vast Atlantic Ocean physically separates him from Sierra Leone, with the Odokoko River in his beloved neighborhood feeding into the ocean, widening the gap between him and his homeland. It is understandable why water is a central metaphor in Koroma's writing, as we are all connected to water somehow.

Koroma's nostalgia transcends physical places, weaving together history, culture, people, and nature to create a mosaic of memories in readers' minds. He achieves this through profound simplicity, lucid fluidity, and resilience, mirroring the recurring water imagery in his poems. For Koroma, nostalgia serves as a dynamic tool to probe and renew the ethos and values of society. His poetry flows like pure water from the mountains of Isale Eko, traversing various social and intellectual streams to become as essential as water in Sierra Leone's literary world. The poet's near-religious adherence to the metaphor of water as a vehicle to convey his ideas makes the collection read like a single poem, with a unified metaphor encapsulating themes of nostalgia, decay, corruption, and longing.

Attributed to Kahlil Gibran, the esteemed American-Lebanese poet, the poem "Fear" beautifully encapsulates the existential trepidation of a river nearing the ocean. As it approaches the vastness of the sea, the river fears losing its identity within the overwhelming expanse. Yet, it cannot turn back:

> The river needs to take the risk
> Of entering the ocean
> Because only then will fear disappear
> Because that is where the river will know
> It's not about disappearing into the ocean
> But of becoming the ocean.

The Moon Rises Over Isale Eko observes the ailing Odokoko River, the ever-flowing Jange River, the diamond-rich Sewa River, and even the humble trickles from gullies and gutters journeying toward the boundless ocean. The rivers face the intimidating prospect of losing their distinct identities and shared histories. However, as the Odokoko River merges with the sea, it symbolizes a universal pursuit of transformation. Koroma has undeniably carved a niche through his poetic odyssey, securing a prestigious place as one of Sierra Leone's most formidable post-war poets. By celebrating the interconnectedness of life's many facets and highlighting water as an essential element, Koroma leaves readers contemplating: Are we interbeings or one being on an eternal journey toward becoming a single ocean of existence?

Works Cited

Bangura, Saidu. "A Roadmap to Sierra Leone English: A Sociohistorical and Ecological Perspective." PhD Thesis, Universidad de Las Palmas de Gran Canaria. 2016. https://accedacris.ulpgc.es/bitstream/10553/17690/3/0724891_0 0000_0000.pdf. Accessed 17 September 2024.

Frost, Robert, "The Road Not Taken," in George McMichael, J.C. Levenson, Leo Marx, E. David Smith, Mae Claxton Miller, and Susan Bunn, *Concise Anthology of American Literature* (Upper Saddle River, NJ: Prentice Hall, 1998).

Gibran, Kahlil, "Fear" (n.d.; available at https://www.tennesonwoolf.com/fear-khalil-gibran. Accessed 17 September 2024).

Gibran, Kahlil, *Sand and Foam* (New York: Knopf Doubleday, 1926).

Holman, C. Hugh, and Harmon, William, *A Handbook to Literature* (New York: Macmillan, 1986).

Koroma, Ahmed, *Along the Odokoko River* (Freetown: Sierra Leonean Writers Series, 2016).

Koroma, Ahmed, *The Moon Rises Over Isale Eko* (Freetown: Sierra Leonean Writers Series, 2019).

Koroma, Ahmed, *Of Flour and Tears* (Baltimore: PublishAmerica, 2019).

Osundare, Niyi, *Poetry and the Human Voice* (Ibadan: Kraft Books, 2022).

Shakespeare, William, *Macbeth* (Glasgow: Geddes and Grosset, 2006).

Chapter 3

English Language Learning and Intelligibility: Idiomaticity, Sierra Leonean English and Sierra Leonean Fiction

MOMODU TURAY

Barely four years after Sierra Leone attained its independence, Eldred Durosimi Jones called for the codification of its English by asking teachers of English to study specimens of both spoken and written English in Sierra Leone in order to decide what 'our' standard is (1965, 38). Sierra Leoneans have heeded this call as is shown in the works of Bubuakei Jabbi (1972), Joe Pemagbi (1989), Miriam Conteh-Morgan (1997), Saidu Bangura (2015), and Momodu Turay (2017). However, these teachers-cum-linguists have generally paid more attention to the lexical features of the variety with little or no attention given to its idioms which could help give the variety its Sierra Leonean stamp. This chapter seeks to examine the idioms that have emerged among Sierra Leonean writers. The focus is on the idioms that have been modified from Standard British English, those that have been influenced by the indigenous languages to express Sierra Leoneans' views of the world. The study further examines the implications of these idioms in the learning of English in Sierra Leone.

The most recent study on idioms in the country is Turay's *A Survey of Sierra Leonean English* (2017) which examines, among others, the phonological, lexical, grammatical, and discoursal features that are typical in the English usage of educated Sierra Leoneans. However, the idioms discussed in that study are not given a detailed treatment because they are sub-categorized under lexical features. Moreover, the data was collected from the media which has shared the blame for the deterioration in the standard of English in the country (Conteh, I. 1999; Osho 2022). The present study involves Sierra Leonean authors, most of whom are university graduates with a better exposure to English, and their English usage is therefore expected to get a positive response from native and non-native speakers of English.

An idiom is defined as 'a group of words whose meaning cannot be explained in terms of the habitual meanings of the words that make up the piece of language' (Todd 1987, 86), or as 'a number of words which when taken together, have a different meaning from the individual meanings of each word' (Seidl and McMordie 1988, 12–13), or further still, 'an expression whose meaning cannot be inferred from the meanings of its parts' (Cruse 1986, 37). A common rule found in all English idioms is the rule of fixed collocation. In other words, the group of words that constitutes an idiom should be fixed. This is what Katie Wales means when she states that English 'phrases are characteristically fixed in COLLOCATION' (1997, 231).[1] Platt et al. (1984, 107–10) present a brief overview and several examples of the emerging idioms in the new Englishes. These idioms follow specific patterns which include the combination of two idioms to form one new idiom, variance of existing idioms in speech or writing that are due to pronunciation difference in that particular variety, lexico-grammatical variance of existing British or American English idioms, expressions combining elements from English and indigenous languages, loan translations of idioms from indigenous languages, and creative forms of idioms.

The idioms that will be discussed in this study demonstrate some of the patterns mentioned above. The data was collected from twelve texts. The researcher read each of them paying attention to expressions that are modified, and those that are translated. To check the identified samples which are modified, the following idiom dictionaries published by British establishments were used: *Oxford Dictionary of Idioms* (Siefring 2004), *Cambridge International Dictionary of Idioms* (White 1988), *Oxford Advanced Learner's Dictionary* (10th ed., Hornby 2020), *Longman Pocket Idioms Dictionary* (Lee 2001), and *Dictionary of Phrasal Verbs* (Sinclair 1989). The data was collected from the following texts: *Who Is to Blame?* – WIB (A. M. A. Sesay 2016), *Landscape of Memories* – LM (O. F. Sesay 2015), *The Dream* – TD (Koso-Thomas 2018), *The Diamonds* – TD (J. S. Conteh 1997), *In Search of Sons* – ISS (J. S. Conteh 2007), *So the Path Does Not Die* – SPDD (Hollist 2012), *We're Not Our Fathers* – WNOF (J. L. Kamara 2016), *This Side of Nothingness* – TSN (M. G. Sesay 2015), *The Mouths of the Junction* – TMJ (M. G. Sesay 2017), *Pope Francis, Politics and the Mabanta Boy* – PFPMB (Tarawallie 2019), *Thursday's Child, My Journey So Far* – TCMJSF (P. Foday 2018), and *The Little Apprentice Tailor* – TLAT (M. Kamara 1994).

To achieve clarity, the data are presented in tables (inspired by Kamtchueng's work on non-standard idioms in Cameroon English Literature [2014]) and are divided into two categories, namely modified idioms and idioms from local languages. The modified idioms are identified in relation to Standard British English because it has been the model in schools since Britain declared Sierra Leone as a crown colony in 1808 (Fyle and Jones 1980). Tables 1 and 2 respectively present the modified idioms and the translations from the home languages.

---

[1] Capitals original.

Table 1 shows the modified idioms with the following information: the idioms, their British equivalents, the affected words or morphemes, the modification processes involved, and the sources of the idioms. The modified idioms are created from one of the following processes: substitution, addition, and deletion. Moreover, some of the modified idioms exhibit more than one of the processes through which they are created.

Table 2 presents the idioms from the texts, their equivalents in the local languages, their meanings, the languages involved, and their sources. The local languages are recorded in two ways. First, Krio is recorded because, as the de facto lingua franca in the country, all the authors are expected to be proficient in it. Second, the other languages recorded are some of the authors' native languages. The possibility is that they would have thought about the idioms in their native languages and have therefore attempted to translate them into English.

'Slap in the face' in sample 1 means 'an action that insults or upsets someone' (White 1988, 355). It is written on the data as 'slap on the faces' where the preposition 'on' has replaced 'in'. In sample 2, the idiom 'on his seat' appears in British English as 'in the driving seat' which means 'to be in control' (Lee 2001, 211). The deviation is caused by the substitution of the preposition 'in' and the absence of the particle 'driving'. In sample 3, 'to look in (on somebody)' means 'to make a short visit to a place especially when they are ill or need help' (Hornby 2020, 928). The data indicates the omission of the adverb 'in'. 'Free rein' in sample 4 is an idiom which means to 'allow (someone) ... to develop (his/her ideas or emotions) and not to try to control them' (Hollist 2012, 147). The wrong word in the data can be attributed to the fact that rein and reign are homophones and can therefore differ in meaning and spelling. It would appear that, having learnt a word, the author tends to use it to cover its homophonous partner. This accounts for the contextual error in this sample. Sample 5 shows the idiom 'on behalf' which means 'the representative of somebody or instead of them' (Hornby 2020, 126). Its attachment to 'myself,' therefore, constitutes a collocation breach. The idiom in sample 6 'in your face' means 'aggressively obvious, assertive' (Siefring 2004, 100). The preposition 'before' has wrongly replaced 'in'. A possible factor for this deviation is the transfer of the structure of Krio, Sierra Leone's de facto lingua franca into English. In sample 7, the idiom 'to make a noise' means 'to complain a lot about something' (White 1988, 272). The deviation is as a result of the omission of the indefinite article in the data. To 'look someone up and down' means to 'scrutinise someone carefully' (Siefring 2004, 177). Significantly, the idiom in sample 8 'to look someone up' means to 'visit a person ... after not having seen them for a very long time' (Sinclair 1989, 210). Given that Marc surreptitiously flees abroad after impregnating the fifteen-year-old school-going narrator and that he never admits to being the one who impregnates her justify that the idiom in sample 8 is a deviation from the Standard British usage not only because of the change in structure but also because of the change in meaning. To 'be lost on someone' means to 'fail to influence or be noticed or appreciated by someone' (Siefring 2004, 178). Sample 9 therefore shows the insertion of the 'out' particle in the data.

TABLE 1 Idioms Derived from the Modification of British Expressions

No.	Modified Expressions	British expressions	Words or morphemes affected	Processes involved	Sources
1.	This was a slap on the faces of those who had ridiculed him.	This was a slap in the faces of those who had ridiculed him.	On-in	Substitution	LOM, p.89
2.	He spent very little time on his seat.	He spent very little time in his driving seat.	On-in driving seat	Substitution, deletion	WITB, p.7
3.	At first, they looked … on me with suspicion, as one sent to ensure they worked to schedule without rest.	At first, they looked in on me with suspicion, as one sent to ensure they worked to schedule without rest.	In	Deletion	TD, p.85
4.	Resentment and anger took free reign of her body and she welcomed them.	Resentment and anger took free rein of her body and she welcomed them.	Reign-rein	Substitution	SPDD, p.173
5.	I owe you an apology on behalf of myself and my wife.	I owe you an apology on behalf of my family.	Myself – family	Substitution	ISS, p.189
6.	… they point their guns at you and before your very face take away your sweat.	… they point their guns at you and in your very face take away your sweat.	Before – in	Substitution	TSN pp.67–8
7.	Some children were making noise out in the rain.	Some children were making a noise out in the rain.	The indefinite article	Deletion	TD, p.197
8.	Marc himself paid a visit to Sierra Leone and looked me up…	Marc himself paid a visit to Sierra Leone and looked me up and down.	And down	Deletion	TCMJSF, p.27
9.	… the fact of the existence of African traditional religion was not lost out on President Koroma.	… the fact of the existence of African traditional religion was not lost on President Koroma	Out	Addition	PFPMB p.202

TABLE 2 Idioms Derived from the Tranlation of Indigenous Languages

No.	Expression from texts	Idioms derived	Indigenous language expressions	Meanings	Language	Source
10	...my parents dried their own tears.	To dry one's tears.	fɔ wep yu yay	To console oneself	Krio	TCMJSF, p.16
11.	I don't vomit and lick it.	To vomit and lick something.	Ngeh baali wu nga kɔmi	To renege on what one has said	Mende	TD p.154
12.	She did not have a head for trade.	To have a head for trade.	Fɔ gɛt ed fɔ tred	To have a business acumen	Krio	WNO F, p.75
13.	Bad-hearted people started badmouthing him.	To have a bad heart.	Fɔ gɛt bad at	To be envious of people	Krio	TMJ, p.34
14.	Bad-hearted people started badmouthing him.	To bad mouth.	dà n yàmà	To gossip	Madingo	TMJ, p.34
15.	It was in this place that I ate soil.	To eat soil in a place.	nɔ dɛ di kɔbɔf	To be born and bred in a place	Temne	TMJ, p.67
16.	I can't understand why a son of the soil will be so uneducated in the ways of his people.	Son of the soil.	ɔkɔsu gbeŋ gbeŋ	A true indigene	Temne	LM, p.67
17.	...how can I cook a soup without tasting it?	To prepare a meal that you don't eat.	Yu go kuk sup yu nthat you do	You cannot serve your community without thinking about yourself	Krio	TMJ p.13
18.	Now go and eat that dry rice in the table quickly.	Dry rice.	fɔ it drai rɛs	Rice without sauce	Krio	TLAT

The above deviations show violations in the forms of the original idioms that are found in British English. The authors have modified the idioms either by substitution (as is shown in samples 1, 2, 4, 5, and 6), by deletion (as is shown in samples 2, 3, 7, and 8) or by addition (as is shown in sample 9). The modification of idioms has been attributed to linguistic innovations which emanate inter alia from transfer from local languages, acquisitional limitations, and inadequate teaching' (Kachru 1986, 21–2). However, with the exception of the deviation in sample 8, the structural changes have not changed the meanings of the idioms. This means that the forms of the idioms have changed, but the meanings have remained the same. This finding is related to Cruse's description of an English idiom as 'a lexical complex which is semantically simplex' (1986, 37).

The idioms relating to the home languages show Sierra Leoneans' views of the world. To get pregnant out of wedlock is a disgrace that can emotionally destabilize heads of families (see sample 10); true love comes from the heart as is shown in Finda's response to Gibao's proposal to marry her (see sample 11); human beings are endowed with their weaknesses as is indicated by Ngor Fatty's inability to account for her business capital (see sample 12); envy and engaging in ill-natured talks about people are despicable acts (see samples 13 and 14, respectively); to be born and to be bred in a particular place create an unbreakable bond between one and the environment and its people (see samples 15 and 16, respectively); serving one's community does not preclude one from serving oneself (see sample 17), and an average family can live on rice – the country's staple food – without sauce (sample 18).

Jones' call for the codification of English in order to decide on the Sierra Leonean variety has opened a Pandora's Box with respect to the learning of English in Sierra Leone. For example, a dictionary of Sierra Leonean English and an authoritative grammar that documents the rules and structures of the variety are yet to be a reality. Moreover, the authors studied here are academics ranging from university graduates to accomplished professors of English both in the country and abroad. More importantly, their works are being read in Sierra Leonean schools and colleges. This means Sierra Leonean pupils and students are being exposed to the two categories of idioms discussed above. Of these two categories, the one regarding the modification of idioms appears to be having a negative impact on the learning of English in the country. This is mainly because, in the West African Senior School Certificate Examination, candidates' English Language scripts are graded out of 100 marks for the English Language Paper 2. 50 marks are allotted to the Continuous Writing section which includes 20 marks for Expression, 10 marks each for Content, Organization, and Mechanical Accuracy. Examiners give priority to candidates for the appropriate use of idioms. On the other hand, examiners penalize candidates by deducting points for, among other things, wrong spelling or grammatical errors as well as for wrong use of idiomatic expressions like those shown above. The above 'deviant' idioms can partly account for the poor performance of Sierra Leonean candidates in English Language examinations.

Significantly, it would appear that this deviation type can also be spotted among the setters of the English Language Paper as is illustrated in the substitution of the verb in the following sentence: 'At the last minute, he developed cold feet' (instead of 'he HAD cold feet', West African Examination Council 2015, 9; emphasis added). Language 'experts' in the sub-region have replaced the original British idiom 'to have cold feet' with 'to develop cold feet'. In order to address this problem, priority should be given to the teaching of Standard British idioms in schools and colleges with emphasis on their meanings, forms, and their equivalents in other English varieties. Moreover, the prescribed books for schools and colleges should contain the idioms that have British equivalents. This is important because at the West African Senior School Certificate Examination, candidates are penalized for inconsistency if they use an idiom in British English for example and later decide to switch to its American or Canadian equivalents.

With regard to the idioms in prescribed texts that involve translations of indigenous languages, their meanings should be explained in glossaries and footnotes. This is necessary for the growing trend where the number of foreign pupils and students in public schools and colleges, who are likely not familiar with the meaning of these expressions, is on the increase. The use of glossaries and footnotes can be connected to what Smith (1983) mentions as the intelligibility criterion which is among the three criteria that are to be fulfilled for the English language to continue to grow and evolve. This criterion states inter alia that the speaker (in this case the writer) should make himself or herself understood.

Linguists in the country also have a role to play. This means they should design a national dictionary which will record the words and expressions that are being used by Sierra Leonean writers as well as other academics. They have to do the pioneer work needed before these words and expressions can be recognized within and beyond the country. This is how the *agbada* (a more or less loose-fitting robe worn by men in West Africa) and others like it have found their way in the Oxford Advanced Learner's Dictionary (Hornby 2020, p. 29). At the moment, the evolving Sierra Leonean variety is without a national dictionary and an authoritative grammar to record its rules and structures. However, the increase in the number of Sierra Leonean fiction writers will likely help overcome these obstacles. The authors have illustrated three of the six features of the idioms that exist in the New Englishes (see Platt et al. above). Ultimately, the question remains: if these structures have existed in other non-native English countries, why should Sierra Leonean examination candidates be penalized for using them? It is hoped that, if the number of fiction writers continues to grow, and if the suggestions given above are implemented, the recognition of 'new' idioms, and by extension the evolving Sierra Leonean English variety, will be only a matter of time.

Works Cited

Bangura, S., *A Roadmap to Sierra Leone English: A Sociolinguistic and Ecological Perspective*, PhD dissertation submitted to the Department of Modern Languages (Las Palmas, Gran Canaria, 2015).

Conteh, I., 'Grammerphone', *Concord Times*, 21 May 21 1999, p. 2.

Conteh, J., *The Diamonds* (Warima: Sierra Leonean Writers Series, 1997).

―――― *In Search of Sons* (Warima: Sierra Leonean Writers Series, 2007).

Conteh-Morgan, M., 'English in Sierra Leone: A Description of the Language as used in this West African Country and a Consideration of its Status There', *English Today* 13.3 (1997), pp. 52–6.

Cruse, D. A., *Lexical Semantics* (Cambridge: Cambridge University Press, 1986).

Foday, P., *Thursday's Child, My Journey So Far* (Warima: Sierra Leonean Writers Series, 2018).

Fyle, C. N. and Jones, E., *A Krio-English Dictionary* (Oxford: Oxford University Press, 1980).

Hollist, O., *So the Path Does Not Die* (Mankon: Langaa, 2012).

Hornby, A. S., *Oxford Advanced Learner's Dictionary*, 10th ed. (Oxford: Oxford University Press, 2020).

Jabbi, B., 'Innovative Deviancy in Sierra Leone English Usage', unpublished paper presented at the Conference on the Implications of English for West African Universities, Freetown, Njala University College, 1972.

Jones, E. D., 'Steps towards Standard Sierra Leone English', *SLATE: The Bulletin of the Sierra Leone Association for the Teaching of English* 1.1 (1965), pp. 34–6.

Kamara, J. L., *We're Not Our Fathers* (Warima: Sierra Leonean Writers Series, 2016).

Kamara J. L., 'The Return Migration Theme in the Sierra Leonean Novel', unpublished M. Phil. Thesis, Fourah Bay College, 2019.

Kamara, M., *The Little Apprentice Tailor*, Mactracks Series (Macmillan Education, 1994).

Kachru, B., *The Alchemy of English: The Spread, Function and Models of Non-Native Englishes* (Oxford: Pergamon Books, 1986).

Kamtchueng, Lozzi Martial Meutem, "Non-standard idioms in Cameroon English literature and their impact on English language learning and intelligibility", *Theory and Practice in Language Studies*, vol. 4, no. 8, (2014), pp. 1550–7.

Koso-Thomas, K., *The Dream* (Warima: Sierra Leonean Writers Series, 2018).

Lee, W., *Longman Pocket Idioms Dictionary* (Harlow: Pearson Education ESL, 2001).

Osho, K. O., *Foundation English for Senior Schools and the University* (Warima: Sierra Leonean Writers Series, 2022).

Pemagbi, J., '"Still a Deficient Language" – A Description and Glossary of the "New English" of Sierra Leone', *English Today* 5.1 (1989), pp. 5–17.

Platt J. T., H. Weber, and Ho Mian Lian, *The New Englishes* (London: Routledge & Kegan Paul, 1984).

Seidl, J. and McMordie, W., *English Idioms*, 5th ed. (Oxford: Oxford University Press, 1988).

Sesay, O. F., *Landscape of Memories* (Warima: Sierra Leonean Writers Series, 2017).

Sesay, A. M. A., *Who Is to Blame?* (Pittsburg: Dorrance Publishing, 2016).

Sesay, M. G., *This Side of Nothingness* (Warima: Sierra Leonean Writers Series, 2015).

——— *The Mouths of the Junction* (Warima: Sierra Leonean Writers Series, 2017).

Siefring, J., *Oxford Dictionary of Idioms* (Oxford: Oxford University Press, 2004).

Sinclair, J., *Dictionary of Phrasal Verbs* (London: William Collins Sons & Co., 1989).

Smith, L., *Readings in English as an International Language* (Oxford: Pergamon Press, 1983).

Tarawallie, S., *Pope Francis, Politics and the Mabanta Boy* (Kibworth: Matador, 2019).

The West African Examinations Council. West African Senior School Certificate Examination for School Candidates, English Language 1 (Accra, 2015).

Todd, L, *An Introduction to Linguistics* (Harlow: Longman, 1987).

Turay, M., *A Survey of Sierra Leonean English* (Warima: Sierra Leonean Writers Series, 2017).

Wales, K., *A Dictionary of Stylistics* (London and New York: Longman, 1997).

Walon-Jalloh, A., *Voices and Passion* (Warima: Sierra Leonean Writers Series, 2015).

White, J. G., *Cambridge International Dictionary of Idioms* (Cambridge: Cambridge University Press, 1998).

Chapter 4

The Female Condition in the Novels of Aminatta Forna

SAIDU BANGURA

Literature has always been seen as a window to society and the people that live in that society. Elsewhere, I equate the study of literature to the study of society, culture, people, and the general way we perceive and understand the world and our immediate environment (Bangura 2021, 42). Hence, reading the novels of Aminatta Forna should guide the reader to gaining an understanding of society and the characters she presents in her novels. Aminatta Forna herself states that "literature is about nuance and understanding the intricacies of life" (2015). The "nuance and ... intricacies of life" that I present in this chapter deal with the female condition in Aminatta Forna's *Ancestor Stones* and *The Memory of Love*.

Eustace Palmer's conceptualization of the conditions of women, what I refer to as the female condition in this context – the social, economic, and political hegemony, and the subsequent privileges that men enjoy in contemporary African societies while women are seen as a subaltern group – becomes my primary aim in this chapter. Palmer describes the female condition thusly:

> The received opinion seems to be that the condition of women in Africa is quite deplorable. Women, according to this view, are absolutely subjugated by their husbands who are indisputably the heads of households and whose position as the law giver whose will must be obeyed remains unchallenged. Women have less access to education and consequently fewer opportunities for gaining employment, particularly in the positions that really matter. (Palmer 2021, 191)

Given the above theorization of the condition of women in Africa, I read both *Ancestor Stones* and *The Memory of Love* to understand the "nuance and ... intricacies" of the lives of the female characters of Aminatta Forna. Whereas women's deplorable condition and their subsequent subjugation by their menfolk is a primary objective as I show in my interpretation of Forna's female characters, my secondary aim is to intertwine how female writers are considered and how they create female characters to counter both "the received opinion" (Palmer 2021, 191) about the conditions of women in Africa, and how they portray themselves as female writers who "have been written out" and "rendered invisible in literary criticism" (Stratton 1994, 1). This second aim presents Aminatta Forna's motivation as a writer based on how female writers are considered.

While *Ancestor Stones* looks at the historical trajectory of Sierra Leone from the precolonial to the postcolonial era, *The Memory of Love* is set in the post-independence era and narrates the dark history of Sierra Leone culminating in the Rebel War and its post-conflict effects on Sierra Leoneans and the country (see also Cole 2017). I argue in this chapter that interest in these two novels should neither be about the politics of literature nor that of the literature of politics – although, of course, we cannot read Aminatta Forna without considering the politics behind her writings – but one that deals with the presentation of women in African literature within the historical boundaries under review: precolonial and post-independence Sierra Leone. With reference to what motivates Aminatta Forna to write non-fiction and fiction on Sierra Leone, her *raison d'être* and as her contribution to Sierra Leonean literature, this is what she says:

> The first book I wrote was a memoir of my father, who had been a political prisoner in Sierra Leone when I was a child. I was propelled into writing it by the civil war in that country, my father's country and the place I spent a good number of my childhood years. I wanted to know how the country I had known, seemingly so peace-loving and so beautiful, had imploded into violence. For my country to have a war and for me, a writer, not to write about it seemed to me a gross dereliction of duty. I was propelled into writing by war and I have written about war ever since. (Forna 2015)

Therefore, reading Aminatta Forna without putting into context her motivations and the justifications for writing the way she writes, would be an injustice. We might as well say that what inspires her to write on war is her *cri de coeur* for one of her countries, where her father was born, imprisoned, and killed, and where she lived for a good part of her childhood and where she regularly visits other relatives. But much more than all these factors, Forna tells us that for her country to have a war and for her, as a writer, not to write about it would be "a gross dereliction of duty".

Despite her writing on the war and its impacts on women as evident in *The Memory of Love*, and as I mentioned in the introductory paragraphs, I approach the female conditions in both novels by Aminatta Forna under review for an understanding of the characters she presents in these novels, and the portrayal of her female characters and the conditions they face as women. The otherwise invisibility of female writers and female characters is put into context here. Hence, just as for Forna, it will be a desertion of our responsibility as readers and literary critics not to engage with her writings as affecting us all generally as readers of her magnificent narratives, and as Sierra Leoneans in particular.

Contextualization: African Women Writers and the Conditions of their Female Characters

Considering the number of African male writers – novelists, playwrights, and poets – and how these have presented female characters in their works including literary critics who have ignored women writers by making them invisible in their critical works of African literature, an analysis of Forna's female characters must also include a brief comment on women writers.

For some scholars, the main concerns of West African women writers are not only about the lived experiences of women within their socio-cultural and socio-economic realities, but one that focuses on the conditions of women as narrated in fictional works (Mojola 2017). For others, gender roles in traditional and modern African milieu under the institution of polygamy, traditional cultures and religion must be studied and juxtaposed within the contours of the socio-cultural and socio-economic realities that exist between the genders (Ng'umbi 2017). For others still, while not supporting the examination of literature based on the gender of the writer, the contributions of women writers should be included in order to capture the universality and the diversity of voices and subject matter in the field, especially that dealing with oppression, pain, inequality, and the general conditions of women in society as presented in literature (see Norridge 2013). Considering this, women writers tend to present female characters in their works as a representation of their marginalization and invisibility within literary canons and how they have overcome the oppression, the pain and inequality they have suffered as writers. These exclusionary practices of gendering African literature are what Stratton critiques here:

> In characterizing African literature, critics have ignored gender as a social and analytic category. Such characterizations operate to exclude women's literary expression as part of African literature. Hence what they define is the male literary tradition. When African literary discourse is considered from the perspective of gender, it becomes evident that dialogic interaction between men's and women's writing is one of the defining features of the contemporary African literary tradition. Such a redefinition has important implications for both critical and pedagogical practices. What it indicates is that neither men's nor women's writing can be fully appreciated in isolation from the other. (1994, 1)

Taking into consideration Stratton's position above, the conditions of women writers and that of their characters are almost similar: both work and exist within male-dominated canons and societies; they must conform to the dictates of a male order; there is a hegemonic hierarchical construct – male first, then women. The silencing and marginalization of women writers has encouraged a new crop of African women writers who are challenging the privileged male writers to understand that "neither men's nor women's writing can be fully appreciated in isolation from the other" (Stratton 1994, 1). Aminatta Forna herself has lamented on the tradition of gendering or othering writers which has affected her as a writer as far as labeling African women writers is concerned. She is not considered as an African writer, but rather as a transnational and hyphenated writer not only because of her being the child of a Sierra Leonean father and a Scottish mother, but because she is a woman and a writer: "We hyphenated writers complain about the privilege accorded to the white male writer, he who dominates the western canon and is the only one called simply 'writer' ... I find myself referred to as an African author less often. I have a new label, 'transnational writer'" (Forna 2015; see also Pérez Fernández 2017, 210).

On the disproportionate suffering, disenfranchisement, and invisibility of women in the global south, Annemarie Pabel writes:

> [W]omen, and especially women of colour, have been disproportionally exposed to multiple forms of prolonged and systemic violence, yet the available literature does not fully represent these realities and the underlying layers of disempowerment. Thus, the ways in which women's voices have been silenced have carried far-reaching implications on how trauma is recorded and faced as well as on the survivors' agency. (2022, 1)

Aminatta Forna's recording of women's sufferings, pain and silence is represented in the elderly womenfolk. The younger female characters become the voices through which the stories of their "mothers" are told in *Ancestor Stones*. Equally so, silence becomes the method through which the memory of trauma in post-conflict Sierra Leone in *The Memory of Love* constitutes a link between "history and identity" (Cole 2017, 167). Although I do not intend to read Aminatta Forna's *Ancestor Stones* and *The Memory of Love* under the lenses of "psychological trauma" or the "complex and prolonged experiences of trauma occurring in literature and the ways in which literary forms facilitate such representations" (Pabel 2022, 1), I argue that, and in accordance with Gregory Castle's irrevocable way of reading literature, Aminatta Forna's characterization of her female characters deserves special reading. On this note, my reading of Aminatta Forna's two novels under review is in line with Castle's theory on reading:

> [F]or in the end, the nature of literature and the literary has to do with how we read, and how we read is fundamentally tied to the social, cultural, and political institutions of a given society at a given time. That some ways of

reading have remained constant is less a function of historical continuity than of institutional memory. (2007, 9)

My reading of *Ancestor Stones* and *The Memory of Love* takes into account how Aminatta Forna deals with the condition of women in both the imagined societies in her works as well as the existing social, cultural and political conditions that obtain in real-life Sierra Leone.

The Conditions of Forna's Female Characters

The presentation of women in African literature has elicited many critical opinions and debates with regard to the place of the woman in the African sociocultural milieu in comparison with the presentation of her male counterpart by both male and female writers (see Bangura 2021; Kamara 2001; Stratton 1994; Ogundipe-Leslie 1983; others). Forna's *Ancestor Stones* and *The Memory of Love* are set in Sierra Leone within different socio-cultural, socio-historical, and socio-political contexts. Given male priority and hegemony over every aspect of human existence in society, the complementarity of men and women depicted in Forna's novels is seen as abnormal. A careful reading of her novels demonstrate that she is challenging the established norms and order of male privileges and supremacy in society while presenting a case for a reformation of the traditions that have oppressed women in Africa.

Let us consider two preliminary positions. First, while we may be tempted to understand Stratton's critique that "critics have ignored gender as a social and analytic category" which "operate[s] to exclude women's literary expression as part of African literature" defining only "the male literary tradition", Forna and other women writers have demonstrated that "dialogic interaction between men's and women's writing is one of the defining features of the contemporary African literary tradition" (Stratton 1994, 1). The erstwhile marginalization and invisibility of women writers in literary criticism is no longer possible in African literature given women's inescapable presence on the literary scene. Like their male counterparts, women writers have dealt with complex socio-cultural, socio-political, and socio-economic issues in their writings. In schools and university literature syllabuses, works by women writers have equally occupied an important place and treatment. Second, whereas writing and criticism of literary works were considered as an absolute area for the man, the shifting of the domains of influence initially wielded by women in traditional African societies now played by men (see Palmer 2021) and the consequent deterioration of the living circumstances in modern Africa, such dignified roles are now the sole right of the man. Male domination persists in all forms as Palmer (191) tells us. Palmer further states that:

> the condition of African women in the modern period has been largely the legacy of these three essentially outside forces: Islam, Christianity, and imperialism. This is not to say that the traditional African situation was perfect, or that forces in modern African society have not contributed to the African woman's condition. It is merely to state the nature of the situation and to say that these outside forces should bear the greatest share of the responsibility. Since independence, various African countries have been taking measures to improve the condition of women. There have been some spectacular successes, but a lot still needs to be done. (199)

Forna's contribution as a female writer and the roles her female characters play in the two novels under review should be seen as a suggestion of ways "to improve the condition of women" and to counter those three "outside forces" in giving credence to African traditional values and religion as Palmer states above.

To demonstrate this point further let us borrow from Ogundipe-Leslie's thesis which states, among other things, that African women carry six burdens that weigh them down:

> (1) oppression from outside forces (foreign intrusion, colonial domination, etc.); (2) heritage of tradition (feudal, slave-based, communal); (3) her own backwardness, a product of colonization and its concomitant poverty, ignorance, etc.; (4) her men, weaned on centuries of male domination who will not willingly relinquish their power and privilege; (5) her race, because the international economic order is divided along race lines; and (6) herself. (Ogundipe-Leslie 1983; quoted in Kamara 2001, 216)

Given the roles women play in Sierra Leone's socio-economic and socio-cultural milieu, this chapter engages the following questions as we analyze Forna's presentation of her female characters: (1) does Forna present her female characters within the contours of African cultural civilization, or does she create her female characters to cut across Western and African cultural *modus operandi*? (2) how does change in socio-political, socio-economic, and socio-cultural contexts affect the women in Forna's novels? and, (3) what does it mean to be a woman in a country struggling with a rebel war where violence (physical and psychological) is used as a weapon against women and other vulnerable members of society?

Aminatta Forna's Female Characters in *Ancestor Stones*

Forna's four female protagonists in *Ancestor Stones* are all without husbands: Asana (widow), Mariama (who later becomes Mary, a spinster), Hawa (husband's whereabouts unknown), and Serah (divorced). They tell their stories in a male-dominated and patriarchal society, stories that culminate in the political history of Sierra Leone (see also Cole 2017, 125). Through the voice of the narrator, Abie, their niece, who we understand to be the author of this compelling narrative in the prologue ("The Women's Gardens I") and epilogue ("The Women's Gardens II"), Palmer's (2021, 191) characterization of the condition of the African woman is symbolically presented: hard work is all done by women. Cole (123–4) provides for us the Biblical connotation of the metaphorical Garden of Eden, this beautiful place, Sierra Leone, that Forna presents. This should also set the pace for our understanding of how Forna deals with the female condition in this novel, and hence Sierra Leone. Polygamy as an institution, which is the bedrock of the life of the community, is presented as a normal fact of the socio-cultural reality of traditional Sierra Leone contrary to the monogamous Garden of Eden of Adam and Eve as presented in religious books and literary works. This Sierra Leone, the Garden of Eden, was a land of peace whose inhabitants could live off the land. Women are significant in this process of production and peaceful co-existence with their male counterparts. As the story progresses, this Garden of Eden, Sierra Leone, deteriorates, as decadence creeps in; the stifling of people's rights, especially those of women (the departure of Mariama's mother); the destruction of cultural values (the destruction of the seventeen ancestor stones by the husband of Mariama); the invasion by foreign religion in the form of Islam and Christianity and the death of traditional life and religion.

Tradition, as Cole (2017, 138) points out is used "to exploit and oppress women in society". Cole's position here is in consonance with Ogundipe-Leslie's "heritage of tradition" burden. Forna debunks or deconstructs certain aspects of tradition. For example, her handling of marriage for women gives an interesting postcolonial reading. The women have an option of staying in marriage or divorce their husbands when the relationship becomes abusive or does not favor the woman, as we see in Hawa's case. In fact, our four protagonists in *Ancestor Stones* are all single through different circumstances.

Ancestor Stones is centered around the Kholifa family with Gibril Umaru Kholifa as the head of a polygamous household made up of eleven wives and several children. The Kholifa family symbolizes a wealthy and prosperous family. Poor men cannot afford to marry more than one wife within the socio-economic parameters of the polygamous family institution as we see in the case of Hawa and her husband. Hawa has to abandon the relationship because her husband refuses to marry a second wife.

Surprisingly perhaps to some readers who may have expected to encounter entirely uneducated characters given the traditional setting of the plot, the novel opens with a letter by Alpha Kholifa to Abie, his cousin. Abie, the narrator, a woman, is educated and lives in London. Abie is being asked by her four aunts to return home and take care of the family coffee plantation at Rofathane, the name of their hometown in Temne which translates as "The Resting Place". Abie is also told in the letter about "the dislocations and hardships of the war" and her support in helping to solve the family's economic difficulties is solicited. Interestingly, Abie, a woman, is now looked up to as someone who can take over the family business and ease the financial difficulties faced by the family. This interpretation goes in agreement with Cole's contention that the social relationship between men and women are spaces where gender and power are negotiated (2017, 121 citing Massey 1999). The kitchen and the bedroom are gendered spaces. Women decide what happens in the kitchen and deal with what goes into the pot. The bedroom is the domain of the man who can punish and violently dominate or deprive the woman of sex within the socio-cultural milieu of traditional Africa. In this space, when the woman says no to the man, she is deemed to be rebellious, and hence unfaithful. The woman's body is a space for a man to exploit within the confines of the bedroom. However, with changing gender roles, women now have greater negotiating power.

The six burdens as theorized by Ogundipe-Leslie (1983) mentioned above are being made lighter, and are challenged, contested, and reformulated by Aminatta Forna in *Ancestor Stones*. One of the reasons for this is that the traditional spaces occupied by women have been changed through education and women's economic power to change the lives of others. Abie, an educated woman is now asked by other women to take up responsibilities traditionally known to be that of men. Even Asana tells us:

> I wanted to come to this world, to the place where things happen. I didn't want to stay where I was. I always had big eyes for this world and I was born with them open. My mother never feared for me. There are some children – you can tell the ones – born with a hunger for life. (*Ancestor Stones*, 16)

Asana has set the tone on how the negotiation of gender roles has been set right before she was born, the reason why her mother, who could have passed on the traditional roles of womanhood and culture, does not fear for her. Changes have been silently taking place: a novel which begins with a strong institution of polygamy as the norm of family life advances to seeing divorces and widowhood as empowerment of women and encourages them to undertake other professional activities traditionally performed by men. Polygamy, as an entrenched traditional institution, is given its historical narrative and brings us to the present generation where it is no longer viewed negatively but is rather reinterpreted to fit the present era and generation. Hawa's husband's situation, in which he is considered poor for not being able to afford more than one wife, becomes a disadvantage to Hawa, for all the workload in the family rests on her shoulders (*Ancestor Stones*, 179–80). The husband's incapacity to marry a second wife has reduced her to a servant. This also tells us that polygamy has an economic value in traditional African societies. Apart from the fact that the polygamous husband must have money to marry more than one wife, having more wives also means less work for each co-wife and more income for the family. Hawa's failure to convince her husband to be polygamous and her being overwhelmed with heavy work leads her to divorce her husband, which consequently translates into empowerment through gender role negotiation. Hawa, who is a product of the polygamous family structure and knowledgeable about its advantages and disadvantages, becomes the one who explains what co-wifehood really means. She wants a continuation of this family institutional life – for it makes the lives of women less burdensome and malleable. Hawa provides us with a definition of "polygamy" or co-wifehood according to the Mende culture:

> The women who share your husband with you. The women with whom you take turns to cook. The women you give whatever is left over in your own pot. The women who are the other mothers of your children, who suckle your baby when your own milk has dried up or unexpectedly soured. (*Ancestor Stones*, 65)

Does this understanding of co-wifehood by Hawa lead her to assist Khalil to marry Zainab for her husband? How do we explain Asana's marrying Osman and becoming the man's third wife? Aminatta Forna, through Hawa's explanation, reinforces the power of tradition. Contrary to Ogundipe-Leslie's theorizing tradition as a burden to women, Forna's narrative demonstrates the significance of tradition in women's empowerment and liberation. Hence, we need to see the roles of both Hawa and Asana within the discourse of the restructuring of the institution of polygamy in the modern age. Aminatta Forna's *Ancestor Stones* seems to redefine women's role in society. She is showing how deeply rooted she is as a writer in her tradition and how significant it is to inject a new lease of life into these old practices that have held Africa's traditions intact. Rather than destroy them, the writer is suggesting that these cultural practices need to be reformed and reinvigorated. Hence, even in polygamous family structure, and in situations where women are denied a voice as in the case of the eleven wives of Gibril Umaru Kholifa, women are able to express themselves:

> Women are no longer marginalised; they can speak their voice to challenge the patriarchal hegemony. As such, the four narrators, while embracing the indigenous, as Nnaemeka would have argued in the context of negro-feminism, attempt to reconfigure the institution of polygyny according to the needs of the twenty-first century Africa where negotiation between the two opposing powers (patriarchy and matriarchy) has taken centre stage. (Ng'umbi 2017, 91)

For Gibril, who can afford to marry eleven wives, the institution of polygamy makes the lives of his wives enviable and easy, Hawa is telling us in her interpretation of the Mende "Ores" family culture (*Ancestor Stones*, 65). There is a division of gendered labor. However, what is the role of the senior wife in a polygamous family structure? Gibril's senior wife, Ya Namina, distributes the responsibilities to the junior wives not only in matters relating to looking after their husband but in designating the workload as far as the family's economy is concerned. The senior wife is the arbiter of justice, the symbol of harmony, the harbinger of decency in the family, and the person who holds the family together. At the death of their husband, Ya Namina decides to stay and marries the younger brother of her late husband for the continuity of the family she has joined in marriage, Abie tells us (*Ancestor Stones*, 16).

Forna's *Ancestor Stones*, therefore, demystifies and debunks widely held beliefs about polygamy as a deterrent to individual, family, and societal development. Instead of behaving as rivals, Forna's women in the polygamous family institution cooperate and live as sisters. They all take care of the children as if they were all each other's children. Aminatta Forna's role here as a writer and a pseudo-personified character in the character of Abie, the narrator, "whose life in many respects parallels that of Aminatta Forna" (Cole 2017, 122) does not only signal change in what and how African women writers tell stories, but how they make their characters to depict the change in gender roles: "*Ancestor Stones* provides a nexus between past and present with the aim of eschewing the historical past that was built on patriarchal power dominance and gender inequality. The contemporary generation of African women writers began to advocate new changes" (Ng'umbi 2017, 87–8). Patriarchy and its modus operandi are being challenged by writers like Aminatta Forna in the way she gives agency to her fictional female characters. Female writers, just as their female characters, negotiate and assume the responsibility of changing patriarchal power structures. Asana, Mariama, Hawa and Serah's stories about their mothers, who are silenced, is a testament to Forna's interest in injecting new life into the roles of women in order to change patriarchal power and its stranglehold over women. Aminatta's female characters who, like Hawa, confront patriarchy through discourse creation (for example, Hawa's definition of "polygamy" or co-wifehood grounded in Mende culture (*Ancestor Stones*, 65), could be seen as second co-authors of *Ancestor Stones*. Just as the woman writer, the stories the four women tell in *Ancestor Stones* represent modernity and change.

Aminatta Forna's Female Characters in *The Memory of Love*

Contrary to *Ancestor Stones* whose protagonists are four women struggling to survive and unshackle themselves from the grips of male chauvinism, the protagonists in *The Memory of Love* are three men and their relationships with their female counterparts: Adrian, a British psychologist who volunteers with the city's mental health services; Kai, a local orthopedic surgeon overwhelmed by nightmares and recollections of the war; and Elias Cole, a hospital patient remembering the exploits of his younger days as he surrenders to terminal illness. Although Forna's *The Memory of Love* is a fictional story, for most

Sierra Leoneans who experienced the horrors of the Rebel War, directly or indirectly, the story is real. According to Norridge, "Forna is writing fiction, but her subject matter – living with the aftermath of the enduring conflict in Sierra Leone – is very real" (2013, 172). The weapons of war were not only AK47s, RPGs, machetes, and grenades; there was also the conscription of young boys as child soldiers, and hunger, as well as the abduction and rape of girls and women. Rape was the most powerful weapon used, mostly against girls and women, but also against boys and men. Kai's ordeal in *The Memory of Love* being beaten and stripped naked in the following scene is a vivid demonstration of the use of rape as an instrument of war:

> "Fuck her or I fuck you." First spoken and then screamed into his ear, combining with the ringing in his head to make him dizzy. "Fuck her or I fuck you."
>
> The gun was removed from his temple. Kai tried to force himself to think. He was helpless. He felt something – the gun barrel – being pushed between his buttocks, heard the laughter, felt the end of it being rammed into him. The pain was acute and rippled through his body. Clapping. Cawing laughter. The gun barrel was thrust further into him. He flopped forward and was forced up, back on to his hands and knees. He was aware of Balia only peripherally, as she lunged, the sharp report of the gun, the shallow arc described by her body in the air as she fell backwards. (*The Memory of Love*, 433)

As a narrative of memory, not of love but of the trauma of war, the above excerpt describes the sexual abuse and painful conditions women are made to undergo in armed conflicts. The excerpt equally illustrates the torments and inhumane treatment men face in such circumstances just as women's bodies in situations of conflict are seen as fields to be exploited and violated: rape becomes a weapon used by men to dehumanize and demoralize women. Balia has not only been raped by armed men before being killed, but Kai is also invited to sexually abuse her or suffer rape because of his refusal to participate in the exploit. Their bodies are treated as booties of war. Kai is made to feel the excruciating pain of sexual violence that women feel. This experience has a negative impact on Kai's reaction to Nenebah, his partner's, sexual overtures (*The Memory of Love*, 287). Before Kai's painful experience of rape during the war, he and Nenebah used sex as a way to express their mutual desires and pleasures:

> War gave new intensity to their lovemaking. On the floor, facing him. Nenebah with her legs around Kai's waist. He, inside her, a nipple in his mouth. One hand squeezes the surrounding breast, his tongue flicks back and forth, round and round. The fingers of his other hand, in the warm V of her thighs, imitate the same motion. Her breathing rises and quickens. As

she comes, he holds on to her, an arm around her shoulders, pressing her down on to his cock. With the slowing of her shudders he rolls Nenebah on to her back, his fingers in her hair, moving forward and back until he loses himself. Afterwards he lies, still inside her, slowly softening, her hand stroking the back of his neck. In time they both sleep held in the same position. (*The Memory of Love*, 235)

While the foreign psychologist and the local doctor are busy looking after their patients and concentrating on the current situation, Mamakay, one of the female protagonists, tells the reader that irrespective of the violence that is going on, the past, and symbolically the scars that the current violence leaves, cannot be erased as she tells us: "People think war is the worst this country has ever seen: they have no idea what peace is like. The courage it takes simply to endure" (*The Memory of Love*, 282). It will be an uphill task to erase the psychological and physical scars left by the war, the one left by sexual violence. Michela Wrong (2010) maintains that "Aminatta Forna's magnificent second novel is not really about love. Its themes are far grittier, and all the more compelling for it: war, loss, and how a society emerging from civil strife must reinvent its own history" (quoted in Norridge 2012, 19). Violence, post-violence healing, emotional attachments and psychological wounds and their memories, and the explicit description of their intimate relationships are all part of what the characters must live for in post-conflict Sierra Leone, Forna seems to tell us. "Through Mamakay the landscape of the city has altered for Adrian. For the first time since he arrived, the city bears a past, exists in another dimension other than the present" (*The Memory of Love*, 255). Whether this is Freetown that is being described or the body of Mamakay, one thing remains clear: we are shown how the intimate relationship between Adrian and Mamakay has coalesced into oneness. Norridge offers the following interpretation regarding this coalescing of bodies in sexual intimacy: "*The Memory of Love* probe[s] the ways in which sexual encounters can increase self-awareness and a sense of (imperfect) connection with other cultures" (2012, 22). These bodily and intimate pleasures do not establish a permanent relationship with the people involved. They only create a momentary "imperfect" connection with the people involved, not their cultures as represented by Mamakay and Adrian.

Forna presents in *The Memory of Love* this desire of outsiders to exploit and to get connected with other cultures and pleasures (see also Norridge 2012, 22). This is vividly presented in Kai's reflection in the following excerpt:

It was errantry that brought them here, flooding in through the gaping wound left by the war, lascivious in their eagerness. Kai had seen it in the feverish eyes of the women, the sweat on their upper lips, the smell of their breath as they pressed close to him. They came to get their newspaper stories, to save black babies, to spread the word, to make money, to fuck black bodies. (*The Memory of Love,* 218)

The body of the woman is not only exploited by her local male counterpart, but by foreigners who see African women's bodies as a potential landscape of sexual exploitation. Irrespective of these interpretations of sexual appeals and encounters between outsiders and African women, we learn that Adrian is somehow able to understand the true sufferings of the people he meets and "serves" through sex. A case in point is his relationship with Mamakay. While Forna's women's reaction to the sexual exploitation they suffer from outsiders is visible in their eyes, on their lips, and in their bodily odor, the trauma they suffer from both their African male counterparts and outsiders is silently endured. Silence is Agnes' own form of enduring trauma, a condition Cole considers as "historical amnesia to avoid re-traumatization of the body politic with a resurgence of hostilities" (2017, 169). Agnes's silence then becomes an example of how people struggle to hide the scars of their trauma which feeds into the legacies of post-conflict Sierra Leone. Silence and secrecy become the mechanism characters use to hide the scars left by the war. There is also a secret complex web of romantic relationships and entanglements all pointing to the sexual desires of men for their female counterparts. Interesting examples to consider include Elias's romantic attraction to Saffia, the wife of his colleague, Julius, while Vanessa is in love with Elias, who hardly notices Vanessa since he is blindly in love with Saffia. At the death of Julius, Elias proposes to Saffia, ignoring the mores of society.

The female body becoming a site for sexual exploit and the satisfaction of men's desires is strongly explored by Forna. The picture she presents to us at the opening of the novel is a case in point:

> This is how it is when you glimpse a woman for the first time, a woman you know you could love. People are wrong when they talk of love at first sight. It is neither love nor lust. No. As she walks away from you, what you feel is loss. A premonition of loss. (*The Memory of Love,* 1)

Elias is not only talking here about what goes on in his mind when he sees a woman and the intensions of "love" or "lust" at the very first sight, but about "loss" of that opportunity to interconnect with that woman, or the separation of the bodies after sexual intercourse. The momentary nature of love, lust, and loss all point to the idea of the female body becoming a site for sexual exploitation. This picture is further reinforced in the sexual encounter between Kai and Nenebah as remembered by Kai:

> They'd been lying in bed, spooned against each other, he was still inside her, savouring the slipperiness of semen and sweat. Once she described for him the sensation that followed his withdrawal from her body if it happened too soon, his *abandonment* of her body. Loss, she said. It felt like loss. (*The Memory of Love,* 260; italics original)

While Elias Cole imagines "a woman you know you could love" (1), Kai and Nenebah are "savouring the slipperiness of semen and sweat" (260). In *The Memory of Love*, apart from the secret entanglements of the sexual desires and appeals, we also witness Balia being raped and killed by rebels after both Kai and Balia were kidnapped (431–4). Note the description provided below:

> The first person Kai helped down from the tailgate was a woman, both of whose hands were almost entirely severed, they flapped from her wrists like broken wings. He'd seen a man, hopping, clutching his own amputated foot in both hands. There were dozens of them, men, women, children. Some had survived for days in the bush. In the theatre Kai worked harder, faster and more furiously than he had ever done in his life. And afterwards, if you had asked any of the survivors how they had managed it, they would not have been able to tell you. It was as if those days in the forest, the escape to the city, had passed in a trance. *The mind creates an alternative state.* (*The Memory of Love*, 325; italics original)

While it is true that men, women, and children suffer in the fictional world of Aminatta Forna as seen in the excerpt above, the violence, both physical and psychological, meted out on women is much more negatively impactful than that inflicted on men.

Conclusion

I have asked elsewhere and proffered suggestions on how African women can remove the six mountains on their backs as hypothesized by Ogundipe-Leslie (Bangura 2021). As argued above, writers, especially women writers, have a huge responsibility in demystifying and debunking the tradition and burdens women inherited by simply being women in Africa. Aminatta Forna's two novels studied here depict female characters whose stories dismantle and demystify certain held beliefs. *Ancestor Stones* and *The Memory of Love* do not present women within the same context and perspective both in terms of settings and in comparison with other African novels.

Aminatta Forna, in her attempt to reform certain traditional practices such as polygamy through her novels, presents us with female characters who challenge the traditional marriage institution. The four female narrators in *Ancestor Stones* are all single through various means, including divorce, which cannot be considered an alternative that women can opt for given the socio-cultural and socio-economic demands of the traditional African society. The older generation of women are unable to pass on some of the traditional practices to the younger generation given their silence and passive presence in *Ancestor Stones*. Foreign cultural influences like Islam, Christianity and education could not make the younger generation kick against their traditional practices. Abie's role to take care of her family and the family's agricultural business in *Ancestor Stones* is a case in point. Gender roles are changing to the advantage of the girl-child and the woman, thanks to education and women writers like Aminatta Forna who write with a reformative perspective of Africa's traditions that have held women down. That notwithstanding, male domination persists. In *The Memory of Love* women suffer the consequences of conflicts. They are violently raped and killed. Their bodies are treated as spaces to be sexually exploited by both their African counterparts as well as foreigners who come as expatriates but with a hidden agenda. On this note, sexual violence in this case is not just restricted to war zones. The dynamics of sexual violence can happen wherever there is a male sex predator and a woman. Some of the women in *The Memory of Love* use silence as a way of expressing the traumas they are going through.

While we acknowledge Ogundipe-Leslie's (1983) theorization of the six burdens women face in Africa and the negative presentation of female characters by male writers, reading Aminatta Forna's *Ancestor Stones* and *The Memory of Love* has provided sufficient narratives to believe that the conditions of women in Africa, both as writers and characters, are changing. Gender roles are now being negotiated with women taking the lead in the process. Women writers are now taking the lead in writing the stories of other women and challenging the established canons in a field that has been dominated by men for so long. The female condition in the two novels reviewed here deserve further study so that both women writers and their female characters can be better appreciated within the context of the creation of a new world where men and women can be seen as equal partners in society.

Works Cited

Bangura, Saidu, "Literary Perspective," in A.K. Bangura (ed.), *Black Lives Matter vs. All Lives Matter: A Multidisciplinary Primer* (Lanham, MD: Lexington Books, 2021), pp. 41–60.

Castle, Gregory, *The Blackwell Guide to Literary Theory* (Malden, Oxford, and Carlton: Blackwell Publishing, 2007).

Cole, Ernest, *Space and Trauma in the Writings of Aminatta Forna* (Trenton, NJ: Africa World Press, 2017).

Forna, Aminatta. *The Devil that Danced on the Water* (London: HarperCollins, 2002).

——— *Ancestor Stones* (London: Bloomsbury Publishing, 2006).

——— *The Memory of Love* (London: Bloomsbury Publishing, 2010).

Forna, Aminatta. "Aminatta Forna: Don't judge a book by its author," *The Guardian*, 13 February 2015 http://www.theguardian.com/books/2015/feb/13/aminattafornadontjudge-bookby-cover. Accessed September 11, 2022.

Kamara, Gibreel M., "The feminist struggle in the Senegalese novel: Mariama Ba and Sembene Ousmane," *Journal of Black Studies* 32.2 (2001), pp. 212–28.

Massey, Doreen, *Space, Place and Gender* (Minneapolis, MN: University of Minneapolis Press, 1999).

Mojola, Yemi I., "The onus of womanhood: Mariama Ba and Zaynab Alkali," in Newell, S. (ed.) *Gender, Popular Culture and Literature in West Africa* (London: Zed Books, 2017), pp. 126–36.

Norridge, Zoe, *Perceiving Pain in African Literature* (Basingstoke: Palgrave Macmillan, 2013).

Norridge, Zoe, "Sex as synecdoche: Intimate languages of violence in Chimamanda Ngozi Adichie's *Half of a Yellow Sun* and Aminatta Forna's *The Memory of Love*," *Research in African Literatures* 43.2 (2012), pp. 18–39.

Ng'umbi, Yunusy Castory, "Re-imagining family and gender roles in Aminatta Forna's *Ancestor Stones*", *Tydskrif vir letterkunde* 54.2 (2017), pp. 86–99.

Ogundipe-Leslie, Molara, "African women, culture and another development," *Journal of African Marxists* 5 (1983), pp. 77–92.

Pabel, Annemarie, *Women Writing Trauma in the Global South: A Study of Aminatta Forna, Isabel Allende and Anuradha Roy* (New York: Taylor & Francis, 2022).

Palmer, Eustace, *Africa: An Introduction* (New York: Routledge, 2021).

Pérez Fernández, Irene, "Emotional (un)belonging in Aminatta Forna's *The Memory of Love*", *Complutense Journal of English Studies* 25 (2017), pp. 209–21.

Philips, Deborah, "The politics of literature and the literature of politics," in Deborah Philips, and Katy Shaw (eds.) *Literary Politics: The Politics of Literature and the Literature of Politics* (Basingstoke: Palgrave Macmillan, 2013), pp. 1–14.

Stratton, Florence, *Contemporary African Literature and the Politics of Gender* (New York: Routledge, 1994).

Wrong, M., "When Words Fail," *The Spectator*. 8 May 2010. https://www.spectator.co.uk/article/when-words-fail (2011). Accessed 13 September 2024.

SECTION II

LEGACIES OF WAR AND PANDEMIC: LITERATURE AS WITNESS TO VIOLENCE, TRAUMA, AND RESILIENCE

Chapter 5

Syl Cheney-Coker's *Stone Child and Other Poems*: A Graphic Exploration of War Trauma

EUSTACE PALMER

In previous collections such as *Concerto for an Exile* (1973), *The Graveyard Also Has Teeth with Concerto for an Exile (1980)* and *The Blood in the Desert's Eyes* (1990), Syl Cheney-Coker has demonstrated unrivaled adroitness in the exploration of suffering. The collection *Stone Child and Other Poems* (2008) continues this preoccupation and is largely a presentation of the horrific suffering of the people of Sierra Leone during the Civil War of 1991–2002. From one's own personal experience in talking to the victims and from Cheney-Coker's presentation, this suffering can only be described as traumatic, although a strict adherence to the postulations of some leading proponents of trauma theory might point to a different conclusion. However, if the experience so graphically presented by Cheney-Coker in *Stone Child and Other Poems* is not traumatic, one wonders what could be and whether the people's suffering could be described accurately in any other way.

The earliest proponent of Trauma theory was Sigmund Freud who contended that trauma is the impact of an event or experience on the mind. In other words, trauma, from Freud's perspective, is entirely psychological, not physical, emotional, or social. The impact of the traumatic experience results in nightmares or hallucinations. Before Freud, the received wisdom was that trauma generally resulted from physical injuries. In a sense, Freud put paid to the idea that trauma was caused by the physical and from now on the emphasis was on the psychological and the impact of experiences on the mind. It was Cathy Caruth who established trauma theory as an important component of literary critical activity, and she remains the leading proponent of the traditional model of trauma theory, building on the postulations of Sigmund Freud. In other words, trauma for her is almost completely psychological. In her seminal work, *Unclaimed Experience: Trauma, Narrative and History* (1996), the work in which the term "trauma theory" appears for the first time, she claims that trauma is an event that fragments consciousness. It is a wound inflicted, not on the body, but on the mind (Caruth 1996, 3). The traumatic experience inevitably does tremendous damage to the psyche. It causes a breach in the mind's experience of time, the self, and the world. The reference to time here is important. Caruth is concerned with the relationship between trauma, or the traumatic experience, and time. The traumatic experience, unlike a physical wound, does not heal with time; it becomes permanent, because it is a psychological wound. Indeed, a very important aspect of trauma is the continuous recapturing of the past and of the traumatic experience. This could take the form of nightmares, dreams, or hallucinations. According to Caruth, we can understand the nature of trauma by studying its causes and its effects on the victim.

Caruth also emphasizes the relationship between trauma and language. She suggests that Freud in his analysis turns to literature because it is only through literature that such traumatic events could be narrated, and language is therefore essential in the representation of trauma. Whether language and literature constitute the only medium through which trauma could be represented is debatable, but the fact remains that literature has played an enormous role in its expression and representation. Hence the importance of writers like Syl Cheney-Coker. The use of the appropriate language (both by the writer and the sufferer in some cases) can be therapeutic.

Caruth can therefore be seen as being instrumental in the promulgation of trauma theory, especially in so far as it relates to literature, but there are problems with her postulations, some of which have been pointed out by other scholars. In the first place, her scheme is much too Eurocentric, concerned as it largely is with trauma in the Western world, and failing to give adequate attention to the differing spatial/temporal manifestations of trauma. The causes and effects of trauma might differ in various societies and communities. The effects will almost certainly differ if only because, over time, various societies have developed various methods of coping with trauma. It is almost certainly true that the effects of trauma in African countries differ from those in European countries. Caruth suggests that the traumatic wound can never be healed, and the traumatic experience keeps on being recaptured. As far as Europe is concerned, she is probably right, because one hears trauma victims claiming that they still have nightmares and bad dreams decades after the event, and can still not trust anyone, or go to certain places, or that their metamorphosis into serial killers or disturbed individuals is due to that traumatic event. One hardly hears this about African victims, and the peoples of Africa have certainly had their own share of trauma, as Cheney-Coker's poems copiously illustrate. Could it be that because of effective support services or certain ritual practices or other therapeutic methods developed in certain societies the therapeutic wound can be healed, though it cannot be forgotten?

The view, deriving from Freud, that trauma is only psychological, is also problematic. Ultimately, every traumatic event is bound to affect the mind, because the mind will apprehend it, think about it, or recall it, but that does not mean that the impact is only psychological. Let us consider some events that actually happened in real life during the Sierra Leone Civil War and are recaptured in the poems of Cheney-Coker. When a mother sees her child killed before her eyes by being pounded on a stone with another slab of stone, this is surely trauma, and the impact is psychological, but it is also surely emotional. When a boy of eleven is asked to lay his hand on a stone and the hand is hacked off with a machete, the impact is both psychological and physical. Indeed, it is possible to argue that Cheney-Coker plays down the psychological but emphasizes the emotional, social, and physical.

Some studies suggest that trauma is a largely twentieth-century phenomenon, and it is quite clear that these proponents are mainly thinking about the Jewish Holocaust, which must have been one of the most traumatic events ever. There can be no denying the traumatic impact of the Holocaust, but surely there have been other events throughout history whose impact has been equally traumatic and devastating. One thinks about slavery, the Hundred Years' War, the Black Death, the Spanish Inquisition, the aftermath of the French Revolution, the Rwandan Genocide, and so on. The present-day suffering of the people of Ukraine surely also suggests the continuation of trauma into the twenty-first century. Trauma knows no boundaries of time or place.

Because of all these problems and issues, particularly with Caruth's traditional model of trauma theory, other alternatives have been adduced, effectively displacing her model and establishing a more comprehensive model of trauma theory. Studies by Forter, Mandel, Cvetkovich, and Hungerford suggest the multiple causes, effects, and methods of representation of trauma, and Morrissey investigates the nature of trauma in history and historical literature. Inspired by his experience in studying the Anglo-Saxon epic poem *Beowulf*, Morrissey was led to explore the traumatic suffering of those Nordic peoples at the hands of the monster Grendel and its representation in literature. Perhaps Roger Kurtz is the most interesting for our purpose here. Through a detailed analysis of various traumatic events that happened in Africa, such as the Nigerian Civil War, he shows how literature can influence our understanding of trauma and the transformation that can result from it. He shows that trauma can be transformative and that it is possible to be healed after the experience. Kurtz also shows the resilience of the African who can re-emerge from the experience bruised or even battered, but not out for the count. This kind of framework is very important for our study of Cheney-Coker's representation of trauma.

For further understanding of trauma, it may be necessary to look at the definition of trauma. Here is the Webster Dictionary's definition, wherein it refers to three main categories: "1a: an injury to a living tissue caused by an extrinsic agent; b: a disordered psychic or behavioral state resulting from mental or emotional stress or physical injury; 2: an agent, force, or mechanism that causes trauma." In other words, trauma can refer not only to the injury or wound inflicted by an external agent, but also to the suffering, whether physical, emotional, or psychological, resulting from such an injury, as well as to the cause or the agent inflicting or responsible for such horrendous suffering. This is an inclusive view of trauma, which is similar to the comprehensiveness shown by Forter, Mandel, Cvetkovich, Hungerford, Morrissey, Kurtz and others. It even goes beyond them to suggest that the agent inflicting or responsible for the suffering is itself a part of the trauma. It is the argument of this chapter that all these categories are dealt with in *Stone Child and Other Poems*. In this attempt to explore and understand Cheney-Coker's latest poems and his representation of trauma, we will therefore reflect this comprehensive and inclusive trauma model, paying attention to the multiple causes and agents of trauma which can be regarded as a part of the trauma; to the traumatic wound or experience itself which could be physical, social, or psychological; to the consequences of trauma which could include the psychological, emotional, or social; and to the nature and effects of trauma in non-European and non-Western societies. The chapter will therefore consider the agents or causes of the horrendous suffering during the war, agents and causes which are themselves part of the trauma; the nature of the actual injury caused and the horrendous experience itself; and the emotional, physical, or psychological suffering it entailed. It will also be obvious from the discussion that Cheney-Coker's use of language and imagery is uniquely effective in the evocation of the intensity of the suffering.

Let us start by looking at the agents or the causes of this unprecedented suffering. It might be supposed that Cheney-Coker would highlight the human agents, that is the rebels and others of all ages who killed, maimed, or raped thousands of their countrymen and women. Cheney-Coker certainly has these in mind, as will appear later, but he primarily locates the cause of the war and the suffering precisely where it belongs: the stone, or the diamond. The diamonds that should have been a blessing to the country became a curse. The diamond could thus be seen as a symbol of both economic prosperity and economic deprivation, the difference between the "haves" and the "have-nots," which has always been one of the major causes of civil strife, not just in Sierra Leone, but in Africa as a whole. In the case of Sierra Leone, the war was, in the view of many, quite simply about who should control the nation's diamond resources. It is quite significant that, as a result of one of the many accords that sought to put an end to the strife, Foday Sankoh, the leader of the rebel Revolutionary United Front (R.U.F.), was placed in charge of the nation's mining activities, and one of the main objectives of the R.U.F. was the capture and control of diamond-producing areas, with the aid of Charles Taylor, the then Liberian Head of State. Also, in an attempt to defeat the R.U.F., the government of Captain Valentine Strasser had an agreement with a group of dubious mercenaries for their military assistance, in exchange for the diamonds the country produced. Diamonds were therefore at the heart of the war, and the "stone" in "Stone Child" not only suggests the acts of brutalization and exploitation and the suffering they entailed, but also the cause of that suffering. The diamond was itself the trauma.

In poem after poem Cheney-Coker contemplates the paradox and ambivalence of the stone. He wonders how something that could appear so beautiful on a woman or that could make a woman so beautiful and even desirable, could also be the cause of so much bestiality and suffering. Indeed, the poet continually compares the gemstone to a highly desirable and beautiful woman, roughly equivalent to the lady in medieval courtly love poems, who is placed on a pedestal and adored and on whose behalf hordes of admirers are prepared to perform extraordinary feats of courage; it is also compared to the damsel in distress that needs to be rescued from a monstrous or evil force.

One of the poems is appropriately entitled "Our Lady of Diamonds", like "Our Lady of Lourdes" or "Our Lady of Guadeloupe", a force that is not only worthy of worship, since in herself she is beautiful and innocent, but also has the charisma that compels men to worship and adore her. The diamond is thus a variant of the Madonna figure. However, the Madonna and Child figure of "Homage to Stone Child" can easily degenerate into the figure of the madam, the whore, or the prostitute, like the Biblical "Whore of Babylon." Thus, the figure of the Madonna and that of the prostitute become conflated. In "Homage to Stone Child" the poet calls the gem a "trollop," a cursed stone for whom the child was killed. In "Our Lady of Diamonds" the gem has become a "stone woman," naked and sensual, dancing fandangos with the butcher of Huambo, and for whom the karate mosquito kills in Sierra Leone (9).

The Lady of Diamonds has thus degenerated into a "shameless stone," "a bloodletting woman," whom the poet cannot love but would rather give up to the "fevered lust of the world." The pursuit of the stone is thus equated with the most depraved forms of lechery and lust. Of course, the diamonds were obtained, not just by digging deep into the earth, but by "panning" in the rivers, and so the river becomes a pervasive image in the collection. Two of the poems are entitled "The Meaning of Rivers." Cheney-Coker suggests in "The Meaning of Rivers (1)" that Sierra Leone's rivers have become conduits of death:

> Relentlessly using our insane verbs,
> We panned the stone rivers in inflammable brawls,
> Before entering the slaughterhouses.
> The bewildering beds of death were waiting for us there (13)

This is a reference to the brutal scramble for the diamonds in the rivers and the inevitable slaughter of each other that was a fact of life among the men who panned for the diamonds. Counterpointing with the image of rivers or water is the image of fire, suggesting another cause of the trauma: the war itself and the internecine strife within the land. Thus in "The Meaning of Rivers (1)" the poet says, "we panned the rivers in inflammable brawls," and in "The Meaning of Rivers (2)", "we let the cursed minerals set the tipsy ferns ablaze." In "Letters from Home", "the Prima Donna, our lady of diamonds shat her own cannonball of fire," and in "When the Dead Talk," "the Dead woke up like fiery vowels and metaphors of spitfire and bent the raptures of the wind to the cutting edge of their vengeance." Fire thus becomes simultaneously a metaphor for the war and the cause of the trauma as well as literally one of the effects of the war. It should be recalled with horror that some people were burnt alive, locked up in their houses, and swathes of land were set on fire.

However, the poet assuredly suggests that the people of Sierra Leone themselves, through their greed, corruption, materialism, and incompetence, were a cause of the war and therefore part of the trauma. Sierra Leoneans were themselves the inveterate murderous brutes who embarked on this fratricidal strife and set the country on fire. This is the main focus of the powerful "New Year in Freetown, 1999," which suggests that even while Sierra Leoneans were preparing to honor the Christian God at Christmas, they were secretly planning the most horrific and mindless attacks that resulted in carnage and wanton destruction. At the dawn of the century, a fratricidal hatred was raging in people's hearts. The dawn of a new century and of a new year suggests ideas of birth, rebirth, and renewal, and the poet goes on to deploy images related to these very skillfully. However, there will be no rebirth for Sierra Leone, given the "dissonant notes." The various factions in Sierra Leone are compared to Siamese twins, joined at birth and nursing at the same mother's breasts, but eventually turning on each other when left to themselves, like Cain and Abel. The image of the Siamese twins simultaneously suggests the natural closeness, originally, of the warring factions, but also the monstrous birth, rather than rebirth that occurs. The image of birth is continued in the reference to "primitive obstetrics." Left to themselves after the birth (independence), Sierra Leoneans fell on each other like animals, unmindful of the noble example of Nelson Mandela, and turned the country into a blasted desert, all because of the love of gemstones, the "shameless woman" whose eyes are as repulsive as "the Medusa's."

In "The Meaning of Rivers (1)," the poet talks of the people's greed, their sycophancy and naivety that made them hurry to crown a new leader who was mainly anxious to unveil an ancient lust. Lust here is carnal lust, the lust demonstrated by so many African leaders, including those of Sierra Leone, for the most beautiful women. "Someone was saying a new king deserves vestal virgins, white roosters, the finest harvest, a crest on his head, woven by the sea-maidens" (13). However, "lust" is also lust for wealth and the proprietorial enjoyment of the country's resources. Thus, the complicity of the people in setting up leaders who eventually become dictatorial predators is underscored. The leader then proceeded to deceive them, and before they were aware of it "a bloody palm tree fell on our hope" and they declined from being the "Athens of West Africa" to the "Wretched of the Earth." Above all, Cheney-Coker suggests the complicity of leaders all over the world in bringing about Sierra Leone's suffering. Arabs, other Africans, Europeans, Jews, Gentiles, Hindus and pagans, because of their unquenchable desire for the gemstone, have contributed to the suffering and should be held accountable. They, too, are part of the trauma.

Second, there is the actual injury itself caused by the external agent. This could take the form of a physical maiming or abuse or even death, but it could also be any form of brutalization, or corruption resulting from the action of the agent, or exploitation of any kind. Some would say that this is the actual trauma from which the abused suffers. Suggestions of actual maiming or killing are rife in Cheney-Coker's collection. The fourth stanza of "Homage to Stone Child" goes like this:

> Being human was only a cup away from our lips,
> which was not too much for God to ask of us,
> so I dare not imagine your misery, when the rain falls
> on your immature grave, although I need your watery gaze to learn
>   how you died, after we ceased to be human. (2)

"Immature grave" suggests the child prematurely killed and buried in a stone grave, or a grave covered with stones. The poet looks at the grave and reflects on the inhuman circumstances that brought the child there. The image of the stone recurs in the next stanza where there is a reference to "a mother's scream loud in the air about how a stone fell on her breasts." The stone connotes something hard and utterly destructive and life-denying as contrasted with the breasts that connote fruition and nourishment; one almost sees the visual picture of a mother screaming as her child is battered by the stone. The next stanza continues like this:

> Amongst the Dead, that woman was looking for her son.
> Innocent, no girl had kissed him yet; his heart was fragile
> when they selected him, Mother, his soul was crushed
> that morning, you were not there to hear his cry
> as he waited for the stone to give him a name. (3)

Here the child could be a literally dead child whose mother was searching for him amongst the other dead bodies, but also a metaphorically "dead" child, an innocent youngster who has been abducted to fight in the war and whose soul and entire personality have been crushed by the war and by the stone. In fact, in the ranks of the combatants he will be literally branded like an animal, "crying out loud as he waited for the stone to give him a name," he will be robbed of his previous identity and given a new identity and personality. This boy's soul was crushed as surely as his mother's breast was by the stone. The stone is both a literal stone, a branding iron, but also, of course, the diamond. In other words, as a result of the struggle for the nefarious gems, youngsters lost their identity, their selfhood and their souls. In the next stanza the stone is explicitly referred to as the "Gemstone" and compared to a highly desirable woman that everyone in the world wants, and who thus becomes a "cursed stone" and a "trollop" for whom the child was killed. The poem continues:

> His blood on the other stone
> was too hot for his mother to cuddle in her arms;
> the sun was drained of its colour; it had the face of that
> woman: a lunatic raving about how the men
> severed her son's hands for the stone. (3)

Stone here refers to the stone on which the child was killed or on which the child's hand was placed before it was severed from its body, a reference to the numerous children whose hands were deliberately amputated in the war. In the next stanza, which is addressed to the "innocent child," the stone becomes the sinful harvest, a hard destructive thing contrasted with the nourishing bread the harvest should make available. It is the chaos and suffering caused by the war. Stone is thus used in several senses: the cursed gemstone, the slab of stone or heap of stones on the child's grave, the stone that crushed the mother's breasts, the stone on which the child was killed or on which its hands were amputated, the stone that was used to crush the child's soul and bring about his loss of personality and identity, and the chaos resulting from the war.

Indeed, the image of the severed hand permeates the collection, as do various other parts of the body such as bellies, breasts, and heads that have either been slit open or battered, or whose functions, in many cases, have been subverted. Thus, bellies are usually split open or swollen, and heads have been converted to skulls, thereby reminding the poet of stilted and abnormal growth. Summer has been transformed to autumn and, though crickets stir, ravens call the poet to the woods.

Cheney-Coker clearly suggests that a very important aspect of the injury inflicted on the people was the subversion of a number of aspects of the nation's life and their transformation from the normal to the abnormal. This can be regarded as a social injury and is already hinted at in "The Meaning of Rivers (2)," where the poet suggests that the rivers have become polluted and diverted from their pristine innocence and capacity for nurturing. They are now "gem rivers" or "damaged rivers" and their songs are barbarous because the people injected a murderous syringe into the country. The image of pollution or infection is very pronounced, and the dominant note of deliberate corruption or even sacrilegious rape of something that was once innocent cannot be missed: "the rivers offered their breasts that we devoured endlessly" (15). Earlier in the poem the poet had referred to "the breasts of some young girls responding to our smiles" (15). There is thus a contrast between innocence and corruption. Even the gem itself was originally innocent – a Madonna – before it became corrupted by greed and materialism and became a whore. Similarly, the rivers were also innocent and held their secrets in their bosoms like the succulent, innocent, trusting breasts of the young girls. But then came corruption, seduction, exploitation, and betrayal of trust and innocence. It is also significant that the image of rape is pervasive here, rape which is one of the most important and repellent forms of trauma and a weapon of war deployed in the war.

The subversion of important aspects of the country's life or the transformation from the normal to the abnormal applies particularly to religion. Religion is never far away in the poetry of Cheney-Coker. Ernest Cole (2014), for instance, draws attention to Cheney-Coker's preoccupation with religion and his religious attitudes and concerns (72). Generally, Cheney-Coker's attitude to religion and the Christian God is sarcastic at best. In this respect, the collection *Stone Child and Other Poems* is no exception. The sarcasm can already be detected in the poem "Our Lady of Diamonds" where the usual connotations of the Madonna are subverted. In the collection as a whole the poet seems to be asking where God was when all this butchery was taking place. At best, God seems to have been indifferent to the people's suffering both before and during the war. In other words, religion which should have nurtured, sustained and even protected the people turned a blind eye. The poem that most compellingly presents this idea is "The Golden Chalice." Here are the first three stanzas:

> Without those lustful diadems of diamond
> to crown, majestic, our sinful heads,
> the pestilential hunger dies, our carnality is sheathed,
> and the gem diggers sleep quietly in the now peaceful rivers.
> still the cup of life tastes sour in the orphans' mouth:
>
> Children of your creation, all, God, their last hope
> was your golden chalice. Now it is bitter and inchoate,
> even as they pray for your great presence.
> Fervent believers all, they were singing those meandrous songs
> that did not reach your ears: it was a ritual. Ah, *the Wretched
> of The Earth* – those not so very innocent children of Sierra Leone!
>
> Waking up from those persistent nightmares
> they went seeking your hands, but all they saw, sculptured
> in skeletal form, was this new frieze that stinks!
> Proud profiles: the earth shook from the beating of their chests;
> becoming children once again, they adorned their foreheads
>   to look innocent; but a rogue leader sold their laurels to a Sahara
>   desert,
> where a djinn swallowed them when no saints were watching. (24)

The chalice is, of course, the cup with which the wine is given to the communicants during the Christian sacrament of Holy Communion, and it is supposed to contain the blood of Christ with its hope of salvation. It should normally be a life-giving force suggesting hope and prosperity. Here, however, this "cup of life" tastes sour in the orphans' mouths. All these poor people were children of God's creation; they were all fervent believers, good Christians all who trusted in God's protection, and whose last hope was, in fact, the Christian God who promised protection and salvation through his son. But the sacrament of Holy Communion became nothing but an empty ritual; the people's cries did not reach the ears of God and they experienced neither the protection nor the salvation they had been led to expect. In fact, they became, in Fanon's phrase, "the wretched of the earth" (1961). In the third stanza there is the implied reference to the hordes of disillusioned youngsters who took refuge in the camps of the R.U.F. out of frustration, but who were, in turn, betrayed by their new leaders (the rogue leaders), another pervasive motif in the poems. In their rage, these stone children had allowed themselves to be enticed by a rogue leader who "sold their laurels to a thirsty Sahara." This could be a reference to the training the young men received in Libya and neighboring countries. Instead of the salvation and prosperity promised by the chalice, all they had were the empty cups of dreams. The indifference of God and Christianity to the plight of the young in particular, and the people in general, is surely suggested in "when no saints were watching" and "Christ sat watching their profuse deliriums."

However, there is a suggestion in this collection, that the blame lies not so much with religion or God, as with the people themselves who have perverted or subverted religion. The transformation of religion and the subversion of religious practices is an aspect of the trauma, a trauma caused by the people themselves in their materialism and obliviousness to all that is sacred. In "New Year in Freetown, 1999," which explores the brutal rebel invasion of Freetown in January of that year, the poet refers to the pointless and essentially godless Christmas celebrations that immediately preceded the infamous attack:

> We were sanguine during that drama of insidious intent,
> and rushed like relentless gladiators to honour that god,
> remorseless and sangfroid, even as we professed innocence.
> Afterwards, the world waited for our icons of war
> so perfect, a forger could not have copied them.
> Tragedy-prone, we painted these God-denying images,
> rituals of derangement, before pulling out our hairs
> over what was more important: maiming our children
> at Christmas, or celebrating that Coptic-Jew. (6)

The poet registers the religious hypocrisy inherent in celebrating Christmas, which, after all, is a period of "peace on earth and good will towards men," while during this time Sierra Leoneans were meditating on and planning a savage and brutal attack on their countrymen. It was all a drama of "insidious intent," honoring Christ even as we coldly and deliberately planned to do battle like "relentless gladiators." We were blood-thirsty and made plans for war even as we professed innocence. Maiming our children at Christmas was more important than celebrating that "Coptic-Jew."[1] The poet implies tremendous religious insincerity and hypocrisy and avers that if God seems to have deserted the people, it is entirely their own fault, for "after the way we killed the stone child, no Christ will ever visit Sierra Leone again." In a bid to dramatize the repulsiveness of the injuries inflicted by Sierra Leoneans on fellow Sierra Leoneans, the poet deftly counterpoints images suggesting the natural and human with those suggesting the abnormal, thus implying that the culture presented has subverted everything from the natural and human and converted them to the abnormal and the monstrous. Thus, breasts which should naturally connote fruition, procreation and nurturing are counterpointed with stone. Images from the world of vegetation are counterpointed with images of destruction. In "Homage to Stone Child" the harvest is a harvest of stone; bread in the oven becomes a "bitter candour of death"; and yeast tastes of "severed hands." Furthermore, water images which are normally benevolent in literature take on a completely different coloring in this collection. The river, as we have seen, has become a conduit of death, and rain has become a terrible thing. In "Homage to Stone Child" it registers the grief of the mother whose child's hands have been cut off, and it also suggests the continuing anarchy and terror in the country. It is seen as a savage rain that "baptizes" the child. As for the sea, it is imagined in the poem "The Breasts of the Sea" as a creature (a woman) that has been oppressed over the years, an abused mother who can therefore produce no more islands:

> After our bloody century, the sea will groan
> under its weight, somewhere between breasts and anus
> filled with toxins, her belly will not yield new islands. (19)

Finally, we'll look at Cheney-Coker's presentation of the third aspect of the trauma, the actual suffering and misery of the people on whom such horrendous injuries have been inflicted and the numerous consequences of such injuries. To a certain extent, this has already been implied in the discussion so far. It might take the form of the extreme agony of mothers who witness the amputation of their children's limbs, or see their children battered to death with stones. It might be the screams of those being burnt to death in houses

---

[1] While the poet uses religion, Christianity more specifically, to buttress his critique of the "ungodliness" of the war, this does not mean that 1) Sierra Leone is a predominantly Christian country, or 2) that those doing the killings were all or mostly Christians. The Civil War in Sierra Leone, a Muslim dominant country, was a free for all, regardless of religion, region, or ethnicity.

in which they have been locked up. It might be the long-term damage done to the psyches of people who have witnessed such atrocities, or who have themselves suffered rape, or who have been forced to fight and kill friends and relations against their will and who, on their return to their societies at the end of the war, find that they are rejected and ostracized by those they love because of their activities during the war, and, even if accepted, find that they cannot fit in.

The Stone Child of the title is the child whose entire fate has been adversely affected by the war (largely caused by the stone, the diamond) and whose character has been everlastingly conditioned by the circumstances of the war. During the war, thousands of very young boys and girls were abducted[2] from their homes (some of them after having witnessed the killing of their elders), mostly by the rebels, and the boys were introduced to hard drugs and induced to fight mindlessly, killing relations and friends in the process, while the girls were used as sex slaves. Many of the boys became drug addicts and many of the girls gave birth to "bastard" children that they would rather not have had. At the end of the war those who survived discovered that they could not return to and be accepted by their homes and families because of the atrocities they had committed during the war, or, in the case of the girls, because they were seen as polluted. The girls, in particular, had to live with the stigma of having been raped or having given birth to "bastard" children. In a sense, these abused participants in the war are the "stone children" of Cheney-Coker's collection. It is of such children that the poet says in "Homage to Stone Child":

> Sex slaves, orgies: outraged guttural ancestors:
> the images are sacrilegious, but do not compare
> with you, nameless child, whose innocence
> lights a candle in our tenebrous age. (2)

And later,

> Mother, his soul was crushed
> that morning, you were not there to hear his cry (3)

Cheney-Coker surely hints at the traumatic disorder during the aftermath of the war in "Out of the Abyss" when he suggests that

> We emerged, worn-out from the abyss, a broken country,
> the women less tender, the men wounded, their children gone crazy,
> and the innocents raving naked on the night's brutal highways. (27)

---

[2] To be sure, many of the boys and girls who became child soldiers joined the fighting of their own accord. This is part of the ongoing debate in child-soldier studies about the agency of children and child soldiers.

No other words could have more forcefully rendered the continuing psychological impact of the war on men, women, and children.

As we have seen, poem after poem registers the suffering of mothers whose children have been killed or abducted. We hear the scream of a mother as she sees her child ripped from her breast and battered with a stone. We feel the agony of the mother looking for her son among the dead, her son who has been abducted and whose soul has been destroyed even before he reached adolescence. There is also the compelling vignette of the mother who has gone mad, raving about how her son's hands were amputated. But the agony is not just individualized, it is general, for even the poet himself has nightmares in which he dreams about those "lost hands."

Syl Cheney-Coker's *Stone Child and Other Poems* brilliantly encapsulates all three categories of Webster's definition of trauma: there is the stone which is the ultimate cause of the suffering as well as the people who in their drive for the stone perpetrated such horrors on themselves; there is the actual injury and the brutal experience and suffering of all the inhabitants of the country, signified particularly by maimed children and raped women; and there are the multifarious effects of this mindless and brutal maiming. This was Sierra Leone's trauma.

Works Cited

Caruth, Cathy, *Unclaimed Experience: Trauma, Narrative, and History* (Baltimore: Johns Hopkins University Press, 1996).

Cvetkovich, Ann, *An Archive of Feelings: Trauma, Sexuality, and Lesbian Public Culture* (Durham: Duke University Press, 2003).

Cheney-Coker, Syl, *Concerto for an Exile* (London: Heinemann, 1973).

—— *The Blood in the Desert's Eyes* (London: Heinemann, 1990).

—— *The Graveyard Also Has Teeth* (London: Heinemann, 1980).

—— *Stone Child and Other Poems* (Ibadan: Heinemann, 2008).

Cole, Ernest, "The Poetry of Syl Cheney-Coker: *The Blood in the Desert's Eyes*", in *Emerging Perspectives on Syl Cheney-Coker* (eds.) Eustace Palmer and Ernest Cole (Trenton, NJ: Africa World Press, 2014), pp. 71–8.

Forter, Craig, "Colonial Trauma, Utopian Carnality, Modernist Form: Tony Morrison's *Beloved* and Arundati Roy's *The God of Small Things*", in *Contemporary Approaches to Literary Trauma Theory*, ed. Michele Balaeo (New York: Palgrave Macmillan, 2014), pp. 70–105.

Freud, Sigmund, *Beyond the Pleasure Principle* (London: Norton, 1959/1920).

Hartman, Geoffrey, "On Traumatic Knowledge and Literary Studies," *New Literary History* 26.3 (1995), pp. 557–63.

Hungerford, Amy, *The Holocaust of Texts: Genocide, Literature, and Personification* (Chicago, IL and London: University of Chicago Press, 2003).

Kaplan, Ann E., *Trauma Culture: The Politics of Terror and Loss in Media and Literature* (New Brunswick: Rutgers University Press, 2005).

Kurtz, Roger, *Trauma and Transformation in African Literature* (New York: Routledge, 2020).

Mandel, Naomi, *Against the Unspeakable: Complicity, the Holocaust and Slavery in America* (Charlottesville: University of Virginia Press, 2006).

Mish, Frederick C. (Editor in Chief), *Merriam Webster's Collegiate Dictionary* 10th ed. (Springfield, MA: Merriam Webster Inc., 1993).

Morrissey, Ted, *The Beowulf Poet and His Real Monsters: A Trauma-Theory Reading of the Anglo-Saxon Poem* (New York: Edwin Mellen Press, 2013).

Tal, Kali, *Reading the Literature of Trauma* (New York: Cambridge University Press, 1996).

Chapter 6

Space, Trauma, and Healing in Delia Jarrett-Macauley's *Moses, Citizen and Me*

OUMAR CHÉRIF DIOP

In his article "Of Other Spaces," reflecting on the mirror as a placeless place, Michel Foucault leads us into the unreal, virtual space behind the mirror where we are but also are not. That utopian, unreal space allows us to see ourselves where, in fact, we are not. "Starting from this gaze that is, as it were, directed toward me, from the ground of this virtual space that is on the other side of the glass, I come back toward myself; I begin again to direct my eyes toward myself and to reconstitute myself there where I am" (1986, 24). This affordance of the mirror to help us turn our gaze to ourselves and reconfigure ourselves is paramount to shaping or reshaping our identities. Foucault also draws attention to the fact that "the space in which we live, which draws us out of ourselves, in which the erosion of our lives, our time and our history occurs […] is also a heterogeneous space delineated by a set of relations irreducible to one another and not superimposable on one another" (22). Thus, in a social context, the mirror redirecting the gaze in the process of construction or reconfiguration of selfhood must be considered in relation to spatial heterogeneity and to the relations that define, structure, and shape that space. The intersubjective relations the subject entertains in various networks and the outward gazes they involve contribute to processes of self-discovery and identity construction or reconfiguration. Thus, an analysis of space must consider the social networks, power relations, and conflicts pertaining to each situation.

In post-apartheid South Africa, post-genocide Rwanda, and post-civil war Sierra Leone, Truth and Reconciliation Commissions (TRCs) were set up to facilitate the return to self that we mentioned in the quote from Foucault above. In that vein, the TRCs were spaces designed to allow victims and perpetrators of violence to redirect their eyes toward themselves and to reconstitute themselves from where they are. Arguably, in these public venues, testimonies of victims and confessions of perpetrators can contribute to establishing relatively accurate records of countries' pasts to learn from them and avoid repeating them, and to help in the healing process and promote national reconciliation. However, according to Tim Kelsall (2005), referring to Sierra Leone,

> witnesses did not generally accept the idea that the Commission was a platform upon which to enact grief, catharsis and healing, either for their own benefit or for that of the nation. The drama of healing through public confession and grief, which enlists a number of tropes in the Christian imaginary, such as suffering, martyrdom, and resurrection, and explains in part the widespread fascination with truth commissions, was a story in which most participants seemed reluctant to be enrolled. (371)

The fact that public truth-telling lacks deep roots in the local cultures of Sierra Leone explains the witnesses' unwillingness to testify at the TRC. To the TRC's public venues, Delia Jarrett-Macauley's *Moses, Citizen and Me* suggests alternative spaces where various activities emerge and allow the return of the gaze. Using Michel Foucault's analysis of the mirror in his article "Other Spaces" and Henri Lefebvre's concept of "spatial practice", I will focus on how healing processes occur in such spaces.

In Delia Jarrett-Macauley's *Moses, Citizen and Me* (2006), the main protagonist, the thirty-year-old Londoner Julia, returns to Sierra Leone. One of the neighbors of her bereaved uncle Moses asked her to come and comfort him. His eight-year-old grandson, Citizen, had murdered his wife Adele and led Moses and his friends to the mangrove swamp where the "big soldier man" ordered him to commit the unspeakable act. Adele was shot several times in her back with her hands tied behind her back and her legs bound together. When Julia got to Uncle Moses's house, Citizen was outside the yard wandering around a tree, his eyes fixed on the dusty ground. A little bit later, perched high on the balustrade, Citizen "looked more burnt and more punished than a plantation worker ever did. His eyes were red. His short hair was unclean; his cheekbones stood out prominently and suggested poise" (7). Citizen's physical appearance bespeaks desolation, and his hesitancy in the yard contrasts with how comfortably and purposefully the neighbors Anita and her daughter Sara make use of that space. Progressively, under Sara's guidance, Citizen finds his bearings in the yard and partakes in outdoor activities: "Citizen and Sara, in shorts and barefoot, were on their hands and knees planting some shoots in the earth she had dug up that morning and rearranged elsewhere." In their cooperative venture, they joined hands "clearing holes, putting in the shoots, and patting down the earth" (45). Responsive to Sara and enthusiastic about their endeavor, Citizen shows the first reassuring steps toward reintegrating the family circle, which surprised Uncle Moses' neighbors, Anita and Julia. From where they were spying on the two children, they reacted: "'Thank God,' said Anita. 'Amen,' replied Julia" (45). They both agreed that that plot of land "should be reserved for them, a site for neighbourly endeavors" (45).

These collaborative "neighbourly endeavors" were in stark contrast to what happened days earlier when Julia, Anita, and Sara visited Citizen at the ex-child soldiers' Doria camp where there were hundreds of them as young as six years old. Sara shared with Citizen her drawing and her story of a snappers' quick counterattack against whales plotting to take over their waters.

> When the snapper heard this, they organized themselves into a brave army and put the most potent, fattest snapper in front. They spread the sea floor with poisonous weeds that the whales could not resist, and as the whales became sleepy and drugged from eating the weeds, the snapper laughed at their faces and swam away. (41)

The words she whispered in Citizen's ear might have stirred a painful memory that plunged him into a somber mood. When Julia approached and touched him to comfort him,

> [h]e whimpered and slumped to the floor. I went to stand by him, reaching out to touch him. Without warning, he jumped to his feet, shouting into the air, hitting and punching in a way that suggested combat with several ghostly enemies. Sounds emerged from his lips, but nothing we could make sense of, no actual words – just noises and grunts that until that moment had been beneath his tongue. Alone he battled, then cautiously straightened as though in fear of being hit back. Finally, he was done and slumped on the floor. (42)

The resolution of Sara's story demonstrates that one must use unsuspected resources one harbors not to surrender to fear and brutal force. The potency of the drug used by the snapper is proportional to the power of the snappers' imagination and indomitable will to resist their bully's assaults. Furthermore, the story suggests that the more victims are intimidated to the extent of assuming their powerlessness and caving in, the more powerful they make their attackers. Going beyond the entertaining aspect of the story to underscore its didactic dimension, the story's coda that Sara might have whispered in Citizen's ear, resurrected a painful memory that points at his weakness, cowardice, and guilt. Sara's whisper and Julia's touch trigger the traumatic memories expressed through his incomprehensible, non-verbalized reaction. They emerge spontaneously in situations that recall the original traumatic condition and are produced by the mechanism "Janet called *restitutio ad integrum*. When one element of a traumatic experience is evoked, all other elements follow automatically. Ordinary memory is not characterized by *restitutio ad integrum*" (Van der Kolk and Van der Hart 1991, 431). Thus, Citizen's kinetic, bodily, and iconic forms of expression are tantamount to traumatic stress, which

> interferes with consolidating a verbalizable explicit memory but does not affect implicit sensory, motor, or affective representations of the traumatic

> event. Furthermore, such implicit representations are deeply imprinted in memory under high adrenaline levels and other stress hormones. They can intrude on consciousness through annoying sensations, images, feelings, and motor activities. (Shobe and Kihlstrom 1997, 72)

Undoubtedly, Citizen is still under the tyranny of a past whose memory he cannot organize into a narrative. Therefore, compulsive and terrifying elements of the trauma flood his consciousness. He continues to re-experience somatic anxiety reactions the way it happened during a hide-and seek game when Moses found him, and he let a soul-tearing scream that cut through the house (78). However, Sara's story and Julia's reaction had a dual effect on Citizen. On the one hand, they triggered painful traumatic memories. On the other hand, they allowed him to catch a glimpse of his other self without the terrifying background scenes laden with corpses and burnt huts and trees. Such sights made him relax and gave him the urge to speak after being silent for a whole year.

In contrast to the episode at Doria camp, Citizen became accepting of people's proximity after being immersed in gardening in the yard, under Sara's leadership. As a result of such an experience, after watching Anita scrub Sara clean and shampoo and condition her hair, Citizen jumped into the tub naked and let Julia bathe him. In the tub, he joyfully splashed the water and played with the hippo brush while Julia rubbed ointment into the number 439K cut in his back. He then allowed Julia to wrap him in a towel, and for a moment, he was in her arms. Eventually, Julia watched him lie in bed calmly and sleepy and wished him sweet dreams. The closeness to Sara, the maternal care from Julia, and the intimacy in the yard and the rooms help Citizen reach a significant emotional milestone in reconquering his childhood. The gardening experience was part of his early childhood before the murder of his parents Kole and Agnes, and his abduction. They owned a plot upcountry where they grew and sold vegetables. His work with Sara in the garden reconnected him with that blissful period of his life when his enthusiastic involvement with his parents' farm as a toddler earned him the name "First Citizen of the Farm." That was a period in his life when during the festive harvest, special parties were organized for children.

Thus, the process of reclamation and reintegration of the yard through collaborative gardening with Sara, under the benevolent eyes of Anita and Julia, presents Citizen with a mirror that is neither cracked nor turned against him. Instead, it welcomed him and reflected on him a soothing and relaxing image he was eager to embrace. The change in Citizen's emotional and mental conditions is a result of the relations the yard had been imbued with. Like thousands of children aged 8–14 years, Citizen was exploited and forced to be a child soldier by both the Revolutionary United Front (RUF) and the Sierra Leone army during the Civil War in Sierra Leone. Many of the child soldiers ended up in the Gola rainforest between Sierra Leone and Liberia. The RUF rebels strategically used this isolated and underdeveloped region in their plans to invade Sierra Leone from Liberia. As the RUF guerilla warfare spread in the Gola Forest, the communities were subject to violence and unspeakable atrocities, and children were abducted and conscripted into the RUF army. The child soldiers lived under dire conditions and committed heinous crimes wherever they went:

> The bitter cold air was relentless, just as the sun always left them weary on their day searches for food. Abu tried to get up, but he could not. He rolled about to ease the pain brought on by "eating too much fruit on an empty stomach. I'm very cold," Abu kept mumbling. After hunger, no proper food. After fighting, no rest. (58)

Citizen joined number-one-burn-house "unit" whose mission was to rush into "crowded villages with fire in their hands, wreaking devastation on homes, land, and people they compared to insects running for their lives" (59). After creating such mayhem, Citizen, under the influence of drugs, remained fearless and unperturbed. Ibrahim, the unit commander, had been involved in the most horrifying scenes of violence, seeing "people defecating like wild beasts in terror, parents burnt alive in front of their children, every ugly death; multiple rapes, single rape, gang rape, rape of pregnant women, daily rape, rape over a fortnight" (53). Like Ibrahim, Thomas, the "trigger-happy" twelve-year-old boy, who just got back from the front, was remorseless. He bragged gleefully about the ten or eleven people he killed (63). As for their companion Viktor, he shared how afraid he was the first time he killed someone, and how, after drinking, he killed many people indiscriminately. These boys have been burning and ruining villages, killing people, and raping girls and women. Bemba G, a senior member of the Gola community, pledged to put an end to their terrible ways (86). Bemba G successfully reclaimed the Gola Forest as an intimate, safe healing space for child soldiers who were victims and perpetrators of the worst acts of cruelty.

Bemba G's participatory and interactive pedagogy helped former child combatants learn applied math and encouraged them to participate in games, drama performances, and storytelling as a means of remembering and reconnecting with their humanity. Patiently, Bemba G helped some child soldiers deal with the trauma memories they experienced during intense emotional stress or fear, and re-experience them through flashbacks, nightmares, or overwhelming physical sensations. He helped others remember their fragmented memories. These are examples of the processes of re-membering Susanne Buckley-Zistel debates in her 2008 *Conflict Transformation and Social Change in Uganda: Remembering after Violence*. According to Buckley-Zistel, remembering "the past differently is to re-member" because when a community previously exposed to violence remembers the past, it "re-members the members of this community," meaning it re-organizes social life by re-assembling differently the community and its members (50). Under Bemba G's tutelage, the Gola Forest was no longer a place of terror to be feared as it used to be under the control of RUF. Instead, Bemba G's Forest culture is shaped by "crop rotation, which plants and shrubs to use for medicinal or recreational purposes ... forest lore, the details of rice cultivation, the value of elephant-dung rice ... shape-shifter stories about men and elephants" (Z'étoile 2017, 139).

Bemba G's transformation of the Gola Forest to help the former child soldiers heal confirms that space and time are always socially produced and result from the dynamics of the relations that bind its occupants. Diachronically, the new Gola space is marked by the recent history of violence, the knowledge of which allows Bemba G to design efficient strategies to attain the goals of self-redemption and to endeavor toward reconciliation collectively. As noted above, Bemba G was able to get everyone involved to create a safe and congenial system resulting from the articulation and connection of intellectually and emotionally engaging activities. Furthermore, Bemba G fostered a symbolic dimension of space with processes of signification emanating from the stories being shared in the reformed Gola space. By telling their stories and getting involved in the rehearsal and performance of Thomas Decker's *Juliohs Siza*, a Sierra Leonean Krio rendition of William Shakespeare's *Julius Caesar*, the participants can see and confront their former child-soldier identities and embrace their recovered child or adolescent identities. For example, with the help of Julia in a chosen spot in the Gola Forest, "he [Citizen] worked hard and fast, producing a deep hole in the ground. Then he took the block and buried it. Its descent was quick and clean. Citizen pushed back the soil, putting it down until 439K was covered" (164). The next day, he slept all day long, and when he woke up, "there was a glow on his face." After eating some fruit and nuts, he fell asleep again. Standing next to him, Julia saw in what appeared to be a dream scene and his smile that he became "a child again, afloat in a world of mother's making" (165).

In Jarrett-Macauley's *Moses, Citizen and Me*, processes of transformation remind us of Foucault's aforementioned reflection on the virtual space behind the mirror where we are but also are not. That unreal space, as Foucault argues, allows us to see ourselves where we are not. In many instances in the novel, this affordance of the mirror helps child soldiers turn their gaze to themselves and reconfigure themselves. Earlier in the novel, Sara's story triggered what appeared as Citizen's first self-evaluation. Because he saw his former self in the story, his mood changed, and soon after, he was overwhelmed by traumatic memories.

> Eventually, his breathing softened. He had just caught a glimpse of himself, the familiar frayed shorts and dusty top reflected in the window. This mirror, like a giant petal, welcomed him in. He hesitated, uncertain whether to trust

it or not, but it neither cracked nor turned against him. It did not introduce terrifying background scenes: corpses on the road, trees burnt black. Seeing his own face, Citizen relaxed, his image soothing him. (42)

For the first time, Citizen could see himself in a new light out of the terrifying alleys of his past. The ensuing feeling reassured him that he was in a safe environment. From then on, he became closer and closer to Sara and Julia.

In the Gola Forest, the use of drama by Bemba G helped the child soldiers embark on a process of self-discovery. The narrator comments after a rehearsal:

> What happened next took only two seconds to experience but would take hours to describe adequately. In appearance, nothing changed. The child soldiers held their positions, and the life in the forest continued, but something else was being transmitted. Call it end of amnesia, if you like, or some collective unconscious that I did not know existed. But the child soldiers got it, meeting themselves in the play. They understood their place in the scheme of things. (159)

This is an instance where liminality is on display. The situation is tantamount to a threshold in the ritual of border crossing. It signals entry into a different "law" for those who find themselves there and take on new identities. Bemba G's achievement at the psychosocial level demonstrates his astute management of the spatial practice in the Gola Forest.

In his 2008 article "Henri Lefebvre's theory of the production of space: Towards a three-dimensional dialectic," Christian Schmid expounds on Henri Lefebvre's definition of spatial practice as the material dimension of social activity and interaction. As such, it denotes the system resulting from articulating and connecting elements or activities. According to Caroline Levine, such activities can operate as powerful means of control and subjugation or be used strategically to effect transformative political ends. Whether imposing a temporal order on bodies or labor, sounds or machines, a rhythmic form can potentially do serious political work (49). In the Gola Forest, child soldiers are compelled to perform tasks that contribute to controlling their minds and bodies. Their daily routines condition them to become the vicious agents of death and destruction that they turn out to be.

A typical day for the child soldiers would begin with their leader Ibrahim shouting, "we are number-one-burn-house-unit!" And thereafter, he would ask for the rations they brought back from ransacking villages. They would lay before him the paltry supplies they had filched. He would take the oranges after rebuking them for their meager loot. After taking their daily dose of the drug, the child soldiers would embark on their mission, setting fire to villages.

Instead of this dehumanizing cycle of violence and trauma the child soldiers were caught in, Bemba G offered them a safe shelter, good stories, good food, entertainment, and education, all regulated by daily schedules with defined goals. After their math lessons, children listened to or told stories, played games, rehearsed for the upcoming performance of *Juliohs Siza*, or built shelters, which they did willingly (134). The other aspect of the mirror used to help turn the child soldiers' gaze to themselves and reconfigure themselves is the use of intertextuality. In *Spaces of Fiction / Fictions of Space: Postcolonial Place and Literary DeiXis*, Russell West-Pavlov argues that "intertextuality [...] offers a model of reality-construction: texts serve as explanatory templates to deal with emergent social situations" (85). In *Moses, Citizen and Me*, the incorporation of *Juliohs Siza* allows characters to see their past from another perspective. In that vein, intertextuality necessarily entails a process of reflection upon the ways in which the protagonists are implied within the process of socio-historical meaning-making by reaching back into the past and looking forward to the future. The self-reflexivity of their storytelling sessions and the rehearsal and performance of *Juliohs Siza* help them foreground and engage their lived experiences. Such an exercise is crucial to how they confront the demons of their past and reposition themselves. The play, in its therapeutic role, plays a significant part in the healing process. It acts as a vehicle for self-discovery and a catalyst for introspection. By functioning as a conduit for emotional release, it provides a controlled space for child soldiers to express their pent-up feelings and traumas. The play's intense sentiments and conflicts, reflecting the children's experiences of violence, enable them to confront and process their emotions. Through the play's fictional setting and the characters and their struggles, the child soldiers can express their traumatic experiences indirectly and deal with their own pain and confusion. While helping to reduce the psychological burden of their past gradually, this process fosters the children's grasp of different perspectives and the complexities of human behavior. For instance, grappling with Brutus' and Caesar's motives and actions helps them probe into their own experiences and decisions during the conflict and reassess them.

Weeks of rehearsals of *Juliohs Siza* culminated in the performance attended by the villagers across the river, Freetown elites, representatives from international agencies, journalists, British and American soldiers in uniform (201),

> the crowded dance floor, with boys and girls slipping over the earth, occasionally colliding into one another, rang out with singing. They moved freely. When the excitement took over, they shook their bodies or threw their arms into the air. Couples danced politely and gracefully. They touched the rhythm of joyful abandon. They danced into new relationships. (184)

Bemba G's redemptive pedagogy based on a spatial practice designed to cater to the psychosocial needs of the child soldiers has allowed them to see themselves from both where they had been and where they were not to be able to reclaim new identities. By telling their stories, they were able to face the demons of their past as a prerequisite to re-membering. By acquainting the former combatants with a new temporal order, the resulting rhythmic form helped in the re-membering process. Citizen eventually breaking his silence and speaking to Julia in the forest is an eloquent illustration of the potency of such rhythmic forms. The compounding effects of Julia's interventions, Sara's supervision in gardening, and Bemba G's expert designing and interconnecting of didactic and ludic activities resulted in the new rhythmic forms in Citizen's life that paved the way to his healing. To use Foucault's formula, Citizen and former child soldiers came back toward themselves; they began again to direct their eyes toward themselves and to reconstitute themselves there where they were. They touched the rhythm of joyful abandon because their psychosocial rhythms changed under Bemba G's guidance. After Sara and Julia helped Citizen reconnect with the domestic sphere, Bemba G's reconceptualizing, rehumanizing, and reconquering of the Gola Forest contributed significantly to transforming the child soldier from a victim and perpetrator of violence to a potential harbinger of peace and care.

Delia Jarrett-Macauley's *Moses, Citizen and Me* suggests a deployment of strategies that help reconfigure spaces affected by and associated with acts of violence and trauma to trigger healing processes. Former child soldiers' reintegration into such spaces helps them reconnect with their pre-war selves and regain the sense of community they lost during the war. Citizen, the main protagonist, reintegrates the home's domestic sphere after Sara progressively reintroduces him to gardening. Concomitantly, Julia's nurturing care helps reintroduce him into the house. Thanks to Bemba G's transformative pedagogy, the Gola Forest is reconfigured from a site of violence and trauma to a healing space prone to the intellectual and emotional growth of the former child soldiers and their social reintegration. The novel underscores the importance of designing post-war approaches to trauma that help community members re-member, re-organize, and re-assemble.

Works Cited

Buckley-Zistel, Susanne, *Conflict Transformation and Social Change in Uganda: Remembering after Violence* (Basingstoke: Palgrave Macmillan, 2008).

Foucault, Michel, "Of Other Spaces," *diacritics* 16.1 (1986), pp. 22–7.

Jarrett-Macauley, Delia, *Moses, Citizen and Me* (London: Granta, 2006).

Kelsall, Tim, "Truths, Lies, Ritual: Preliminary Reflections on the Truth and Reconciliation Commission in Sierra Leone," *Human Rights Quarterly* 27 (2005), pp. 361–91.

Levine, Caroline, *Forms: Whole, Rhythm, Hierarchy, Network* (Princeton: Princeton University Press, 2017).

Schmid, Christian, "Henri Lefebvre's Theory of the Production of Space: Towards a Three-Dimensional Dialectic," in *Space, Difference, Everyday Life: Reading*

Henri Lefebvre, (eds.) Kanishka Goonewardena, Stefan Kipfer, Richard Milgrom, Christian Schmid (New York: Routledge, 2008), pp. 41–59.

Shobe, Katharine Krause, and John F. Kihlstrom, "Is Traumatic Memory Special?" *Current Directions in Psychological Science* 6.3 (1997), pp. 70–4.

Van der Kolk, Bessel A., and Onno Van der Hart, "The Intrusive Past: The Flexibility of Memory and the Engraving of Trauma," *American Imago* 48.4 (1991), pp. 425–54.

West-Pavlov, Russell, *Spaces of Fiction, Fictions of Space: Postcolonial Place and Literary DeiXis* (Basingstoke: Palgrave Macmillan, 2010).

Z'étoile, Imma, "Rewriting the SLTRC: Masculinities, the Arts of Forgetting, and Intimate Space in Delia Jarrett-Macauley's *Moses, Citizen and Me* and Aminatta Forna's *The Memory of Love*," *Research in African Literatures* 48.2 (2017), pp. 129–51.

Chapter 7

Learning How to Smile Again: Ebola, Resilience, and Sierra Leonean Fiction

JOYA URAIZEE

Disease in Literature

"Only YOU can stop Ebola!" "Wi go 'Was' Ebola!" "Ebola! E Du So!" These words screamed out at me as I walked past a small compound on Guard Room Spur Road in the heart of Freetown, Sierra Leone. It was a warm morning in July 2015, and I was on my way to meet a couple of contacts I had at the Ministry of Social Welfare, Gender & Children's Affairs. If words could kill, I thought, these surely would. Painted in bold red letters against a pale painted blue background, they called out to passers-by like me that even death could be made to halt in its tracks. The reality, however, was very different. The 2014–2016 Ebola epidemic killed thousands of Sierra Leonean men, women, and children, all of whom died in horrible circumstances.[1] Ebola ravaged West Africa five years before COVID-19 spread its trail of devastation across the world, and like COVID, it seemed, at least initially, impossible to control.

Even to my untrained eyes, Freetown in July 2015 looked different from the way it did in 2014, when I was there last. Besides these ever-present billboards at every busy intersection and even at the airport, complete with graphic pictures of people in the throes of the disease, there were also repeated instructions to wash one's hands before entering any public buildings. Many large establishments provided visitors with canisters of chlorinated water, and also placed hand sanitizers on sidewalks and outdoor patios. Visible too were health

---

[1] According to the World Health Organization, the 2014–2016 West African Ebola outbreak was the largest in history. The West African death toll was 11,308, with 4,809 deaths in Liberia (out of 10,675 cases), 3,956 in Sierra Leone (out of 14,124 cases), and 2,543 in Guinea (out of 3,811 cases). In addition, there were 8 recorded deaths due to Ebola in Nigeria, and 6 in Mali ("Ebola Virus Disease"). The Centers for Disease Control reported that Liberia was declared Ebola free in May 2015, Sierra Leone in November 2015, and Guinea in June 2016 ("2014–2016 Ebola Outbreak").

care workers armed with thermometers and charts, rushing around measuring everyone's temperatures. How is this possible, I wondered, here, of all places, where specters of the Civil War (1991 to 2002) still haunt the present? How were the people of Sierra Leone going to survive this ordeal, coming as it did so soon after the war? Would any survivors remain? As I was to find out, many Sierra Leoneans not only survived the epidemic, but also achieved a level of resilience that enabled them to rebuild their communities. From the early years of the twenty-first century, Sierra Leonean writers have depicted unique, transformative forms of resilience against various forms of trauma. In what follows, I will briefly outline the obstacles that actual survivors like Yusuf Kabba had to overcome in order to achieve resilience, namely, lack of knowledge about the virus, poor quarantine facilities, and the fragmentation of social support structures. I will then examine, in more detail, fiction written both before and after the epidemic that reflects this resilience in creative ways. Such resilience can be seen in fictional characters like Mariama, my name for the nameless female survivor in Véronique Tadjo's *En compagnie des hommes* (2017); Mariatu, in Mohamed Kamara's "Pregnancy in the Time of Ebola" (2018); Moses, in Delia Jarrett-Macauley's *Moses, Citizen and Me* (2005); and Agnes, in Aminatta Forna's *The Memory of Love* (2010).[2] Their transformative resilience, like that of Yusuf Kabba's, is communal, embodied, and spiritual; thereby including the healing of minds and bodies on individual and social levels.

Ignorance as a Barrier to Healing

From the Civil War onwards, Sierra Leonean writers have described the way civilians suffer through conflicts and epidemics, more than they have depicted how they heal. As Ernest Cole has shown, for some Sierra Leonean writers, "bodily disfiguration[s]" within their fictional characters became symbols of ravages in the "body politic"; more specifically, post-war amputees were, to them, not just traumatized survivors, but symbols of the physical and emotional "amputation" of the nation (2019, 33). For other writers, however, war trauma, particularly greed for diamonds, consumed the collective soul (42). In the period between the war and the epidemic, only a few writers focused on recovery. Healing can, of course, take many forms. On the one hand, storytelling, music, theater and the other arts have long been recognized as therapeutic activities for survivors of trauma. On the other hand, culturally sensitive representations of, and theorizations about, trauma can, in and of

---

[2] In subsequent paragraphs of this chapter, Tadjo's *En compagnie des hommes* will be referred to as *Company*; Kamara's "Pregnancy in the Time of Ebola" will be "Pregnancy"; Jarrett-Macauley's *Moses, Citizen and Me* will be *Moses*; and Forna's *The Memory of Love* will be *Memory*.

themselves, be beneficial. As Stef Craps puts it, "an inclusive and culturally sensitive trauma theory can expose situations of injustice and abuse, and open up ways to imagine a different global future" (2013, 8). In either case, narrating the trauma, whether that is done privately within a family circle, or publicly, within the culture at large, can help traumatized people heal. As Boris Cyrulnik suggests, trauma survivors, particularly children, can build resilience most effectively when they are incorporated into what he calls an "open affective clan constellation" which is, itself, part of a larger "constellation of peers" (2008, 29). However, building resilience within peer or kin groups is a slow process. It works most effectively, according to Cyrulnik, when it takes the form of "feelings provided by the group and meaning transmitted by the narratives" (35). In essence, resilience is produced when affective and narrative "constellations" work together to provide meaning to a traumatic event.

Yusuf Kabba was severely traumatized by his encounter with Ebola, as he has stated eloquently in the many interviews he gave, after he became National Chairman of the Sierra Leone Association of Ebola Survivors (SLAES). Much of the trauma that Ebola survivors like him experienced arose from witnessing horrifying deaths against which they were powerless to intervene. According to the American Psychiatric Association's *Diagnostic and Statistical Manual*, traumatic events are those that involve "actual or threatened death or serious injury, or a threat to the physical integrity of self and others"; that produce "intense fear, helplessness or horror"; and that may result in distortions in human memory (1994, 427, 428). The shock of trauma is so debilitating, according to some theorists, that survivors tend to push out of their conscious minds detailed memories of their horrifying experiences (Piers 1999, 58). Even when they are able to recall some details, they typically do so only in the form of "somatic sensations, behavioral reenactments, nightmares, and flashbacks" (van der Kok and van der Hart 1991, 172). Given these circumstances, then, how were Sierra Leonean Ebola survivors going to describe their experiences? Would they even want to? Part of the answer to these questions was supplied by other trauma experts, who argued that high levels of stress hormones in the brain do not always impair its memory functions (McNally 2003, 180). Therefore, the reluctance of survivors to describe their terrifying experiences is often, they argue, the result of choice rather than ability (Pederson, 334). Theorist Richard McNally suggests that trauma survivors can describe their traumatizing events; and that even if they alter some of the narrative detail, this does not mean that they cannot remember the events themselves (2003, 184). By way of example, McNally points to the sense that trauma survivors have, that during the trauma, time was slowing down, or that everything appeared unreal (93). These insights notwithstanding, Sierra Leonean Ebola survivors did experience significant difficulties while articulating their experiences. This is because, according to theorist Stef Craps, aesthetic practices that represent trauma via "fragmentation and aporia" are frequently over-valued by scholars, while other narratives, particularly those created by survivors outside of North America or Europe, are often under-theorized (2013, 46). Many such survivors, like Agnes in *Memory*, cannot be clinically "desensitized" to trauma because of the indignities of their daily lives, in which they are often forced to live alongside the killers of their loved ones. Therefore, they perform what Ryan Topper has called "an embodied memorialization of ... constitutive trauma," in which they use their minds and bodies to cope rather than to heal (93). Contemporary theorists like Jill Bennett, Roseanne Kennedy, and Roger Luckhurst, have pointed out that in cultures outside of North America and Europe, trauma frequently arises not from a single, catastrophic event (like the Holocaust), but instead, from everyday, ongoing forms of oppression and powerlessness that are systemic and difficult to alleviate (Craps 2013, 50–1). As the following paragraphs will show, the resilience achieved by real survivors like Yusuf, and fictional ones like, Moses, Agnes, Mariama, and Mariatu, suggests, that for them, traumatic events (like wars or epidemics) were large, life-changing, and catastrophic, while also causing small everyday recurrences of powerlessness and oppression. Their healing processes were therefore embodied, spiritual, and communal, resulting in transformative resilience.

A year after the epidemic had officially ended in Guinea, Ivoirian novelist Véronique Tadjo published *En compagnie des hommes* (2017), an eloquent poetic novel about the virus. It was translated into English in 2021. Tadjo wrote *Company* after writing two other novels, namely, *The Shadow of Imana* (2000), about the Rwandan genocide, and *Queen Pokou* (2005), a historical novel. *Company* describes, in vivid detail, the terrible human and environmental toll of the epidemic, using multiple voices and viewpoints, such as, those of survivors, trees, bats, and even the virus itself. In the early part of *Company*, an ancient Baobab tree informs us that it is "the first tree, the everlasting tree, the totem tree. My roots reach deep into the belly of the earth. My crown pierces the sky. I seek the light that brightens the universe" (Tadjo, *Company*, 26). Near the end of the narrative, when the epidemic is waning, the everlasting Baobab rejoices, knowing that now younger trees will start growing in the forest, "reborn from those young seedlings. / The wheel of fortune and disaster never ceases to turn" (140). A year after Tadjo published *Company*, M'Bha Kamara's short story "Pregnancy" was published in *African Literature Today* (2018). Kamara followed that up with *When Mosquitoes Come Marching In* (2021), a play about the Civil War. In "Pregnancy," Mariatu, a pregnant woman experiencing complications during her labor, gives birth to a dead child, partly because the epidemic made it impossible for her to receive the medical attention she needed. Similar representations appear in fiction about the Civil War.

Moses (2005) is Jarrett-Macauley's debut novel, coming after *The Life of Una Marson* (1998), a biography she wrote of the Jamaican novelist and feminist. In *Moses,* Julia, a British Sierra Leonean woman, tries to heal her traumatized young nephew, Moses, who had been forced to kill his own grandmother. The Civil War also touches the lives of all the characters in *Memory* (2010), which is Forna's third novel, coming after *The Devil that Danced on Water* (2002) and *Ancestor Stones* (2006). In *Memory*, Agnes, a middle-aged traumatized woman, deals with her trauma by repeatedly running away from home.

As this background suggests, both the Ebola epidemic, and the Civil War before it, made it hard for survivors to overcome their trauma, or even articulate it. Earlier in this chapter, I argued that there were three major obstacles that the epidemic created for survivors. The first of these was ignorance. Lack of knowledge about the virus was widespread when it first appeared in West Africa. During the eighteen months that it ravaged Sierra Leone (May 2014 – October 2015), 3,956 of its citizens died ("Ebola Virus Disease"). By contrast, during the eleven-year Civil War (1991–2002), 70,000 Sierra Leoneans were killed (Kaldor & Vincent, 4). Although the war-time deaths far exceeded the fatalities due to the epidemic, the latter were horrifying and at least initially, mysterious. Experts and civilians alike indicated to me that during most of 2014 and the early part of 2015, friends and family members of victims had no idea how to prevent their loved ones from dying or even how to protect their own lives. Hundreds of health care workers in Sierra Leone, Liberia, and Guinea died while treating patients, as did several leading international physicians ("Ebola in Graphics," 2015). Tadjo provides us with a fictional example of this situation when, in one sequence of her novel, a nameless nurse confesses that in the first few months of the epidemic, she and her colleagues began treating Ebola patients "with our bare hands," protected only by their white coats (Tadjo *Company*, 42). In another sequence, a physician admits that he is up against an impossible task since "there is no effective medicine against the virus. So the main thing is to rehydrate the patients" (33–4). Not only was a cure against Ebola unavailable to most civilians, but many were forced to heal in inadequate facilities. As Mariatu, the pregnant protagonist of "Pregnancy" finds out, even when patients were in distress, bystanders often refused to help. When Mariatu begins bleeding before she even reaches the hospital, people around her misdiagnose her condition: "'Ebola. She has Ebola!' One person screamed. People instinctively ran helter-skelter, knocking over stalls and other people as they did so" (Kamara "Pregnancy," 217). This misunderstanding has a fatal effect on Mariatu's baby. After the surgeon operates on her, he presents her with "her still-born child swaddled in simple white cotton cerements" (219). Preventable deaths like these have been described by other Sierra Leonean writers, too. In a sequence in *Memory*, for example, British psychiatrist Adrian watches as a Sierra Leonean physician tries desperately to help a woman in labor. Although the context here is post-war Sierra Leone, the woman seems to be in as much distress as Mariatu was. Even before she enters the operating theater on a stretcher, the attending physician uses "his entire weight – or so it seems – to press down upon the patient's abdomen." The result is a "terrible stillness" with a dead baby "lying there between his mother's legs" (Forna *Memory*, 24–5). By contrast, eight-year-old Citizen, in *Moses,* remains alive after the war, but, because of the atrocities he had been forced to commit as a child soldier, he is deeply traumatized. Unlike his age mates, he roams around his neighborhood at night, chews tobacco, and shows the kind of spirit that is "far removed from anything" the adults who care for him had ever experienced (Jarrett-Macauley *Moses*, 7).

Problems Caused by Poor Facilities

Not only were many Sierra Leoneans unaware of how the virus was spreading, but the media did not always report the death toll accurately. This fact has been pointed out by several scholars, among them, Abioseh Jarrett, then Chair of Fourah Bay College's Social Work Program. Yusuf Kabba lost seven family members and many friends to the virus and almost died himself ("Reminiscences"). In an interview that became part of the Centers for Disease Control's Oral History Project, Yusuf recounts how before he got sick, he did not pay much attention to the anecdotes he had been hearing about a mysterious illness that had surfaced in Guinea. "The whole idea of Ebola was new to us," he said. This sense, that something unprecedented was unfolding in Sierra Leone, had also been his dominant emotion when the war had begun fourteen years earlier, especially because of the numerous evacuations he had had to endure then. "The same traumatic experience continued when the issue of outbreak came," he said. "I didn't want to die."[3]

Yusuf contracted Ebola on October 6, 2014 after coming into contact with an infected physician who eventually died. In the Oral History Project interview mentioned earlier, Yusuf recounted that the physician's ailments were initially misdiagnosed as malaria, and that he had had to wait a long time to get the correct results, by which time he had infected many people ("Reminiscences"). This point, about the delay in test results, is consistent with the observations made by several experts. During the early months of

---

[3] Dying was often on the minds of survivors like Kabba. Unfortunately, in the early years of the epidemic, instructions from elected Sierra Leonean officials were not helpful. Their commands of "ABC" ("Avoid Body Contact") and "APC" ("Avoid People's Compounds"), had the impact, he argued, of putting "a knife into the things that keep us together." This was because they "insulted" centuries-old cultural practices that dictated that if loved ones got sick, family members took care of them until they recovered. As a result, Kabba began to think of Ebola as "an evil spirit" that was out to "destroy the love that was created by God" ("Reminiscences").

the epidemic, blood tests on Sierra Leoneans who had contracted the virus were not made available for weeks on end, resulting in many deaths. The government, which prohibited family members from doing traditional funerals, often took days to bury corpses, despite protestations from family members (Jarrett 2015). As Mariatu, the protagonist of "Pregnancy" finds out, many families, whose loved ones had died of Ebola, buried them "clandestinely" (212). These secret funerals resulted in many deaths, until the government forbade private ceremonies. Along with the pain of not being able to bury loved ones properly, many Sierra Leoneans could not forget the horrors they had witnessed as their family members suffered through their final moments. Mariama, in *Company*, describes these horrors very effectively. For her, the hospital was like an "underworld," an area of darkness, where patients became "disoriented. There's nothing left" (Tadjo *Company*, 71). The same sense of disorientation haunted children who survived the Civil War. In *Moses,* eight-year-old Citizen, unable to cope with the trauma of killing his grandmother, spends his nights roaming the streets of Freetown, often falling asleep from sheer exhaustion (Jarrett-Macauley *Moses*, 18).

The rapid spread of the virus across Sierra Leone meant that the only way it could be effectively contained was through quarantine measures. Poor quarantine facilities, is, in fact, the second obstacle that Yusuf and other survivors had to overcome.[4] Part of the reason for this was the Civil War. In 2002, when the war ended, 3 million Sierra Leoneans had been displaced, 70 percent of the country's educational facilities had been destroyed, and, most importantly, only 16 percent of the country's health care facilities were still functioning (Gberie 6). Twelve years later, the epidemic exacerbated the situation. As a result, the most vulnerable sections of Sierra Leonean society, namely children, pregnant women, and women breastfeeding their babies, suffered the most. Since infected mothers frequently passed on the virus to their children, many children died along with their mothers (Sheriff Interview). Some died in their homes, others in ETUs (Ebola Treatment Units), which were often converted police training schools (Kabba Interview).

As a result of these deaths, doctors and ambulances became sources of fear for the average Sierra Leonean. In one sequence of *Company*, for example, the narrator describes an ambulance as a symbol of a death that "moves quickly" (67). Ambulances typically took the sick to be tested, after which

---

[4] As Kabba indicated in several interviews, the Observational Interim Care Center (OICC) that he was taken to was very dirty. Bodies of the recent dead were lying on the floor because government workers had not removed or buried them. There was blood all over the floor, which was never cleaned up. No one took care of him in that holding center, even when he began vomiting blood, because his test results had not come in. Eventually, a week and a half after he arrived, his results came back and he was taken to an Ebola Treatment Unit (ETU) ("Reminiscences").

they were confined inside Observational Interim Care Centers or OICCs. The sick were often forced into these facilities with little food and no counseling, a situation described by Tadjo as one in which "there was hardly enough time to clean up the traces of death before someone else was brought in ... no one wanted to come near us, so scraps of food were thrown to us from a distance" (Tadjo *Company*, 70). Even the doctors felt overwhelmed, seeing themselves as "trespasser[s] in the kingdom of Death ... like ... astronaut[s] floating in space, a thousand miles from earth" (37). Moreover, patients often transferred their fears on to health care professionals. Part of the problem was that hospitals began resembling morgues or dungeons.[5]

In one sequence of "Pregnancy," for example, Mariatu arrives at a hospital and sees "a rainbow of Wellington boots ... drying out on stakes buried into the ground, soles watching God, as if in supplication on behalf of all the unfortunate souls, dead or alive, who could no longer trust their governors" (Kamara "Pregnancy," 217).[6] During the Civil War, hospitals also became places of dread. In a late sequence in *Memory,* for example, rebel soldiers burst into a hospital in Freetown, and kidnap Kai, a physician, and Balia, a nurse. After forcing them to perform makeshift surgeries on injured fighters, the soldiers also threaten them with physical and sexual violation. Rebel soldiers tell Kai, at gunpoint: "Look how fine she [Balia] is. Why don't you

---

[5] This association between hospitals and morgues was partly a result of the condition of the OICCs or Interim Care Centers (ICC)s. Many of the ICCs were little more than one-room shacks. Those suspected of having contracted the virus were isolated in them, with no treatment, and no one to turn to for help or guidance. If they survived, they remained confined for up to twenty-one days or more. Yusuf was lucky enough to leave after a week and a half ("Reminiscences"). In the Oral History Project interview, Yusuf mentions that it was only after he left the ICC and moved to an ETU that he finally received treatment. In the ETU, he was put on a regular regimen of medicines and food, and slowly recovered. As he recovered, he "managed to smile when I looked at myself in the mirror" ("Reminiscences").

[6] Partly due to this lack of trust, the government of Sierra Leone eventually revised its quarantine tactics. It set up the National Ebola Response Centre (NERC), which was previously known as the Emergency Operations Centre (EOC), with a mandate to contain and end the outbreak ("Report on the Audit," 2). NERC began to centralize its efforts and facilitated the use of the "117" phone number for people to call to report new cases. At this time, the government also took other measures, such as sending information to the OICCs and other holding areas, outlining procedures to follow ("Sierra Leone Emergency," 4–6). NERC also launched the "stay-at-home" campaign for three days in March 2015. During this time, the government began ensuring that response workers were available to people in quarantine, and were providing them with better food and water ("Zero Ebola"). As Health for All Coalition's National Director, Edward Jusu, mentioned in his interview with me, in the early days, infants had sometimes been put in quarantine without access to milk. This new campaign tried to correct some of those errors.

share your girlfriend with us? You tink say because you na big doctor, you deserve better than we" (Forna *Memory*, 430). Kai is only able to escape with the greatest difficulty, after Balia is killed. The memory of her death haunts him for the rest of his life.

Social Fragmentation as an Impediment

Ignorance and poor facilities (which I have labeled obstacle one and obstacle two), meant that when survivors went home, the social realities that they encountered were different than those that had existed when they left. The fragmentation of many of Sierra Leone's social structures was, in fact, the third obstacle that Yusuf and other survivors faced. Yusuf's comments, in his Oral History Project interview, underscore the extent of that fragmentation.[7] The so-called "Ebola Orphans," like the de-mobilized child soldiers during the war, had not always lost both parents. Numbering around 12,000, they were children who had lost either one or both parents to the virus (O'Carroll 2015).[8] Many had to manage with few or no resources and could not even rely on that social mainstay, the extended family (Jarrett interview). Tadjo reflects this state of affairs in *Company*, when Mariama's family refuses to accept her back after she recovers. As a result, she is forced to return to the hospital for her basic needs. There, a nurse suggests that she get involved in the Ebola effort, and she agrees, talking to young patients every day, telling them that "they too, can survive as I did. They have to realize that it's possible" (Tadjo *Company*, 73). Eventually, she finds a new purpose in life and heals herself and others. Many other Ebola survivors, however, were unable to heal. In another sequence of Tadjo's novel, for example, a dying mother recalls seeing pedestrians "disperse rapidly" whenever an ambulance whizzed past them, because they were terrified of it. They knew, she recalls, that "death moves quickly, looking for bodies" (67).

The same situation was true during the Civil War. Many of the young soldiers recruited by both the government and the rebels, could not find jobs after the war ended, having missed years of schooling (Kaldor & Vincent 2006, 12). Other former recruits felt they would not be welcomed back into their communities because of the crimes they had committed as soldiers.

---

[7] Post-conflict recovery in any society often hinges on effective social and personal rehabilitation and healing. After the epidemic, however, the Sierra Leonean extended family system fragmented because of fear of the virus, therefore, children who survived were left with even less support than the former demobilized civil war child soldiers. As Francis Kabia, then Director of Social Welfare within the Ministry of Social Welfare, Gender, and Children's Affairs, indicated to me in an interview (2015), Ebola severely destabilized social cohesion.

[8] Overall, there were about 7,000–10,000 Ebola survivors, both adults and children in Guinea, Liberia, and Sierra Leone ("Healthy Families," 48).

Some used stolen motorbikes as *okadas* (motorbike taxis), thereby scraping together a living. They worked in groups or loosely formed organizations, and frequently clashed with the police due to their recklessness (12–13). I know of several cases after the war, when extended family members took in demobilized children, even if temporarily. However, many of the children became sources of fear for their friends and family and were isolated. After he kills his own grandmother, for example, Citizen, in Jarrett-Macauley's novel, becomes the kind of child that "most people will not … let … near their house … They believe they are little devils. Bad bush" (Jarrett-Macauley, *Moses* 19–20). As a result, Citizen chooses temporary homelessness and isolation over being with his family.

Communal Healing

The social fragmentation that the epidemic caused has also been documented by non-profit organizations in Sierra Leone, such as Advancing Partners and Communities (APC), which was formed by the U.S. Agency for International Development. In a 2019 report, APC pointed out that in Guinea, Liberia, and Sierra Leone, Ebola survivors had many lingering health problems which they could not treat, partly because of fear by their community members and partly because the treatments were unavailable ("Healthy Families Thrive," 11, 48).[9] Some lived in fear, others tried to kill themselves in desperation (O'Carroll 2015).[10] With or without the support of government agencies, survivors like Yusuf had to find their own ways of achieving resilience against the trauma they had endured. As indicated earlier, the resilience they achieved was communal. Yusuf was welcomed back by his community after he recovered and was able

---

[9] As he did his outreach work, Yusuf began to realize that Ebola survivors had a range of long-lasting health problems including miscarriages, severe joint pain, deafness, and blindness (Kabba "Why Ebola").

[10] In general, extended family members did not offer much help to the "Ebola Orphans," because they were often too afraid of contracting the virus (Kabia 2015). This is where organizations like SLAES and APC stepped in. APC even developed a "Post-Ebola Recovery Toolkit" to help survivors get their needs taken care of ("Post-Ebola"). Interventions like these seem to have resulted in some improvements in health care facilities ("Healthy Families" 49). NERC also provided some psychosocial and reunification welfare support to the "Ebola Orphans." It oversaw command centers in every district, provided logistics support to the government and distributed assistive packages to the orphans (Kabia). Unfortunately, however, it also mismanaged funds. As a 2014 report by the Auditor General of Sierra Leone shows, the government spent Le84 billion on combating the Ebola virus ("Report on the Audit," 1). Half of that Le84 billion was spent without proper supporting documents or explanations (4–5). SLAES, under Yusuf's guidance, joined a December 2017 lawsuit filed against the government by two survivors, who were supported by a local nonprofit, the Center for Accountability and Rule of Law, directed by Ibrahima Tommy (Courtright 2018).

to enjoy the company of his family and friends. He was also heartened to hear that the then President of Sierra Leone, Ernest Bai Koroma, had described survivors like himself as "heroes" ("Reminiscences"). Despite this, Yusuf was unable to find a job, since no one wanted to hire him, and he got no financial support from the government (Kabba "Why Ebola"). He went on to chair SLAES, driven, as he indicated, by a "passion for humanity" and a desire to end the stigmatization that survivors often experienced ("Reminiscences"). When Ebola cases were going down in Guinea, Liberia, and Sierra Leone, national survivor networks were created in all three countries, made up of district and regional groups of survivors. When Ebola survivors registered in these networks, they were encouraged to join their local network or chapter, and eventually participate in their national networks. The idea was to "unite people who had suffered from the outbreak" while helping them "overcome the major challenges that they were facing, including the loss of work and livelihood, medical complications, and stigma from colleagues and neighbors" ("Reflection," 1).[11]

Networks similar to SLAES also helped fictional Ebola survivors heal. Mariama, in *Company*, is turned away from home by her relatives, because they believe she is still contagious, and this situation throws her into despair. She hesitates to act, even after the nurse asks her to get involved with outreach. She begins to mourn her dead parents and brothers, until she realizes that she needs to find something else to do. Although she was "still aching from the pain of not being able to do anything to help," she tells herself that community outreach was "my chance to make up for that failure. So I said yes" (Tadjo *Company*, 73). When she begins work at a treatment center, she forms alliances with the other women working there, and they visit different parts of the city each day, "explaining that people like us still have their rightful place in the community" (73). They instill confidence in community members who then seek help for their ailments. In similar fashion, Mariatu, in "Pregnancy," awakens from her surgery to find her husband and mother-in-law standing at her bedside. Although her child is dead, the family draws comfort from the fact that they endured the loss together (Kamara "Pregnancy," 219).

People coming together in order to overcome trauma has also been represented in Civil War fiction. In *Moses,* for example, Citizen attends weeks of group therapy, along with other former child soldiers, in a forest clearing presided over by Bemba G, an old man who resembles a shaman. Despite this therapy being magical rather than real (it takes place inside Julia's head)

---

[11] Along with the creation of survivor networks in Guinea, Liberia, and Sierra Leone, a two-year program was started in all three countries, called the Ebola Transmission Prevention and Survivor Services (ETP&SS). APC (as USAID) helped with its funding, and it was run by JSI Research and Training, under the auspices of the World Health Organization. ETP&SS tried to improve survivor's access to healthcare ("Reflection," 2).

it underscores how effective communal healing in a natural environment can be. Bemba G, "an expert in mind control or teaching" starts his sessions by involving the children in math problems that have real-world applications, and eventually, all the children become "immersed in their own projects ... The compound heaved with activity" (Jarrett-Macauley *Moses*, 90). He provides plenty of opportunities for the children to talk about their war experiences, feeding them with wholesome, home-cooked food, and giving them time to rest or play interactive games (125–37). Bemba G's most effective cure, however, comes from his leadership on a performance of Thomas Decker's *Juliohs Siza,* which the children enact right there in the forest, before an audience of locals and foreigners. As they rehearse, Bemba G shows them how to "stage fight" instead of fighting realistically, and, more importantly, he casts Citizen in the role of Lucius, Brutus' servant, because he himself is playing Brutus (151, 147). He also permits Citizen to sing a Malian love song instead of saying his lines, and this helps Citizen rekindle his love for his murdered grandmother (181). Eventually, all the performers realize that they are "meeting themselves in the play. They understood their place in the scheme of things" (159).

In a similarly charged sequence in *Memory*, British psychiatrist Adrian realizes that in the psychiatric hospital where he works, there are fewer female than male schizophrenic patients because women prefer to heal at home, using "local healers" (Forna *Memory*, 87). Agnes herself is eventually "cured" by one such local, communal effort. After Adrian fails to cure her, a member of Kai's extended family puts him in touch with a number of women, all of whom either know Agnes or were present during her moment of horror. Collectively, they explain to Kai the sources of Agnes' trauma:

> Each person told a part of the same story. And in telling another's story, they told their own. Kai took what they had given him and placed it together with what he already knew ... [the story unfolded] in hushed voices, told behind a curtain in a quiet room and in the eye of the night, from the lips of many. (306)

These chroniclers finally reveal why Agnes had become a night wanderer, disappearing for days every now and then. During a rebel assault on her village, Agnes had been forced to watch as Jaja, a rebel officer, had murdered her husband. She had fled to a neighboring country and had become a refugee. When the war had ended, she had returned to her home village, and had been reunited with Naasu, her adult daughter, from whom she had been separated before her husband was murdered. Naasu, now married, had then introduced Agnes to her new husband who, Agnes eventually finds out, was Jaja himself. Even after that realization, Agnes had been obliged to live in the same house as Naasu and Jaja, because she had nowhere else to go (312–13). Unable to tell Naasu the truth, she had chosen to keep running away for short periods of time, performing the role of a person who is "crossed" by grief (306).

Embodied Healing

Real survivors like Yusuf, and fictional ones like Moses, Agnes, Mariama, and Mariatu achieved transformative resilience via embodied healing, as indicated above. In this regard, they are unlike the civilians in the opening sequence of Edward Zwick's *Blood Diamond*, whose amputations become, as Cole suggests, "a permanent marker and a lasting witness of pain" (2019, 44). Yusuf, for example, joined SLAES, which was established in 2015, and was supported by the Ministry of Social Welfare, Gender, and Children's Affairs. It advocated for access to free healthcare for Ebola survivors ("Reflection," 2). Yusuf believes that the organization's main function is to protect the dignity of the survivors. When I interviewed him, the activities he described doing the most, within SLAES, were counseling and psychosocial support. Even before he chaired SLAES, while he was still recovering from the virus, he had felt the need for a survivor's network. In his ETU, he had led the other patients in singing short songs, which reinforced the idea that it was possible to "kick Ebola" and keep hope alive.[12] He had then started a drama group, which performed humorous skits, some of which were written by him, to make the recovering survivors laugh and relieve their stress. One of his plays, "Early Treatment," showcased how important it was for the sick to get care quickly. He went on to write a series of short pieces that focused on reintegrating survivors and reducing stigma (Kabba Interview). Realizing that orphans and widows, in particular, were very fearful of the virus and of returning to their communities, Yusuf used singing, music, and dancing, to get them to "smile again."[13]

Like Yusuf, Mariama, in Tadjo's novel, keeps her spirits up by doing physical activities. At first, she feels revived by looking at the "huge" and

---

[12] In this regard, Yusuf may have been inspired by Savage and Kuriansky's music video, "Hope is Alive" (2015). In 2015, Dr. Judy Kuriansky, a clinical psychologist and faculty member at Columbia University Teachers College, teamed up with rapper Emrys Savage and others, to create this music video. Kuriansky wrote the lyrics during the outbreak, when she was helping survivors, and taught it to members of SLAES. With its catchy rhythms, its images of survivors grieving, rejoicing, and then dancing together, and its memorable lyrics like "we got to kick Ebola, kick Ebola" or the repeated "hope is alive," it is inspirational and optimistic. Whether or not Yusuf was able to view this video when he was recovering, communal singing became his way of using his body to help heal himself and others. It forced him to pay attention to other voices and melodies, thereby motivating him to challenge his previous assumptions and think positively. The doctors in his facility liked what he was doing and encouraged him to continue ("Reminiscences").

[13] At this time, Yusuf also visited counseled survivors, often traveling all over the country to provide psycho-social support. He secured funding for SLAES from outside donors, and SLAES grew to more than 3,000 members (Kabba "Why Ebola"). He used community engagement techniques that required people to come together in physical spaces to address the need for socio-cultural support ("Reminiscences").

"majestic" baobab tree in the hospital courtyard. The tree's presence gives Mariama strength, even when she feels abandoned (Forna "Document," 6). When she is strong enough to move around, she walks up to the tree, to "thank it for comforting us in the depths of our despair. When I leaned against it, I could sense its life-giving vibrations" (Tadjo *Company*, 71–2). She imagines the tree telling her that she can make it, and she hugs the tree in gratitude (72). The same embodied forms of healing worked for young, Sierra Leonean war survivors. In one sequence of *Moses*, for example, the traumatized Citizen is healed via the movements of his body, as he performs his part in the play, *Juliohs Siza*. Bemba G allows him, and the other child performers, to improvise their lines, and to include the songs, dances, and games that they played in the forest. During rehearsals, the performers realize that the guilt that haunts them is slipping away: "an invisible thread runs between the hungry empty ghosts [their victims] and our earthly selves. As time passes, the veil between our worlds thins" (185). A similar form of embodiment appears in *Memory*. Agnes, the "crossed" woman, copes with her trauma by walking the streets at night and then getting picked up by strangers and taken to the psychiatric hospital. She does this at least once every six or seven months, each time arriving in the custody of strangers (Forna *Memory*, 163).

Spiritual Healing

As the above examples show, the process of achieving resilience is complicated, being at once communal and embodied, besides also taking on spiritual overtones. Ryan Topper has described war survivors as having the ability to develop new "modes of consciousness" that involve "spiritual crossings" and shamanic rituals. They inhabit, as it were, the "African animist imaginary," which, in blurring the boundaries between the human and the nonhuman, the living and the dead, create a "subject-object continuum" (2019, 87–8). In this imaginary, trauma is not a sickness to be cured in a clinical setting, but a "rupture within a network of mutually constitutive life forces always already open to the spirit" (88). Therefore, traumatized persons, who tend to move back and forth between the real world and the spirit world, can only be cured via communal rituals (88). Real and fictional survivors of trauma did, in fact, focus on communal rituals to heal themselves and others. When I interviewed Hawa Sam, another Sierra Leonean Ebola survivor, she pointed out how difficult it was for "Ebola Orphans" to cope. Not all of them were welcomed back into their home communities, as Yusuf was. Hawa joined SLAES and traveled across the country with other SLAES members, focusing her attention on the needs of the young. "They miss their parents and family," she said. She, too, lost many family members to the virus, including her own child, and could not forget her intense feelings of fear and loneliness. During her time with SLAES, she encountered survivors of all ages, but chose to focus on the young, since, as she pointed out, their needs were ignored by many adults who were afraid to come near them. Those neglected children were not aware of how the virus spread, so they took the social ostracization hard. "I tell them my story," she said, "I give them courage." What she did not say explicitly is that caring for the young also helped her heal.

Just as Hawa's storytelling process helped her heal, Mariama, in Tadjo's novel, invents rituals to restore hope in herself and in others like her. She works in a group, developing processes they invent together. They visit different communities, holding hands, "walk[ing] side by side ... showing the others that there's nothing to fear" (*Company*, 74). Likewise, the nameless grave digger in *Company*, invents burial rituals, not only to help him cope with his trauma, but also, to ensure that the souls of the dead make a smooth transition to the next world (Messay 2021, 454). Lamenting the total absence of friends and family at each burial, he provides details of the burial process: bodies are placed in disinfected bags by men in protective suits, who then walk solemnly toward the graveyard, behind the priest-like chlorine sprayer, who waves his "magic" wand. Eventually, the body is lowered into the grave (Tadjo *Company*, 52–3). Despite these rituals, every morning, when the grave digger arrives at work, he is visited by ghosts of the dead, who are "reluctant to leave the earth, hoping we'll let them return" (55). Only the chlorine sprayer can exorcise these ghosts, because he is not just priestly, but is also "a warrior in plastic armor" (56).

In similar fashion, Julia, in Jarrett-Macauley's novel, heals Citizen only after she learns the appropriate rituals. As Topper suggests, those rituals are, essentially, a "reworking" of colonial history (89). The rituals begin with a hair braiding session, during which her head becomes "a map of Sierra Leone, its farmland ... fighters, leaders. Up the smooth dark skin of my neck marched a band of boy and girl soldiers" (Jarrett-Macauley *Moses*, 51). Once Julia allows these sessions with child soldiers to start playing out in her head, she sees sequences of arson, rapes, and killings, playing out in front of her eyes. She also joins the children in their therapy sessions with Bemba G, participating in the storytelling events concerning real and imaginary episodes from the children's pasts (143–9). In one sequence, Citizen shows her a broken-off tree bark into which he carved the identifying number that had been branded onto his back while he was a soldier. As he had carved it, he chose not to look at his work, thinking instead the way it had felt on his skin. He had subsequently reproduced it, Julia suggests, "like a pianist committing a sonata to memory" (163). These ritualistic aspects of healing after war trauma are also evident in *Memory*. Agnes, her family members assume, is a "crossed" person who can move "back and forth between this world and the spirit world ... [and] in between the worlds" (Forna *Memory*, 114, 129). What her family members fail to realize is that Agnes merely performs this role as a means to get away from "intolerable circumstances. Escaping the house, her daughter, most of all escaping Jaja" (326). As the rest of Forna's narrative indicates, Agnes is not alone in trying to escape an "intolerable situation." Kai and Adrian as well as Mamakay, the woman both of them love, are all forced, by war or other circumstances, into finding rituals that will help them deal with their traumatic situations.

Transformative Resilience

During and after the epidemic, survivors were often in need of coping strategies. In late July 2015, when scientists at the University of Liverpool and at the 34th Regiment Military Hospital and Ministry of Health in Freetown developed an experimental technique to treat Ebola involving donations of plasma from survivors, Yusuf was delighted. In his words, "this is an African solution for an African problem. This will give hope to people and encourage them to come for treatment. It could save many lives and serve as a national resource for the future outbreaks of Ebola" ("Ebola Survivors").[14] While it may be true that African problems are best solved with home-grown African solutions, Ebola is not just an African problem. As the havoc wrought by the recent COVID-19 pandemic has shown, finding the resilience to survive traumatic events means much more than training and supporting physicians.[15] The low incidence of COVID cases in West Africa was not solely a reflection of poor reporting infrastructures. It also suggested that Sierra Leoneans may have developed their own forms of transformative resilience. As James Arinaitwe, an Aspen Institute New Voices Fellow puts it, Africans must

> unite to work together across ideological and geographical backgrounds to invest our resources, skills, and ideas to drive our own economic and social agenda. Only then can we ensure that the child survivors of Ebola are born in an Africa where they are not seen as victims or beggars, but as captains of their own fate. (2015)

Arinaitwe's call for Africans to work together to solve problems was echoed by Yusuf who said, in an interview with me, that "[he] who feels it, knows it." Moreover, his leadership of SLAES showcased how his resilience transformed both his life and those of many others ("Reminiscences").

As this analysis has revealed, Sierra Leonean fiction, written both before and after the epidemic, reflects the resilience of survivors in nuanced and creative ways. Both in form and in content, *En compagnie des hommes*,

---

[14] According to the WHO website, Ebola can now be treated with vaccines, which have been used in Guinea and in the Democratic Republic of the Congo (DRC). Also, in late 2020, the US Food and Drug Administration approved monoclonal antibody treatment for Ebola, for use by adults and children ("Ebola Virus Disease").

[15] In February 2021 there was another outbreak of Ebola in Guinea, resulting in 12 deaths ("Ebola: N'Zerekore").

"Pregnancy in the Time of Ebola," *Moses, Citizen and Me*, and *The Memory of Love* contain numerous examples of transformative resilience. Characters, images, and narrative styles in all of these texts represent forms of communal, embodied, and spiritual healing, on individual and social levels. In doing so, they not only provide readers with insights about healing, but also reveal the power that Sierra Leonean fiction has, to transform global theories about trauma. In the words of the ancient Baobab tree in *Company*, during the epidemic, "ordinary men and women" did "extraordinary things" (Tadjo *Company*, 26). The "extraordinary things" that Sierra Leonean writers did was to create complex examples of transformative resilience that has enabled readers to start smiling again.

Works Cited

"2014–2016 Ebola Outbreak in West Africa." Centers for Disease Control and Prevention (CDC), March 8, 2019, www.cdc.gov. Accessed June 21, 2022.

Arinaitwe, James Kassaga, "Ebola Orphans in Africa Do Not Need Saviours," *Al Jazeera*, 28 February, 2015, www.aljazeera.com. Accessed August 13, 2015.

Courtright, James, "The Forgotten Ebola Survivors of Sierra Leone," *Goats and Soda*, National Public Radio, April 25, 2018, www.npr.org. Accessed June 24, 2022.

Cole, Ernest, "Imaginative Representations of Illicit and Conflict Diamonds in the Sierra Leone Civil War: From Paradox and Ambiguity to Traumatized National Psychology," *Journal of the African Literature Association* 13.1 (2019), pp. 31–47.

Craps, Stef, *Postcolonial Witnessing: Trauma Out of Bounds* (New York: Palgrave Macmillan, 2013).

Cyrulnik, Boris, "Children in War and Their Resiliences," in *The Unbroken Soul: Tragedy, Trauma, and Human Resilience*, eds. Henri Parens, Harold P. Blum, and Salman Akhtar (Lanham, MD: Jason Aronson / Rowman & Littlefield, 2008), pp. 21–36.

Diagnostic and Statistical Manual of Mental Disorders, 4th ed. [DSM-IV] (American Psychiatric Association, 1994).

"Ebola in Graphics: The Toll of a Tragedy," *The Economist*, July 8, 2015, www.economist.com. Accessed August 11, 2015.

"Ebola: N'Zerekore, Guinea, February–June 2021" (World Health Organization, 2021), www.who.int. Accessed June 22, 2022.

"Ebola Survivors' Plasma Used in Freetown, Sierra Leone," University of Liverpool Institute of Translational Medicine. *Clinical RM*, July 21, 2015, www.clinicalrm.com. Accessed August 6, 2015.

"Ebola Virus Disease," (World Health Organization – WHO, 23 February, 2021), www.who.int. Accessed June 21, 2022.

Forna, Aminatta, "A Document of Losses" (review of *In the Company of Men*), *The New York Review* September 23, 2021, https://www.nybooks.com/articles/2021/09/23/veronique-tadjo-document-losses. Accessed October 1, 2024.

Forna, Aminatta, *Ancestor Stones* (London: Bloomsbury, 2006).

Forna, Aminatta, *The Devil that Danced on the Water: A Daughter's Quest* (Washington DC: Atlantic Monthly Press; London: HarperCollins, 2002).

Forna, Aminatta, *The Memory of Love* (New York: Grove, 2010).

Gberie, Lansana, *A Dirty War in West Africa: the RUF and the Destruction of Sierra Leone* (Bloomington: Indiana University Press, 2005).

"Healthy Families Thrive: Why Community Health Matters in the Journey to Self-Reliance" (Advancing Partners and Communities, Final Report, December 2019), www.advancingpartners.org. Accessed June 20, 2022.

Jarrett, Abioseh. Personal interview. Freetown, Sierra Leone, July 8, 2015.

Jarrett-Macauley, Delia, *The Life of Una Marson, 1905–1965* (Manchester: Manchester University Press, 1998).

Jarrett-Macauley, Delia, *Moses, Citizen and Me* (London: Granta, 2005).

Jusu, Edward. Personal interview. Freetown, Sierra Leone, July 7, 2015.

Kabba, Yusuf. Personal interview. Freetown, Sierra Leone, July 11, 2015.

Kabba, Yusuf, "Why Ebola Survivors are Suing Sierra Leone," *Al Jazeera* 24 July, 2018, www.aljazeera.com. Accessed June 17, 2022.

Kabia, Francis Mohamed. Personal interview. Freetown, Sierra Leone, July 8, 2015.

Kaldor, Mary, and James Vincent, "Case Study Sierra Leone," Evaluation of UNDP Assistance to Conflict-Affected Countries (United Nations Development Programme Evaluation Office, 2006), www.undp.org. Accessed August 11, 2015.

Kamara, M'Bha, "Pregnancy in the Time of Ebola," *African Literature Today* 36 (Woodbridge: James Currey, 2018), pp. 211–19.

Kamara, M'Bha, *When Mosquitoes Come Marching In* (South Gate, CA: NoPassport Press, 2021).

McNally, Richard J., *Remembering Trauma* (Cambridge, MA: Harvard University Press, 2003).

Messay, Marda, "'Nous étions ici pour durer': Memorialization and Environmental Advocacy in Véronique Tadjo's *En compagnie des homes*," *Contemporary French and Francophone Studies* 25.4 (2021), pp. 450–7.

National Ebola Response Centre (NERC). 2015. www.nerc.sl. Accessed December 11, 2015.

O'Carroll, Lisa, "Ebola Leaves 12,000 Orphans in Sierra Leone," *The Guardian*, March 4,

2015, www.theguardian.com. Accessed August 13, 2015.

Piers, Craig C., "Remembering Trauma: A Characterological Perspective" in *Trauma and Memory* Linda M. Williams and Victoria L. Banyard (eds.) (London and Thousand Oaks, CA: Sage Publications, 1999), pp. 57–65.

Pederson, Joshua. "Speak, Trauma: Toward a Revised Understanding of Literary Trauma Theory," *Narrative* 22.3 (2014), pp. 333–53.

"Post-Ebola Recovery Toolkit." (Advancing Partners and Communities, n.d.), www.advancingpartners.org. Accessed June 20, 2022.

"Reflection: Strengthening National Ebola Survivor Networks: Successes and Challenges." (Advancing Partners and Communities, n.d.), www.advancingpartners.org. Accessed June 20, 2022.

"Report on the Audit of the Management of the Ebola Funds." (Audit Service Sierra Leone, May to October 2014), www.auditservice.gov.sl. Accessed July 8, 2015.

"The Reminiscences of Yusuf Kabba." David J. Sencer CDC Museum Digital Exhibits. (Centers for Disease Control and Prevention, 2016), cdcmuseum.org. Accessed June 18, 2022.

Sam, Hawa. Personal interview. Freetown, Sierra Leone, July 11, 2015.

Savage, Emrys, "Hope is Alive." Music video. Lyrics by Russell Daisey, Judy Kuriansky, Yotam Polizer and Emrys Savage. Freetown, Sierra Leone, 2015, https://www.youtube.com/watch?v=YkLbxn2Irrw. Accessed October 2, 2024.

Sheriff, Brima. Personal interview. Freetown, Sierra Leone, July 7, 2015.

"Sierra Leone Emergency Management Program Standard Operating Procedure for Management of Quarantine." (National Ebola Response Centre, October 2014), www.nerc.sl. Accessed August 13, 2015.

Tadjo, Véronique, *In the Company of Men.* Trans. by the author in collaboration with John Cullen (New York: Other Press, 2021). Originally published as *En compagnie des hommes* (Paris: Don Quichotte éditions, 2017).

Tadjo, Véronique, *Queen Pokou: Concerto for a Sacrifice.* Trans. Amy Baram Reid (Oxford: Ayebia Clarke, 2009). Originally published as *Reine Pokou: Concerto pour un sacrifice* (Paris: Actes Sud, 2005).

Tadjo, Véronique, *The Shadow of Imana: Travels in the Heart of Rwanda.* Trans. Véronique Wakerly (London, Heinemann, 2002). Originally published as *L'Ombre d'Imana: Voyages jusqu'au bout du Rwanda* (Paris: Actes Sud, 2000).

Topper, Ryan, "Trauma and the African Animist Imaginary in Aminatta Forna's *The Memory of Love* and Delia Jarrett-Macauley's *Moses, Citizen and Me*," *English Language Notes* 57.2 (October 2019), pp. 86–98.

van der Kok, Bessel A. and Onno van der Hart, "The Intrusive Past: The Flexibility of Memory and the Engraving of Trauma," *American Imago* 48.4 (1991), pp. 425–54.

"Zero Ebola." (National Ebola Response Centre, March 25, 2015). www.nerc.sl. Accessed August 13, 2015.

Zwick, Edward, *Blood Diamond.* Warner Home Video, 2007.

Chapter 8

War and Social Degradation in Oumar Farouk Sesay's *Landscape of Memories*

ELIZABETH L.A. KAMARA

This chapter examines the themes of social degradation and war in Oumar Farouk Sesay's *Landscape of Memories* (2023). It sheds light on the evils perpetrated by the rebels during the Sierra Leone Civil War and shows how they dragged the country into one of the most brutal wars the world has ever seen. It explores the issue of social degradation and makes clear that although characters degraded others before the eruption of the war, the outbreak of war takes social degradation and abuse to a whole new level. Furthermore, it discusses the dichotomy between the aspirations and achievements of migrants and reveals their pain and suffering in war-scarred Sierra Leone.

Set mainly in Masingbi in northern Sierra Leone and partly in the diamondiferous Kono district in eastern Sierra Leone, *Landscape of Memories* is about the tragedy of a nation and its people caught in the web of violence, evil, lawlessness and degradation during the country's eleven-year Civil War. The novel explores the causes of that war and thoroughly exposes the atrocities committed by the rebels, spearheaded by their leaders, Colonel Ranka (Bomo) and Saybom. Sesay also artfully portrays the harrowing story of the heroine, Adama, an immigrant from Mali, who experiences the trauma of losing both her husband Silakeh and child, Sundiata, in their new home in Sierra Leone. The novelist exposes the evil nature of Colonel Ranka who is directly responsible for the cold-blooded murders of Sundiata and members of the families of Kafri Kamara (the notorious investor) and Konneh (formerly Silakeh's friend), among others. Page after page depict acts of debauchery that the rebels force family members to perform on each other, their destruction of property and desecration of culture and tradition. The novel further traces the dehumanization and degradation of both Laminaroto (an ordinary man who is stripped of his livelihood and dignity) and Kurbalay (the Gambian immigrant), who only want to make life meaningful for themselves.

Social degradation and war are here examined because they are Sesay's major thematic preoccupations. Social degradation is one of the major causes and a key hallmark of the Civil War in Sierra Leone. The lack of freedom of speech, the abuse and dehumanization of the citizens combine to make them frustrated with the status quo. These are some of the issues that lead them to rebel, as will be shown further in this chapter. It is however important to point out that Adama, the heroine, and almost all the major characters in the novel are migrants embroiled in the war and degraded by it. It needs to be said that though most of the degradation stems from the war, there are cases of degradation that are not directly related to the war but essentially reveal the callousness and corruption of human beings. In this work, many of the migrants find themselves on the edge of society, though it is obvious that some of them perform very important roles in their new home.

Migration, the movement of people from within or across borders, is a global phenomenon and is becoming more and more important because of the prevalence of wars, economic crises, political instability, natural disasters, oppression and lack of opportunities in certain countries. Human beings have always lived a nomadic existence and most people migrate either freely or unwillingly. Two prominent migration theorists, Dustmann and Weiss, hold that the twofold reasons for migration are: "economic motives ... and motives related to natural disaster or persecution" (2007, 237). This argument holds for most of the migrants in *Landscape of Memories*, many of whom travel to Sierra Leone from Mali, Senegal, The Gambia, Guinea and the Middle East or internally migrate from one part of Sierra Leone to another, for example, to Kono and Masingbi, in order to avoid oppression as in the case of Baba the imam who comes from Rokupr, or for an economic reason as in the case of Kurbalay, Silakeh and others. People also migrate for education, health and love.

Key among the migrants in *Landscape of Memories* are Adama, the heroine of the story, and her husband Silakeh, a descendant of a powerful warrior clan in Mali, their birthplace. Adama emerges as a woman of substance. Her independence and astuteness come to the fore when she rejects the suitor chosen by her father and chooses her husband, Silakeh on her own. Her father, however, approves of her marriage and when the magic of the diamonds hooks the heart and soul of Silakeh, Adama is left with no option but to emigrate with her husband. This is how they come to Sierra Leone, transit in Masingbi and become a part of everything that is going on around them.

By the same token, migrants often experience a lot of suffering and are sometimes made to feel that they are second- or even third-class citizens. Sesay raises the alarm about the moral bankruptcy and injustice in society exhibited by those at the helm of power. A case in point is when the Prime Minister Shekuna (President Stevens),[1] drives away foreigners from the mining area

---

[1] Shekuna represents Siaka Stevens who was the Prime Minister of Sierra Leone between 1967 and 1971, and President from 1971 to 1984. He was a dictator whose

as soon as he assumes office. This xenophobic policy is a thorough denunciation of the powers that be and reflects how foreigners are often treated in Sierra Leone and other receiving countries. To be sure, this nationalistic policy aimed at curbing the influx of foreigners into Kono became a very potent tool of exploitation by the politicians during the era of Stevens, especially in the 1970s and fed into the history of violence in Sierra Leone. Young migrants without mining permits became *sansan* boys (illicit miners) and the issue of dividend sharing led many into violent conflicts with investors and licence holders. They lived very precarious lives – they could lose their lives if found guilty or suspected of stealing (or swallowing) diamonds. In *Landscape of Memories*, when the military enter Kono, they abuse, brutalize and violate the basic human rights of foreigners.[2] Teacher Conteh (the Head teacher of the Pentecostal Mission School in Masingbi) however saves Silakeh when he tells him about the mandate to expel foreigners from the mining area and prevents him from going to the mines. The quotation below demonstrates that injustice and corruption are at the heart of such xenophobic attacks:

> Middle Eastern nationals with connections to the Prime Minister were not touched … The politicians collected their kickbacks in brown envelopes in the coziness of their offices. The foot soldiers wrenched bribes from the so-called aliens in Kono. In some cases, piles of gravel were washed and equipment stolen and the miners came to Masingbi. (89)

The above is a concrete manifestation of the degeneration and corruption of a nation by people who are supposed to uphold its integrity. The abuse of power, widespread corruption and the oppression of the masses manifested above, are some of the leading causes of the war in Sierra Leone. In fact, control of the diamond mines is also one of the key factors responsible for

---

rule was characterized by mismanagement, corruption, repression and injustice. This led to the moral degradation of many people who found proscribed ways to survive. President Stevens cared more about enriching himself and his cabal than seeking his people's welfare and his policies were largely responsible for the Civil War that ravaged his country. By the time he left office, his successor, President Joseph Saidu Momoh, could hardly stem the tide of the nation's collapse.

[2] Yet, it could be argued that in reality, Siaka Stevens' policies ended up favoring 'foreigners' (Malians, Lebanese, Gambians, etc.) in the country, including in the diamond-rich areas like Kono to the detriment of so-called native Sierra Leoneans. This is especially the case of foreigners who had the resources and willingness to bribe local and national figures of political authority. Tax and permit requirement for entry into Kono, for example, was applied, at least in theory, to those considered to be non-Kono natives. Sometimes, Kono born and bred people fell into that dragnet. It was a free-for-all. Stevens and his cabal of corrupt politicians and their acolytes exploited and brutalized everyone (foreigner or local) who was exploitable or suspected of being an obstacle to their thirst for money and power.

the long duration of the war in Sierra Leone – all the parties involved fought to control the mines not only to procure arms for the war but also to enrich themselves.[3]

Sesay seeks to show that migrants have a lot to offer and should be treated with respect rather than degraded. A good number of them are the foundation on which their respective societies rest and they help to develop and raise the profile of their communities. Baba, originally from Rokupr, near the border with Guinea significantly improves the state of Islam in Masingbi. His push factors are the series of clashes with the chiefs who believe that he is deliberately undermining them and they in turn make the place too hot for him and his talibes.[4] He and his talibes decide to migrate to Kono in order to avoid further conflicts. Like the Silakehs, he transits in Masingbi. He steps in for the former Chief Imam, Pa Sadique during the week of his visit. The chief convinces him to stay and provides him with a wife, accommodation and all that he needs to stay comfortably in Masingbi. This seals his fate in Masingbi, where he becomes the Chief Imam and administers to the social and spiritual needs of his people. He contributes to making his society more humane and the popularity of his Muslim religion is the root of his clash with the esoteric society in Masingbi.

Sesay unveils some of the despicable practices in Masingbi and condemns the killing of Baba's neighbour Raka, by the Masubas (a very powerful fraternity in Masingbi). Baba, the newcomer ponders on the sort of society that could kill a son of the soil merely because he could not pay his debts. In fact, Baba's many questions liken him to the beggar (another immigrant) in Wole Soyinka's *The Swamp Dwellers* who is the first to talk about things that the home-grown are afraid to think or talk about. Here, Baba becomes determined to do something about it and promises himself that no one should ever die in similar circumstances. He thus teams up with the village pastor to bring sanity and regeneration to Masingbi. His friendship and collaboration with the pastor symbolize inter-faith tolerance, specifically the religious tolerance for which Sierra Leone is known.

In his very insightful work "Behavior in Reverse: Reasons for Return Migration" (2019), Oded Stark explores the issue of migration and avers

---

[3] One of the most merciless rebels during the war in Sierra Leone, Sam Bockarie (known as Maskita) was once a *sansan* boy (artisal diamond digger) and he ensured that the rebels focused on controlling the mines.

[4] Talibes are boys from Senegal, the Gambia, Guinea Bissau, Guinea, Chad, Mali, or Mauritania who study the Quran at a Quranic school. In Sierra Leone, the hierarchical order of informal Islamic education begins with the talibes, seekers of knowledge, who have acquired tertiary level education in reading and interpreting the Quran, textual criticism, and Hadith.

that failure is one of the factors responsible for return migration.[5] He asserts that return migrants are migrants who, having been internal or international migrants, return to their place of origin either voluntarily or involuntarily. He argues that: "Migrants will return to their place of origin when at the place of destination, they fail to gain employment, they lose hope that their fortunes will turn around, or they are unable to sustain themselves any longer. Rough living is the mother of return" (120). This is what happens in the case of Kurbalay, whose degradation, trauma and dashed hopes abroad lead him to return to his homeland. However, he does not stay because of the attitude of his siblings. Sesay thus suggests that in certain cases, the attitude of others make it difficult or impossible for migrants to return to their birthplaces.

The opening pages of the novel take us to a world on the edge of collapse. Here, the narrator is a migrant who returns to his hometown, Masingbi, after the war. He grew up in his homeland and is therefore a fitting narrator to talk about his society. He is quick to notice the changes that now hug and deface the town:

> It seemed change had already left a scar on the town ... The decade old war had stripped the town naked and left it bare on the edge of history like a throwback from a less compassionate moment of the human epoch; the once elegant houses were now old and decrepit, like the residents living in them. The structural integrity of the houses had yielded to the tyranny of time just like some of the residents. Time had hung a portrait of dereliction on the landscape; the deformity of form was visible: old houses, mostly made from mud, slouched to the ground in a dust-to-dust ritual. (1–2)

The landscape depicted above is a symbol of the moral degeneration and loss of direction that permeate *Landscape of Memories*. The marks of regression or degradation on the landscape, the houses and people are a reflection of the rottenness that has eaten into the fabric of society and further underpin the view that wars are cancers that should not be allowed to thrive. The atmosphere of death and decay that cleave to the houses is reinforced by the novelist's reference to the "dust-to-dust ritual". The physical structure of the town and the use of diction such as "scar", "decrepit", "dereliction", "deformity", "slouched" and "dust-to-dust" leave readers in no doubt that something terrible happened to the people during the decade old war.

Landscape of Memories employs the traumatic memories of the Sierra Leone Civil War as a sort of frame within which everything is perceived. Sesay writes about the evils of war in this novel not only because they provide nourishment for his narrative but also because he believes that that traumatic

---

[5] This does not mean that migrants who are successful do not return. There are numerous cases of migrants who return to their homelands as success stories.

facet of history should never be forgotten. As Patrizia Violi asserts, conserving memory is not enough: there should be a clear idea about *"whose* memory, memory *for whom*? For whom do we wish to conserve the memory of victims? For their relatives, for the survivors, for the local community, for future generations, for tourists? It is not necessarily the same thing" (3; italics added). The war is part of Sierra Leonean history and identity and cannot be forgotten. Sierra Leonean writers have not forgotten about the war and in all genres of literature they continue to weave the story of the war in their writings, to awaken the memories of their citizens and subtly remind them, never to walk along that path again. Gbanabom Hallowell in *The Road to Kaibara*, Pede Hollist in *So the Path Does Not Die*, M'Bha Kamara in *When Mosquitoes Come Marching in*, Kosonike Koso-Thomas in *Peacekeeper Lover* and a host of others are there to call up memories of those dark days in Sierra Leone's history in which: "God himself / scarce seemed there to be" (Coleridge 1993. 345). Like the aforementioned writers, Sesay believes that it is important to preserve the traumatic memory of the Civil War for the present and future generations. In *Landscape of Memories*, he reminds readers that the system in Sierra Leone in the 1990s was rotten to the core and the war exploded in a way many had never seen before in other countries, with human-on-human cruelty taken to a new height.

In this novel, oppression of the masses (including foreigners), gross violation of the people's basic human rights and the high cost of living contribute to a growing sense of disenchantment. Everything is gradually taken away from the masses and they find it extremely difficult to eat decent meals or take proper care of themselves. Children suffer from malnutrition and teachers could hardly afford decent clothes and shoes. Severe deprivation, degradation, suffering and absence of freedom of speech characterize the lives of the ordinary citizen during this period. These are some of the causes of the Civil War. In fact, before the war erupted in Sierra Leone in 1991, Sierra Leone was in the throes of serious financial quandaries and institutionalized corruption. It was not uncommon for public workers to go on strike because of lack of salaries (often for long periods) and people could not even feed their families (UNHCR 4).

Sesay throws light on the attempted coup by the military to overthrow the government of Shekuna. Corporal Saybom (the notorious Foday Sankoh, founder of the Revolutionary United Front) who is supposed to execute the President on that day, oversleeps and learns too late that the coup is botched. When he goes to the radio station, he and his cohorts are captured, beaten, tried, and flung into prison where he is nourished by a cocktail of hatred, revenge, and ambition. He discovers Bomo in prison and together, their hatred of the President and the rule of law, and the grievances of the masses culminate in one of the most gruesome wars the world has ever seen.

Sesay narrates the start of the war as if it were a made-up story and registers that the war starts with a first shot by a group of men who cross over from

Liberia and kill soldiers on parade at Bomaru, Kailahun district, in the east of Sierra Leone. They then swoop down on the rich fields of Kono like a swarm of locusts, killing, looting, burning houses and leaving in their wake a trail of destruction. Their actions are a doomsday precursor to the widespread mayhem unleashed later in the novel. They brutalize and kill the innocent – even unborn children; rip open the bellies of women to win bets on the sex of their children; perform acts of degeneracy on families; and force their victims to rape others within their families. During their reign of terror, they force fathers to rape their daughters; sons to rape their mothers; they rape women in front of their husbands; and gang-rape women and girls in front of their families. They humiliate and torture the innocent and guilty alike, to revenge for the years of injustice and marginalization that they and their compatriots have suffered. The bitter irony is that the rebels profess that they are fighting for the masses but they release their venom on the blameless and guilty alike. Saybom, Colonel Ranka and their depraved bunch deliberately target women, little children and unborn children, apart from men.

It is important to note that Saybom is a descendant of the people of Rosaeŋh, the village of the cursed ones. According to legend, Saybom's grandfather was caught making love with his father's young wife. In order to cleanse the land spiritually, Saybom's grandfather was required to eat dog meat, dance semi naked in the town square, "smacking the private organ after every dance step" (172) The irony is that both the crime and punishment reek of degradation. Additionally, the sexual depravity of Saybom's grandfather foreshadows the moral degeneracy of his grandson whose atrocities contribute in no small way to the viciousness of the Rebel War.

The rebels' inhumanity is also exposed when they attack the Konnehs in Kono and force all the members of the family – parents, children, grandchildren, their son's wife – to strip naked and rape each other. They kill Pa Konneh's grandson and threaten to crush any scintilla of protest by killing the others. The youngest child Fanta escapes from the rebels by putting on an act and her bravery puts her in a Catch-22 situation – it earns her the admiration of the despicable Colonel Ranka who, with his gun pressed against Pa Konneh's nape, "asks" for her hand in marriage. Mrs Konneh loses her life, but her family members escape to Masingbi and their fates become inextricably intertwined with Adama and Sundiata in whose house they seek refuge. The love relationship between Fanta and Sundiata that blossoms into marriage provokes Colonel Ranka to murder Sundiata for what he calls his three-fold crime – "the man who sent me to prison, the guy who made me drop out of school and has taken my wife" (222). Before he kills Sundiata, he cruelly rapes Fanta in front of her husband. He then narrates a warped account of the Ibrahim and Ismail story[6] and declares his intention to enact

---

[6] The Ibrahim and Ismail story is an allusion to a story in the Quran, in which Prophet Ibrahim had a series of dreams in which God told him to kill his son Ismail.

his version of it by forcing Adama to partake in the brutal killing of her son in a very disturbing scene that reminds Sierra Leoneans about the atrocities committed during the bitter war in their motherland. The vengeful Colonel Ranka puts the knife in Adama's hand:

> He held her arms firmly as he pressed the blade on Sundiata's neck. The feel of the knife in her hands, as it touched her son's skin sent a chill inside her. Every neuron and tissue inside her died. Her entire body went into spasm, like the reversal of the feeling she had felt when she had given birth to Sundiata. To kill what she had given life sent her cells into a frenzy. (232)

The above is a damning indictment of the sadism and lawlessness that characterize the perpetrators of the Civil War in Sierra Leone. It further demonstrates the rebels' capacity to devise new and more horrendous ways to inflict eternal pain on their fellow citizens.

When Colonel Ranka wreaks havoc on the town, even the buoyant, patriotic and patient Laminaroto, a representative of the ordinary Sierra Leonean is not spared. It is however important to point out that the degradation of Laminaroto starts well before the war comes to Masingbi. Laminaroto is a fitting symbol of everyman who finds himself humiliated, repulsed and oppressed by the powers that be. Similarly, he stands for all stoic individuals who have conditioned themselves to survive against the odds. We first meet him as one of the most competent, conscientious and hardworking sanitary officers. He is soon recognized by the central government and presented with an award for his commitment. His days of glory are transient, though, as he is relieved of his duties too soon, which takes him to the nadir of his life; or so we think. His degradation is symbolized by his dilapidated wheelbarrow "made of discarded parts. The elliptical object tied with rags and strings replaced the wheel. A pair of uneven sticks cushioned on edge by rags of many colours mimicked the handle" (89). The degeneration of the nation as a whole is further epitomized by both the wheelbarrow and the life of Laminaroto. His fate is an index of the attitude of the powers that be to the citizens and is actually one of the causes of the war – the wanton violation of the basic human rights of the citizens. Laminaroto's degradation however becomes complete when the rebels amputate his hand (at the wrist), asking him (as they asked the author's countrymen during the war) with their macabre sense of humour whether he prefers short sleeves (to be amputated at the elbow) or long sleeves (to be amputated at the wrist). Yet, he remains stoical in the face of all such disappointments, callousness and suffering.

The evils perpetrated by the rebels and the level of their degeneracy are further underscored in their treatment of Kafri Kamara, the man with the God

---

Ismail was willing to be sacrificed. Prophet Ibrahim blindfolded himself while he performed the terrible deed. When he removed the blindfold, he found a ram lying in place of his son, and the uninjured Ismail standing beside him.

complex who tortures Kurbalay in the Tefaya Forest. As if in punishment for his heartlessness toward Kurbalay and others, the rebels "gang-raped his wife and forced him to participate in the act in the presence of his family. They later killed everyone except him. They let him survive" (178). To be sure, the cruelty of Kafri Kamara and his notorious executioner Timberjack are exposed early in the novel, when they torture Kurbalay who they believe has swallowed a diamond. Kafri ensures that he is beaten and tortured until he almost passes out and given a concoction to drink – laxatives mixed with contaminated water – in the hope that this will purge him to death, and they will find the diamond in his excreta. He undergoes torture for three days and on the third day he does not even have sufficient energy to sit on the bucket, but lies down in his own waste:

> Kurbalay's stomach began to rumble like an angry volcano and when it finally erupted there was excrement everywhere. A team of desperate miners immediately started to scavenge through the excreta for the diamond everyone was convinced Kurbalay had swallowed. The miners had abandoned the gravel they worked for and pinned their hopes on Kurbalay's excrement. (45)

This is among the most distasteful scenes in the novel and is a thorough denunciation of the deep-seated malaise that has eaten into the fabric of society. It needs to be said that this stripping of the dignity and humanity of others (even before the start of the war) is also one of the triggers of the war and foreshadows the stripping away of everything decent and humane that characterizes the rebels' diabolical sway. The above not only underpins the depths of decadence of Kafri and men of like stamp, but further unveils the level of humiliation and trauma that people often experience in the mines. Sesay's point here is that things do not have to be this way. People should not be dehumanized whether they are in their homelands or because they have crossed borders. Similarly, this quote reveals that people's penchant for chasing phantoms has led them to lose sight of the things that really matter.

Kurbalay's ordeal takes him to the brink of insanity and when Kafri frees him, he runs at breakneck speed for days before collapsing on Adama's doorsteps. All his dreams are finally incinerated on the altar of Kafri Kamara's cruelty and greed. His feeling of worthlessness is reflected in the job of digging latrines that he now does for a living. The degradation of Kurbalay demonstrates how people, and in this case, migrants often lose their dignity and personhood in their effort to better their lives. In spite of his menial job however, people hold him in high esteem because of his resilience, humility, loyalty to Adama and determination to eke out a living for himself in an honest way. Baba gives him four shillings as *bora*[7] to initiate marriage proceedings

---

[7] Among the Temnes, *bora* is a token given to family members or people in authority during marital rites as a mark of respect. Other ethnic groups in Sierra Leone also adhere to this practice, though they have their own names for it.

with Adama because of the respect that he and others have for him (Kurbalay). Perhaps this is the lesson readers are meant to learn; that it is better to be poor and free than to be rich and in fetters. Kurbalay has swapped one pit for another, but now he has peace and respect. He rises in our estimation when he meets his nemesis Kafri face to face but forgives him wholeheartedly. This suggests that no matter how people hurt their fellow human beings, healing is possible, if only the victims have a heart big enough to forgive.

Furthermore, Bomo (Colonel Ranka) also deteriorates throughout the course of the novel. He starts to retrogress after his clash with Sundiata and the school – he becomes a drop out, a driver's apprentice, an illicit miner, a thief and a morally barren individual who spikes the drinks of innocent boys to get them into trouble. He finds an outlet for his pent-up rage during the war in which he and other merciless beings demonstrate their depravity.

Similarly, the rebels' determination to destroy everything on their path is reflected in how they desecrate Sandathaka, the sacred bush, home of the ancestral chiefs and symbol of tradition. Before the loss of the forest's sanctity, Nasomayla and Pa Kapri were the only people authorized to enter it at will. But now, the sacred bush is "replaced with a bald land with burnt-out logs piled beside some solitary trees. The mausoleum in which the ancestors were buried, whose powers supposedly protected the land, was no more. The pyramid of their existence was gone by the stroke of a match stick" (198). This is a biting indictment of a society that has lost its cultural heritage to the point that, no facet of their tradition is sacred; no portion of the environment is sacrosanct. The rebels' violation of the forest is an index of how far they have gone to wantonly drive a wedge between themselves and their ancestors. The actions of the rebels demonstrate that they are culturally alienated individuals who have lost themselves in the process of destroying their own people – the very people they claim they are liberating.

From the above, it is apparent that, in *Landscape of Memories*, social degradation is amongst the leading causes and key consequences of the war in Sierra Leone. In fact, social degradation, oppression and injustice combine to fuel an extremely violent war, that spares neither citizens nor foreigners. Sesay is a committed writer with a keen sense of history, and an even deeper awareness of where the country is heading. Regarding the issue of migration more specifically, he establishes the point that migration could be a dicey issue and underpins the view that although some migrants experience the green grass, for others, migration is a fruitless ordeal. Some migrants may be as successful and valuable as Baba and help to change their community, while others may face hell on earth like Adama and Kurbalay. What remains clear is that human beings should be watchdogs. At a time like the current one when there is an alarming rate of outbound migration; when people are stoking the flames of disunity; and when drug abuse and lawlessness are on the increase this novel has relevance. This work spurs all to remain resilient and hopeful in spite of the trials of a dangerous world. It further teaches the reader to be a Laminaroto who never gives up; a Kurbalay who finds a way out of his labyrinth; and an Adama who endures it all. And most of all, it tells the unborn generation about the harrowing Sierra Leonean Civil War, and all that is lost and found before, during, and after it.

Works Cited

Coleridge, Samuel Taylor, 'The Rime of the Ancient Mariner', in *The Norton Anthology of English Literature* (ed.) M.H, Abrams, 6th ed., Vol. 2 (New York: W.W. Norton, 1993).

Dustmann, C. and Yoram Weiss., 'Return Migration: Theory and Empirical Evidence from the UK', *British Journal of Industrial Relations* 45.2 (June 2007), pp. 236–56.

Hallowell, Gbanabom, *The Road to Kaibara* (Freetown: Sierra Leonean Writers Series, 2015).

Hollist, Pede, *So The Path Does Not Die* (Bamenda: Langaa Research & Publishing Common Initiative Group, 2012).

Kamara, M'Bha, *When Mosquitoes Come Marching In* (South Gate, CA: NoPassport Press, 2021).

Koso-Thomas, Kosonike, *Peacekeeper Lover* (Freetown: Sierra Leonean Writers Series, 2021).

Sesay, Oumar Farouk, *Landscape of Memories* Revised Edition (Freetown: Sierra Leonean Writers Series, 2023).

Stark, Oded, 'Behavior in Reverse: Reasons for Return Migration', *Behavioral Public Policy* 3.1 (2019), pp. 104–26.

Soyinka, Wole, *The Swamp Dwellers*, *Collected Plays 1* (London: Oxford University Press, 1973).

UNHCR – UN High Commissioner for Refugees, 'UNHCR CDR Background Paper on Refugees and Asylum Seekers from Sierra Leone', 1 November 1998, available at: https://www.refworld.org/docid/3ae6a6418.html. Accessed 9 November 2022.

Violi, Patrizia. *Landscapes of Memory: Trauma, Space, History,* Vol. 7 of *Cultural Memories.* Trans. Alastair McEwen (Oxford: Peter Lang, International Academic Publishers, 2017).

SECTION III

VISIONS OF THE FUTURE: NEW GENRES, AESTHETICS, AND EPISTEMOLOGIES

Chapter 9

"A Window to Society": The Human Condition in the Context of Interspecies Relations in J.M. Coetzee's *Disgrace* and Aminatta Forna's *The Window Seat*

ERNEST COLE

The Window Seat, Aminatta Forna's recent collection of essays, explores a variety of themes in different geographical spaces and in the context of history, politics, and culture. Deeply reflective of her life's experiences, she examines familiar themes of childhood, race, interspecies relations, violence, and trauma from critical perspectives and depth of treatment that provide new insights into her creative imagination.

In this chapter, I make the claim that *The Window Seat* is a template to read human behavior and society's aspirations and failings. Using human-animal relations as a construct of sight and perspective in both Coetzee's novel and Forna's essay, I argue that Forna demonstrates how mankind's treatment of animals offers a window into the nature of humanity and the societies we live in. I argue that humans' treatment of four types of animals in the works selected – dogs, goats, chimps, and foxes – provides a template to read society's cruelty and ill-treatment of animals, and that our actions and behavior provide a clear indication into human desire for control and domination. Using J.M. Coetzee's *Disgrace* as a framework to analyze the three essays in which these animals are depicted – "The Last Vet," "Bruno," and "Wilder Things" – I posit an ethical frame to read the sufferings of animals and argue that the complexities of human-animal relations are largely informed by anthropocentrism and mankind's desire for control over nonhuman animals. From my reading of these three stories, I contend that human-animal relationships must be configured on a basis of reciprocity and on an ethical consideration of the sufferings of animals, preservation of their lives, and humane treatment of them. I support Forna's assertion that mankind's interactions with animals imply that the least the former can do to them is to ensure and preserve "an independent exchange of services" (149) between humans and animals. As she notes in citing Milan Kundera's test of humanity (1984): "True human greatness can manifest itself in all its purity and liberty, in regard to those who have no power. True moral tests of humanity lie in those who are at its mercy: the animals" (Forna, 167). I contend that human efforts in establishing a reciprocal relationship with animals are indicative of this manifestation of morality. I draw from theorizations on animal rights and African ethics to emphasize that ethical considerations of animals should constitute human relationship with the natural environment, and that moral relationship is established when they are capable of extending ethical rights to nonhuman animals. I argue for the creation of an ethical system of reciprocal relationships that can accommodate and validate animal coexistence with humans on the basis of a humane and compassionate treatment of them.

In pursuing my aesthetics of an "ethics of reciprocity," as manifestation of oral benchmarks in human-animal relations, it is imperative to situate Aminatta Forna's argument, and indeed, her essays on human ill-treatment of animals, in the context of the Anthropocene. In this way, it makes the claim that mankind's contribution to animal suffering is indicative of the characteristics of the elements of human superiority and dominion in the Anthropocene.

In "Encountering the 'Anthropocene': Setting the Scene" (2019), Frank Biermann and Eva Lövbrand quoted Steffen et al. in conceptualizing the Anthropocene as "the unprecedented changes to the earth's biosphere following the industrial revolution and the post-sixty years of economic activity, consumption, and resource use" (11). They further indicated that "the Anthropocene symbolizes the profound and accelerating human transformations of the earth's climate and environment" (1). In this definition of the concept, Biermann and Lövbrand point out human action in the alteration of the natural order and its complicity in the degradation of the environment. Even though the concept remains "an ambivalent and contested formulation," they agreed, citing a range of works, that "in its manifestation in a number of issues including unequal geographics, political-economic relations, insecurities and bodily labors" (2), the Anthropocene invites a rethinking of "the Western division between natural and human history" and has initiated a call to "vitalize traditional concepts of ethics, care, and virtue" (2).

One aspect of the Anthropocene crucial to my argument of an absence of an "ethics of reciprocity" between human and animals is mankind's ill-treatment of animals and the ethical and moral implications of such treatment. I argue that mankind's treatment of animals can be specifically situated in the Anthropocene in recognition of their disregard for animal life, oblivious attitude to their suffering, denial of animal rights and welfare, creation of policies to support their dominion over animals, and justification of a hierarchical system or order of nature that elevates them to a position of dominion and control. Forna's attention to human-animal relations in *The Window Seat* puts the essays in the context of eco-critical tradition in literature and cultural studies.

My contention is that *Disgrace* and *The Window Seat* not only draw from the concept of the Anthropocene in their depiction of animal life, but that they further define human agency in relation to animals as one of anthropocentrism. In the depiction of the dogs, the chimpanzee, and the fox in these texts, Coetzee and Forna question the rationale of anthropocentrism and its dominant motif of elevating humans above all creation and putting them at the center of material and ethical concerns. As the authors explore human-animal relations in their works, it becomes evident that they are calling into question the central concerns of anthropocentrism, and as Eileen Crist and Helen Kopnina state in their critique of anthropocentrism, its "dominant beliefs, values, and attitudes guiding human action [and being] a significant driver of the pressing problems of the day" (387).

I draw from Crist and Kopnina's 2014 analysis to posit three fundamental elements of anthropocentrism – human agency, ontological inversion of the natural order, and a deconstructive approach to anthropocentrism. I use these formulations to analyze Coetzee's and Forna's perspectives of human-animal relations. Crist and Kopnina conceive of human agency as "The Human Center;" the ability of humans to dominate and transform the natural order by "comprehensively categori[zing it] by naming, classifications, surveillances, rules, and framings" (389). They add that anthropocentrism has allowed for an inversion of the ontological order of nature and being which originally presents "[e]arth as inexhaustible, largely unknown, enchanted, mysterious, and more encompassing" with a "man-made ontology of the civilized human [that] has become physically entrenched and certainly conceptually reified" (389). From an inside-out perspective, they conclude that the "self-placement of Man at the Center has disallowed a vantage point from which any need or desire for limiting human expansionism might be discerned" (390).

The roots of anthropocentrism are varied and complex. Eve Nabulya in her 2022 article "Rethinking Human-Centredness and Eco-Sustainability in an African Setting: Insights from Luganda Folktales" traces the origins of the concept to early writings in Western ecological and environmental thought, specifically Aldo Leopold's influential book *A Sand County Almanac* (1949). She notes his influence on other writers on human moral responsibility towards nonhumans. She references the Norwegian philosopher Anne Naess, who is reputed to have coined the term "deep ecology," and from which she situated anthropocentrism along two axes:

> the ecosystem focused approach (ecocentrism) which advocates for the protection of all elements of the natural environment and for the holistic protection of ecosystems, and the human-centred approach (anthropocentrism) which considers the value of elements of the natural environment, and their decisions regarding their preservation as dependent on their utility value. (310)

Eva Nabulya quotes the Ethno-philosopher Edwin Etieyibo on his conception of anthropocentrism: "the natural order is hierarchically structured with humans holding a coveted position, and an ontological and existential divide exists between human and nonhuman nature. Nature is a system of inanimate particles that operate deterministically, human beings alone are intrinsically valuable, and only human beings constitute the moral community" (310). The implications of this view of human and nonhuman relations are deeply problematic, morally challenging, and ethically demanding. Coetzee and Forna explore these concerns about mankind's treatment of animals in their works.

Helen Kopnina et al., in "Anthropocentrism: More than Just a Misunderstood Problem" (2018), argue that anthropocentrism is ethically wrong and is at the roots of the current ecological crises and make the claim that a deeper (ecocentric) environmental ethic that recognizes the welfare of all nonhuman forms is critical to addressing the problem. In this regard, they conceive of speciesism and human chauvinism as fundamental to anthropocentrism. The treatment of dogs in "The Last Vet," and the fox in "Wilder Things" in Forna's collection of essays calls attention to this issue. In "The Trauma of Anthropocentrism and the Reconnection of Self and World" in J.M. Coetzee's *Dusklands*, Susana Onega places the founding metaphor on which anthropocentrism is based on the motif of domination as expressed in the Bible – "the Biblical notion of dominium terrae" (Genesis 1, 26f), that is, the Creator's mandate to human beings to "Fill the earth and subdue it" (Genesis 1, 28). She supports Peter Kunzmann (2005) in his view that the dominion metaphor is "the cornerstone of pure 'anthropocentrism'" (quoted in Onega 2014, 209–10).

To present a historical and cultural context for understanding this relationship, and to offer a critical lens to read the three essays selected for study, I begin with a broad analysis of selected scenes in Coetzee's *Disgrace* that are both reflective of the treatment of animals in Sierra Leone and indicative of my argument of reciprocal acceptance in interspecies relationships. Coetzee's illustration of the treatment of animals in Bev Shaw's clinic provides the critical lens to frame and explore Forna's depiction of animals in the three essays selected for study, and a context to explore my argument that humans have characteristics and capabilities that we share with animals, and that, in fact, human nature and actions are amplified when animals are anthropomorphized. Essentially, mankind's view of animals is largely based on anthropocentrism but the selected works clearly demonstrate that the lives of animals not only offer us a mirror that reflects shared characteristics, they expose our attitudes, choices, and biases towards animals.

Elisa Galgut (2017), Kai Horsthemke (2017), Vida Yao (2019), and Alan Northover (2009) provide additional critical lenses and contexts to situate my argument of ethical consideration for animals' sufferings and a moral system of acceptance of their lives based on reciprocity. From my reading of their theoretical positionings on interspecies relationships, I raise the following questions as critical formulations for my argument: should we assign moral statuses to nonhuman animals? Do humans have a moral responsibility to nonhumans? If so, what is that responsibility and how is it defined? On what basis should it be conducted? Should humans be held as morally superior to animals? Is comparing humans to animals a degrading stereotype? Should mankind's anthropocentric view of animals be contested?

In my engagement with these questions, and as I analyze selected scenes from *Disgrace* and *The Window Seat*, I divide the chapter into two sections: first, I explore scenes depicting animal abuse in *Disgrace* as context to read mankind's anthropocentric relationships with animals. Second, I draw from this analysis to read the three aforementioned essays in *The Window Seat*. I use the theoretical constructs on animal rights and African ethics in the works of Galgut, Yao, and Horsthemke to establish a basis for examination of how an understanding of interspecies relations can foster a better humanity and society.

I begin with the dialog between David Lurie and his daughter, Lucy, in *Disgrace*:

> But it is true. They are not going to lead me to a higher life, and the reason is there is no higher life. This is the only life there is. Which we share with animals. That's the example people like Bev try to set. That's the example I try to follow. *To share some of our human privileges with the beasts.* I don't want to come back in another existence as a dog or a pig and have to live as dogs or pigs live under us.
>
> "Lucy, my dearest, don't be cross. Yes, I agree, this is the only life there is. *As for animals, by all means let us be kind to them. But let us not lose perspective. We are of a different order of creation from the animals.* Not higher, necessarily, just different. So if we are going to be kind, let it be out of simple generosity, not because we feel guilty or fear retribution." (74; emphasis added)

Gail Fincham's "J.M. Coetzee's *Elizabeth Costello*: From Anthropocentrism towards Biocentrism?" is useful in reading David Lurie's conception of human-animal relations in *Disgrace*. His characterization of humans as "a different order of creation from the animals'" reinforces the hierarchical order of creation and the elevation of mankind as the superior being. Coetzee's position on animal rights and welfare significantly conflicts with David's and the interaction between him and his daughter, Lucy, brings out the unattractive elements of an anthropocentric view of life. This aspect of anthropocentrism is explored in Fincham's article where she interrogates not only David's position but also spells out Coetzee's distance from it. Coetzee's distance is reminiscent of his treatment of Elizabeth Costello, a figure that reminds us of David Lurie and his anthropocentrism, especially in the early sections of *The Lives of Animals*. In her changing perspective on anthropocentrism, Elizabeth, unlike David, as Fincham notes, suggests that "Coetzee may be seen to be approaching, through the figure of Costello, a new dimension in human-animal relations" (54). This new dimension refuses to subordinate animals to the power of humanspeech and writing. This move away from anthropocentrism, Fincham posits, could be described as biocentrism. *Disgrace* and *The Window Seat* articulates this view of human relations with animals and the authors' commitment to it. In contrast to anthropocentrism, biocentrism signals a shift from perceiving human beings as "privileged stewards of creation to a worldview in which humans and non-humans equally share the world" (54–5).

In the above excerpt from *Disgrace*, Lucy makes a case for shared existence with animals. Regardless of its connections to reincarnation and the transmigration of the soul, her claim of shared privileges speaks to interdependence and reciprocity. In this positioning of human-animal relationships, an ethical framework for consideration of animal lives is warranted. The claim further gestures to human-animal coexistence in a shared space, and this, in turn, posits interesting and challenging notions of recognition and acceptance of equality with animals. On the other hand, David's response hits at the core of the ethical-moral controversy in mankind's relationship with animals. While he recognizes the need to "be kind to them," he adopts an anthropocentric position in relation to animals by framing mankind's existence as existing on a different hierarchy of being. Hence, "we are of a different order of creation from the animals" (74).

David's perception and ultimate treatment of animals intersect with his religious belief of mankind's superior position and God-given right of dominion over animals. In his view, ethical and moral considerations of the rights of animals should only go so far as what humans are willing to accord them, and not because of any intrinsic worth or value in them or their lives. David raises the question, as earlier mentioned, of whether ethical status should be conferred on animals, and whether in so doing, animals are not unduly elevated over their "predestined position" in the order of creation. Further, David's position attests to relational morality where moral status is a function of one's position in the order of creation and not on any intrinsic characteristic with which one is endowed; regardless of the shared features between humans and animals. As Galgut infers in her essay regarding such positioning, "Animal Rights and African Ethics: Congruence or Conflict," "the first objection [to this line of thinking] is the claim that humans have unique characteristics and capacities that nonhumans do not share" (2017, 179). If David's argument for "order of creation" is posited as a "vital principle", as Galgut defines it, then it is not only unjustified but anthropocentric as well.

Besides its gesture to anthropocentrism, David's view also raises the question of ascribing moral status to animals. As Galgut notes, the question of moral status essentially makes the claim that "*even if* all humans and no nonhuman animals possessed certain abilities, this would still not provide a justification for assigning to lower animals moral status" (180; emphasis original). It is in this regard that she contests the moral superiority of humans and laments the different treatment ascribed to animals. She infers that, "we may have to treat different beings [humans and animals] differently as a way of *respecting* their moral states" (180; emphasis original). As I show later in this chapter, Forna grapples with similar concerns regarding moral statuses of humans and animals.

In the next two scenarios selected for examination, Coetzee points out mankind's cruelty, neglect, and indifference to the pain and suffering of animals. In chapter 9, David attempts to make friends with the old bulldog bitch in his backyard. He enters her cage and closes the door behind him, where Lucy eventually finds him. This is what transpires in the ensuing dialog between David and Lucy. David notes:

> "Poor old Katy, she's in mourning. No one wants her, and she knows it. The irony is, she must have offspring all over the district who would be happy to share their homes with her. But it's not in their power to invite her. They are a part of the furniture, part of the alarm system. *They do us the honour of treating us like gods, and we respond by treating them like things*." They leave the cage. The bitch slumps down, closes her eyes.
>
> "The church Fathers had a long debate about them, and decided *they don't have proper souls*," he observes. "*Their souls are tied to their bodies and die with them*." (78; emphasis added)

Again, while Lucy stresses the need for reciprocity and an ethical response to mankind's relationship with animals, David draws from some kind of theological construct of the soul to make a distinction between humans with "proper souls," and animals "whose souls are tied to their bodies and die with them" as reason for not treating animals humanely and with compassion. As Lucy notes, the sad reality in human-animal relations is that "[t]hey do us the honour of treating us like gods, and we respond by treating them like things" (78). It is in this context that I analyze the sterilization and euthanasia scene in Bev Shaw's clinic; a situation Forna replicates in her depiction of the sterilization of dogs in Dr. Gudush Jalloh's clinic in *The Window Seat* to highlight mankind's inhumane treatment of animals. I use this analysis to further the claim that mankind's relationship with animals offers a window into human nature and society.

In chapter 10 of *Disgrace*, Coetzee presents two scenes that depict animal pain and suffering: the dog with the abscess tooth, and the goat with the swollen scrotum. I take each scene in turn. On David's first day at the clinic, he assisted Bev Shaw in a minor operation on a dog with an abscessed tooth. The excerpt reads:

> "There's an abscess here from an impacted tooth. We have no antibiotics, so – hold him still, *boytkie*! – so we'll just have to lance it and hope for the best."
>
> She probes inside the mouth with a lancet. The dog gives a tremendous jerk, breaks free of him, almost breaks free of the boy.
>
> He grabs it as it scrabbles to get off the table; for a moment its eyes, full of rage and fear, glare into his.
>
> ... Bev Shaw probes again with the lancet. The dog gags, goes rigid, then relaxes.
>
> ... The dog, on its feet, cowers under the table.
>
> There is a spattering of blood and saliva on the surface; Bev wipes it off. The child coaxes the dog out. (81)

The reference to "spattering of blood and saliva" not only calls attention to Bev's professionalism and the conduct of the whole operation, but it also draws attention to her indifference to the suffering of the animal. The clinical, detached, and unscrupulous method of extraction indicates her lack of concern for animal pain and the emotional needs of nonhuman animals. Fincham's article is again useful here in pointing out Coetzee's revulsion at animal suffering. She cites a private confession of Coetzee in which he stated: "I, as a person, as a personality, am overwhelmed, that my thinking is thrown into confusion and helplessness, by the fact of suffering in the world, and not only human suffering" (quoted in Fincham 2018, 56). This emotional scene of animal suffering recalls Costello's concept of the "sympathetic imagination" and, as Fincham notes, is "her most powerful strategy to move human audiences to greater accountability for animal life" (quoted in Fincham 2018, 55).

The scene with the goat is more disturbing. The narrative affirms that "one half of his scrotum, yellow and purple, is swollen like a balloon; the other half is a mass of caked blood and dirt" (82). Its owner informs us that the goat had been "savaged by dogs" and needs urgent surgical treatment. Its "wound [was] alive with white grubs waving their blind heads in the air" because he was brought late to the clinic for medical attention. Without the 500 rand required for surgery and money for antibiotics after the operation, Bev recommends euthanasia:

> She collects herself and gets to her feet. "I'm afraid it's too late," she says to the woman. "I can't make him better. You can wait for the doctor on Thursday, or you can leave him with me. I can give him a quiet end. He will let me do that for him. Shall I? Shall I keep him here?"

The woman wavers, then shakes her head. She begins to tug the goat towards the door.

> "You can have him back afterwards," says Bev Shaw. "I will help him through, that's all." Though she tries to control her voice, he can hear the accents of defeat. The goat hears them too: he kicks against the strap, bucking and plunging, the obscene bulge quivering behind him. The woman drags the strap loose, casts it aside. Then they are gone. (83)

Like the scene of the tooth extraction, this scene illustrates the indifference to animal pain. This time, however, the goat's response is clearly articulated – he kicks against the strap, bulking and plunging – as indicative of resistance to mankind's inhumane treatment of him. Coetzee affirms that "the goat hears them too." In giving human qualities to the goat, Coetzee anthropomorphizes the animal, and in so doing brings his suffering close to us. Unfortunately, Bev and David do not recognize this construct of shared sensibility with the animal. Bev brushes aside the animal's acute sense of discomfort in the same way she does with the dog – merely wiping off the splatter of blood and saliva on the surface of the table and continuing her conversation with David.

As Helen Kopnina et al. emphasize:

> There is nothing in human moral-thinking that should prevent us from realising that nonhumans are not mere objects, without personhood. While we agree that we can discuss the wants and needs of nonhumans, we also believe it is hard to deny that any animals feel fear, pain, and have emotions akin to our own. (121)

Kopnina et al.'s position recall Costello's response to O'Hearne (in many ways Lucy's response to David, and Forna's response to her countrymen) regarding the importance of animal life: "Anyone who says that life matters less to animals than it does to us has not held in his hands an animal fighting for his life" (quoted in Fincham 2018, 61).

In her analysis of Elizabeth Costello's lecture in J.M. Coetzee's *The Lives of Animals*, Vida Yao makes a significant statement regarding human response to animal suffering: "we are not as different from nonhuman animals as we hope. They are not simply irrational or nonrational, but more importantly, even if they were, it would not matter when it comes to the moral significance of the suffering we bring to them" (quoted in Yao 2017, 327). Yao admonishes us to take our moral duties and responsibilities to animals seriously.

This position becomes all too important when one realizes that a lot of the sufferings brought upon animals stem from human desire for convenience or control over animals. One way in which humans strive to ensure domination over animals is to control their population. In *Disgrace* and *The Window Seat*, sterilization or the neutering of animals is one way of effecting this control. Bev Shaw, like Gudush Jalloh, conducts regular surgical operations to sterilize animals. As she tells us, the clinic "offer[s] free neutering service, and get[s] a grant for that" (84). Neutering or the sterilization of animals is part of an organized system or mechanism of control and domination of animals.

Unapologetically, Bev Shaw justifies the practice of animal sterilization. She tells us:

> "The trouble is, there are just too many of them," says Bev. "They don't understand it, of course, and we have no way of telling them. Too many by our standards, not by theirs. They would just multiply and multiply if they had their way, until they filled the earth. They don't think it's a bad thing to have lots of offspring. The more the jollier. Cats the same." (85)

The excerpt reveals an interesting truth: animal's similarity to mankind and the refusal of the latter to extend to nonhumans the same right of procreation that they so jealously guard for themselves. In fact, resentment is directed at animals not because they are different from us but that they look too much like us. The irony in the excerpt is clear: it echoes the Biblical mandate in Genesis 1:28, for mankind to exercise dominion over all other animals and to procreate, "multiply and subdue the earth." Bev ascribes dominion as the exclusive right of humans and denies its extension to nonhuman animals. Her rationale for this denial is based on the Christian mandate of anthropocentrism and the text calls into question its moral and ethical position. Nonetheless, it is important to point out that animal rights is a controversial issue. As Yao asks, "What's the ethical status of the suffering of nonhuman animals? Does the fact [that suffering is bad] on its own yield reasons for all of us to do something about it? Does it give rise to obligations and rights?" (335).

Perhaps a close look at the incineration of the corpses of dead animals in *Disgrace* would help shed light on this controversy of duties, obligations, and rights on animals. First, in the yard outside the clinic, David finds "not Lucy's well-groomed thoroughbreds, but a mob of mongrels filling two pens to bursting point, barking, yapping, whining, leaping with excitement" (84). At their deaths, whether by euthanasia or natural causes, David tells of the disposal of their corpses: since Bev Shaw is the one who inflicts the needle, it is he who takes charge of disposing of the remains. The morning after each killing session he drives the loaded kombi to the grounds of Setters Hospital, to the incinerator, and there consigns the bodies in their black bags to the flames:

> On his first Monday he left it to them to do the incinerating. Rigor mortis had stiffened the corpses overnight. The dead legs caught in the bars of the trolley, and when the trolley came back from its trip to the furnace, the dog would as often as not come riding back too, blackened and grinning, smelling of singed fur, its plastic covering burnt away. After a while the workmen began to beat the bags with the backs of their shovels before loading them, to break the rigid limbs. It was then that he intervened and took over the job himself. (144–5)

What stands out in these instances of incineration is not the process itself, but rather the desecration of the corpses after they had been incinerated. The attitude with which the procedure was conducted and its implication for respecting the lives of animals is seriously called into question. As David comes to confess, he hopes "[f]or the idea of the world, a world in which men do not use shovels to beat corpses into a more convenient shape for processing" (146).

The Window Seat contains essays that focus on human-animal relations that offer us an opportunity to perceive human behavior and the nature of the Sierra Leonean society through the treatment of dogs in Freetown. In the opening statement of "The Last Vet," Forna points out the physical presence of dogs in the city, a presence that is noticeable in part due to the number of them roaming the streets. This proliferation of street dogs is an indication of neglect and the absence of a national policy on animal control in the country. It also hints at the cultural values associated with the way animals are perceived and their relationship with humans defined. The narrative emphasizes a gap between the realities of human-animal existence and the neglect and abuse of the animals. Forna notes that in Freetown, "the people and the dogs exist on separate planes" (144).

In "The Last Vet," Forna sheds light on the atrocities inflicted upon dogs in Freetown through the local vet, Dr. Gudush Jalloh, whose work with street dogs offers us a window into the dysfunction that characterizes Sierra Leonean society. In first meeting Dr. Jalloh, the reader is given a window seat into a post-mortem operation he is conducting on a pup. The operation in all its grotesque form mirrors the current situation in the country. First, it is a post-mortem examination – the pup is already dead and this parallels the demise of the society. Given the destruction occasioned by the eleven years of the Civil War, as well as the neglect and the corruption that permeate post-war Sierra Leone, the image of the dead dog not only captures the state of the society, it also functions as a premonition of the future.

More revealing of society is the anatomy and physiology of the dead pup. Forna writes:

> The body cavity was a huge fluid-filled sac, devoid of vital organs ... Dr. Jalloh prodded at the dead puppy with a long pair of tweezers and declared this second instance of such abnormality he had seen ... a second pup suffers the same deformity. Another was stillborn. Four survived. (145)

The corpses of the pups reveal anatomical deformities and abnormalities that symbolically indicate political and socio-economic dysfunction in the society. The implications are that Sierra Leone's future is doomed. It is a society that lacks the vital organs for life, and hence, a revitalized and reconnected post-war Sierra Leone was either a stillborn or a deformed child, plagued with social and economic abnormalities.

In addition to the post-mortem examination, the street clinic provides another window into Sierra Leonean society. This medical activity, conducted regularly by Dr. Jalloh, provides free sterilization to street dogs in the capital, and, at times, vaccination and neutering. While the objective could be justified in terms of controlling the animal population, it nevertheless points to the extent to which humans can go to accomplish their desire for comfort and control. The sterilization of dogs unveils mankind's treatment of defenseless animals. Dogs are neutered, and in some cases, like in Thailand, indiscriminately killed, just to fulfill mankind's desire to dominate what is in fact a shared space with animals. Dogs perform many services to mankind, and yet, the latter fail to recognize and appreciate their loyalty and companionship. In fact, we ought to realize that stray dogs are present because of our inadequacies – we have street dogs because streets are dirty and devoid of proper refuse and disposal systems. As the local vet notes, "the dogs performed a function and service by offering security and protection" (148) and, as Forna asserts, there had been "no systemized rubbish collection in the city for decades" (148).

Gudush Jalloh's sterilization of dogs in his clinic recalls Zoher Lederman et al. in their article "Stamping Out Animal Culling: From Anthropocentrism to One Health Ethics." I use this article as a frame to read sterilization, like culling, as human action geared towards controlling animal population. While its objective is clear, its ethics is questionable, troubling, and certainly indefensible. Sterilization and culling lack clear ethical reasoning, privileges human interests above the animals', and occludes animal pain and suffering. Lederman et al. have not only questioned the ethics of the practice of animal control, they have also pointed out its lack of effectiveness and indirect cost to humans. By a study of the effects of culling of badgers in the UK to prevent the spread of rabies, they point out the direct harms to the animals killed, the extreme cost of the procedure, and the harm to humans in indirect ways. Animal sterilization, like the selective slaughter of animals to control their population, is inhumane, unscrupulous, and anthropocentric. It devalues animal life and denies nonhumans the benefits of ethical reciprocity in the recognition of their being, and by implication, their emotions and well-being. The decision to embark on a plan of sterilization and culling is a weighty one and must involve a thorough consideration of its effectiveness, but also of its ethical and moral implications.

Forna's use of sardonic and ironic humor to depict the sterilization of stray dogs in the street clinics is very effective and powerful. The humor reveals both the cruelty of humans and the helpless resistance of dogs to their treatment. I cite two sections of the essay to explore this assertion. First, is her description of the atmosphere in the street clinic:

> We arrived late. It is nine o'clock. Outside the school building, people and dogs wait beneath a steady drizzle. The dogs are collarless, held on a length

> of electric cable, nylon rope or string. A woman in pink holds onto a brown and white dog. A boy cradles a furious pup. A man arrives with a large black and white dog, which leaps and twists at the end of a long rope. Another man leads his dog on its hindlegs, holding on to the front paws, like a dancing bear. Inside the school room, a line of people and dogs wait upon a bench and impressively watch a technician gently shave the balls of a sedated dog. (147).

The humor is certainly palpable in this excerpt, but so too is the underlying sympathy and perhaps discomfort the reader feels about the way the whole process unfolds. One cringes at the helplessness of the dogs as they are forced to undertake the procedure, and the human ingenuity at making this possible is humorous, but also stunning in its determination for execution. Professionalism is again called into question as one wonders about the medical efficiency or etiquette for shaving the balls of a sedated dog.

The other excerpt I cite for analysis is the one depicting the neutering process itself:

> Four, then five, then six freshly neutered and comatose dogs lie in a new row, the paw of one lies across another, strange babies sharing a bed. An assistant tattoos the ear of each dog. There is a general air of understated chaos. Dogs roam the room. Outside a circle of children gather to watch as recently anaesthetized dogs stagger, circle and crash to the ground. The technician with the tattoo machine clips the ear of a reclining dog, which, for being sedated, is merely sleeping. The astounded animal jumps to its feet and stalks humbly away. Elsewhere, a technician attempts to inject a dog. It tries to bite him. (149)

The excerpt illustrates the cruel and unprofessional procedures employed by the so-called technicians in the neutering of dogs. Human action clearly indicates a lack of regard for the life of animals, and their ill-treatment is a violation and transgression of their rights as animals. The whole process of neutering the dogs has been transformed into a spectacle where onlookers gleefully watch "freshly neutered and comatose dogs" lying needy in a row "like babies sharing a bed," or "recently anaesthetized dogs stagger, circle and crash to the ground." Even though the excerpt hints at the lack of resources to professionally conduct such a procedure, a lack that the author explores in subsequent pages of the narrative, one wonders whether the technician's ill-treatment of the animals is solely due to poor training or lack of resources. I argue that the passage suggests otherwise; that it brings out the character of individuals and society's perception and treatment of animals; and that the underlying motive of such depiction of cruelty by the author is a call for an end to such practices. In comparing the comatose dogs to sleeping babies, Forna is anthropomorphizing the dogs and it is in such narrative technique that the full force of the inhuman treatment is amplified and manifested. In this anthropomorphizing of the dogs, the author is making a case for resisting anthropocentrism – mankind's desire for dominance and control over animals, regardless of ethical implications and consequences for animal life.

In other sections of the essay, Forna devotes time to simply highlighting the instances of mankind's cruelty and ill-treatment of animals: the dog that "wandered and late one evening returned, his hind quarters split open to the bone by an axe wound" (150); the smuggler from Colombia who abandoned his dog upon his departure from Freetown, and who now lives with dogs that are "flea-ridden and one has a skin infection" (153); the rabid dog who died because the vet, either out of incompetence or cruelty, refused to admit its ailment, as well as the one with the paralysis of the lower jaw symptoms put down by Dr. Jalloh (151); and the "NGO dogs" abandoned in the streets of Freetown after the expatriate owners departed.

Lest her criticism of inhumane animal treatment is perceived as pertaining only to African societies, Forna also cites parallels with Western societies. She points out the "solipsistic sentimentality" of the West in their warped relationship to dogs, evidenced in the American lady who refuses to donate money to Dr. Jalloh's clinic to help bolster his program but could spend $3,000 to transport a single adopted dog to the States. She further highlights the lack of commitment of international agencies like WHO in not making animal welfare a priority in society; the international companies who would offer Dr. Jalloh vast sums of money to "exterminate the strays" rather than provide care for them; the Western practice of breeding dogs "beyond the point of deformity for the show ring and the fashionable" (158); the slaughter of factory-farmed animals in Britain, where animals are "strung up by a single hind leg, inch along the conveyor belt to the screams of those who went before, emerging stripped of hair and skin, wrapped in cellophane" (158); and the dog fights and fortune of animals in England (158). Mankind's cruelty to animals transcends geographical borders and temporality – it is a function of human nature and the nature of society.

Forna points out "the link between the physical abuse of animals and the physical abuse of children" (158). This cruelty is manifested in: the manner in which animals are sacrificed for ritual purposes, "a man presses a knife against a bull's neck, croons as he looks the animal in the eye and slits its throat" (157–8); the revolting picture of "street dogs [that] grew fat feasting on corpses" on the streets of Freetown after the mayhem of the rebel invasion of the city in January 1999; the humble images of Mathilda, the author's dog hit by a car, that had "two dislocated hind legs and … a broken pelvis" (165); and the gruesome discovery of a "litter of puppy corpses in the bathrooms of a collapsed bungalow" (159).

Despite mankind's ill-treatment of dogs, Forna is at pains to show animal service, loyalty, and devotion to humans. Drawing from her personal experiences in childhood, she points at the crucial role dogs played in her life. Given the instabilities and insecurities engendered by a life in motion, dogs provide a sense of deep love, companionship, and friendship to her. She states:

> I loved only the dogs for reasons too complicated to elaborate upon, and yet also painfully obvious. In a time of lies, I found honesty and loyalty among the dogs. And, if the memory of particular dogs has grown unreliable, then the memory of what they offered me in that time has become indelible: a retreat from the mutability of the human world, a place of safety. (147)

Dogs provided a therapeutic effect to the "benign neglect" stemming from the turbulence of her childhood, especially the repeated arrests and detention of her father. Convinced of the service of animals to mankind and the moral obligation of humans to reciprocate such loyalty and devotion, Forna goes into history to establish a case for a symbiotic relationship between humans and animals. She cites Konrad Lorenz's *King Solomon's Ring* and later, J.M. Coetzee's *Disgrace*, as works that validate human-animal relationships based on a "covenant" of reciprocity and on an ethical consideration of preservation of their lives and human treatment of them. She emphasizes mankind's obligation to animals and, as noted above, suggests that the least the former can do to them is to ensure and preserve "an independent exchange of services" (149). She calls for a radical reform of the culture that devalues the work of vets in Sierra Leone, and implicitly advocates for the creation of policies that protect them and for the enactment of laws to ensure this protection. The narrative further gestures to the need for resources and training to care for and treat animals. A rethinking of human-animal relationships in both Western and developing nations is needed.

In conclusion, Forna makes an ethical plea to humans for rethinking our relationship to animals by citing Milan Kundera's test of humanity: "True human greatness can manifest itself in all its purity and liberty, in regard to those who have no power. True moral tests of humanity lie in those who are at its mercy: the animals" (167). Forna sees the efforts of all those involved in saving the lives of the street dogs as critical to this manifestation of morality. As she notes, "What I saw was compassion, a sense of community, the sweetening of a soured spirit. In other words, I saw hope" (167).

"Bruno," another essay that focuses on mankind's relationship with animals, offers another window into Sierra Leonean society. In this essay, Forna explores the nature of animal life through Bruno's resistance to a caged existence. The essay depicts the life of a chimpanzee at the Tacugama Chimpanzee Sanctuary in the outskirts of Freetown. Forna describes the life of the apes as one of captivity and trauma and suggests that the holding of apes at sanctuaries for human spectacle is not only unjust, but also dangerous. She attributes the caging of animals in sanctuaries as another attempt of humans to enforce dominion and control over animals, the basis of anthropocentrism, which she ascribes to the rise of Christian evangelical ideology of creation and mankind's endowed right of dominion over all animals. Mankind's efforts to restrict the freedom of animals have led to deterioration in human-animal relationship. Animals are now suspicious of humans and treat them as untrustworthy partners. In some cases, suspicion turns into anger, resistance, and violence.

In the opening sections of the story, Forna notes that Bruno does not like people and that he throws rocks at them. In fact, so profound is his hate of humans that he has collected "a pile of rocks, stacked like cannonballs," that he uses to attack visitors at the sanctuary. Bruno's actions constitute a resistance to its caged existence and a desire for freedom.

In the early sections of the story also, Forna points out a critical factor in the chimps: the essence of their being. We read that Bruno was "smart, affectionate, and inquisitive, [but] ... was also destructive, possessive, and territorial" (215). These attributes of the chimp are also human and remind us of their natural similarities with us. Cuba, the other chimp, is given to mood swings and unpredictable actions, just like humans. In the frightening incident in which he grinds the knuckles of the author in his grip, while staring at her unflinchingly, we are reminded of their attempt to not be intimidated by humans and to stand up to our desire to control them. Again, like humans, they exhibit signs of grief and trauma when held in captivity. Forna notes that in Cuba, as with other species, when held in cages, they masturbated a great deal and that "[e]xcessive self-stimulation, including fervent masturbation, is one of the behaviors denominated by captive chimps, who also exhibit signs of trauma and depression similar to humans" (216–17).

Citing Jane Goodall, Forna attests to this idea of the chimpanzee as a being "whose emotional states are quite similar to our own and who is capable of feeling pain, sorrow, happiness; a being who can trust and whose trust is very easy to betray" (219). She concludes:

> Like us, chimps form close and enduring friendships, their families held together by bonds of affection. In addition to their intelligence and apparent humor, those qualities that make people want to turn them into pets, chimps are, like us, warmongering and homicidal. There are more attacks on humans by captive chimps than wild chimps, though the answer may rest in relative proximity and thereby opportunity ... who knows if throwing rocks at human visitors was just the behavior of a protective alpha or bound to some deeper distrust of humans? (219)

Yet, in spite of the indisputable evidence of similarities between humans and animals, and of other aggression to humans only when held in captivity and traumatized from depression, humans continue to hold animals in cages in sanctuaries for spectacle. In fact, Forna suggests that it is precisely because animals remind us of our humanity like theirs that we seek to control them. They are held in captivity simply because they look and behave like us. Three of such animals – the dog, the chimp, and the fox – as I argue in this chapter, reflect mankind's humanity and exposes mankind's desire for control.

And so, mankind continues to subdue animals either by domesticating them as pets, locking them up in cages as objects of spectacle, or neutering them to control their population. In some instances, they are directly attacked, hurt, and killed with impunity. At times, humans encourage them to participate in human folly and debauchery – Bruno was taught to smoke cigarettes as entertainment for human visitors. When he is not entertaining visitors, he would spend "hours of his day chained to a pole frame from which he swung, one hand on the bar, the other gripping the chain around his neck that otherwise threatened to strangle him" (216). The human rationale for such inhumane treatment was that "[r]returning a formerly captive ape into the wild almost never works" (218). The apes are held captive for life. In revolt against this treatment, the chimps, led by Bruno, staged a breakout, and Bruno escaped, never to be found. One of the guards at the sanctuary, Issa Kanu, was killed, "his face and throat torn away" (221).

Bruno's story reveals an indisputable truth: animals desire autonomy just like humans, and attempts to deny them their innate desire for freedom, would lead to resistance, sometimes with deadly consequences. The narrator demonstrates interesting parallels between the lives of humans and animals, and offers us a template to read human behavior and the nature of society. What Bruno's escape teaches us is that: "We crave freedom even from those who love us and whom we love in return; it is a never-ending conflict of the soul" (224). As humans, we not only want to be free from those who love us and we in return, but like Bruno, at times, we want to throw stones at them.

The vixen is the third animal that Forna uses to show how the lives of foxes offer a window into human behavior. "Wilder Things" opens with men's efforts to subdue urban foxes – destroying the vixen's den in an attempt to keep her away from the author's garden. This act of humans is a motif in the essays and illustrates Forna's exploration of the theme of anthropomorphism in her later novel, *Happiness*. Like the chimp and the dog, the vixen also demonstrates human traits: she longs for a mate and when she sees one she likes, she chooses him as a partner. In this way, like the chimps, they are anthropomorphized. More interestingly, urban foxes accentuate the idea of the earth as a shared space with animals. They are not intimidated by humans and some are "quite unfazed by the humans with whom they share the city" (232). Like humans, they are territorial and possessive in their love relationships. They become aggressive when another vixen trespasses into her male's territory.

As in "Bruno," Forna emphasizes that it is partly because of these similar traits with humans that animals are despised and ill-treated by mankind. Like chimps, if they are not caged, "foxes cause very little bother to the human inhabitants of the city and virtually no threat" (234). In fact, the narrator suggests that it is human action and neglect that invite and encourage foxes to dwell in urban spaces. In the absence of proper refuse disposal, foxes thrive in cities where food is available in open dust bins. In abandoned sections of the city, foxes have found spaces to live; occupying neglected gardens occasioned by downward economic trends. As such, "[f]oxes have been drawn to and living in cities like London for many decades" (237).

What Forna suggests is the bone of contention between humans and urban foxes is their refusal to be intimidated, domesticated, or controlled by humans. She argues that the idea of the city represents mankind's attempt to deny animals the privilege of living in a shared space with us and this puts mankind at the center of control. Cities are constructed to not only bring order into the chaos of human life, but to show our dominion over animals. Again, since they reflect and remind us so much of our being, and oftentimes we feel vulnerable about this, we desire to keep them away. That is why we cage them, tame them, eat them, and we kill them – to show our dominion over them. Forna writes:

> What bothers people about foxes is that they will not be controlled and humans are control junkies. We love an ordered environment and there is none more so than the city ... the great metropolises represent man's dominion over whatever in nature might cause us hurt or harm or discomfort ... we do not care to be reminded that we are living beings, for that is to remember that we are vulnerable. (235)

The lives of animals offer us a window into human behavior.

As Forna concludes, she points out that what should be a symbiotic relationship between two species in a shared space is a one-way act of domination and control because mankind hates mutualism and can "tolerate animals only on our own terms" (233). In the scheme of things, the fox stands to be ill-treated because she "chooses to live close to animals but refuses subordination, has submitted neither to domestication nor taming, will not bend to anyone's will. The urban fox possesses a seeming irreverence for both humans and our safe spaces" (235–6).

Forna explores the theme of human-animal relations and how the life of animals offers a window seat into human nature and behavior. I argue in this chapter that mankind's treatment of three animals – dogs, chimps, and foxes – provides a template to read society's cruelty and ill-treatment of animals; actions and behavior that provide a clear indication into human desire for control and domination. Here, the foundations for Forna's larger treatment of the themes of anthropocentrism and anthropomorphism in later novels like *Happiness* are laid. In this way, Forna explores concepts such as the city as a sacred space between humans and animals, environmental degradation and conservation, violence and trauma, childhood, adulthood, and life.

I cite the following excerpt as a fitting conclusion to my analysis of the human-animal relations:

> The more I talked to people about the animals who live in our cities, the more I came across a particular stance which made me uncomfortable. The people most exercised cite all the threats these creatures supposedly pose to us and to our safety, but not one has ever offered evidence of having been so threatened themselves, they only tell me what they have

read or heard ... They hated the animals simply for being in places which these people thought they owned and the animals had no right to be. (257)

Coetzee's *Disgrace* and Forna's *The Window Seat* offer us, from the vantage position of the lives of animals, a window seat into human behavior. Mankind's treatment of animals in these texts are indicative of our desire for control; a desire that finds expression in anthropocentrism and animal ethics in African societies. In the works explored by Forna and Coetzee, we see the pitfalls of an anthropocentric approach to life versus a biocentric one that recognizes an ethical reciprocity between human and nonhuman animals.

Works Cited

Biermann F. and E. Lövbrand, "Encountering the 'Anthropocene': Setting the Scene," in F. Biermann and E. Lövbrand (eds.), *Anthropocene Encounters: New Directions in Green Political Thinking* (Cambridge: Cambridge University Press, 2019), pp. 1–22.)

Coetzee, J.M., *Disgrace* (New York: Penguin Books, 1999).

Crist, Eileen and Helen Kopnina, "Introduction: Unsettling Anthropocentrism," *Dialectical Anthropology* 38.4 (2014), pp. 387–96.

Etieyibo, Edwin, "Anthropocentrism, African Metaphysical Worldview, and Animal Practices: A Reply to Kai Horsthemke," *Journal of Animal Ethics* 7.2 (2017), 145–62.

Fincham, Gail, "J.M. Coetzee's *Elizabeth Costello*: From Anthropocentrism towards Biocentrism?" *English Academy Review: A Journal of English Studies* 35.2 (2018), pp. 54–70.

Forna, Aminatta, *Happiness* (New York: Atlantic Monthly Press, 2018).

Forna, Aminatta, *The Window Seat: Notes From a Life in Motion* (New York: Grove Press, 2021).

Galgut, Elisa, "Animal Rights and African Ethics: Congruence or Conflict?" *Journal of Animal Ethics* 7.2 (2017), pp. 175–82.

Horsthemke, Kai, "Animals and African Ethics," *Journal of Animal Ethics* 7.2 (2017), pp. 119–44.

Leopold, Aldo, *A Sand County Almanac* (New York: Ballantine, 1949).

Kopnina, Helen, Haydn Washington, Bron Taylor, and John J. Piccolo, "Anthropocentrism: More than Just a Misunderstood Problem," *Journal of Agricultural and Environmental Ethics* 31 (2018), pp. 109–27.

Kundera, Milan. *The Unbearable Lightness of Being* (New York: Harper Perennial, 1991 [1984]).

Kunzmann, Peter, "Biblical Anthropocentrism and Human Responsibility," *Konferencja Chrzescijanskiego Forum Pracowników Nauki Nauka–Etyka–Wiara* (2005), pp. 1–5.

Lederman, Zohar, Manuel Magalhães-Sant'Ana, and Teck Chuan Voo, "Stamping Out Animal Culling: From Anthropocentrism to One Health Ethics," *Journal of Agricultural and Environmental Ethics* 34.27 (2021), pp. 26–40.

Nabulya, Eve, "Rethinking Human-Centredness and Eco-Sustainability in an African Setting: Insights from Luganda Folktales," *Journal of African Cultural Studies* 34.3 (2022), pp. 308–24.

Naess, Arne, "The Shallow and the Deep, Long-Range Ecological Movement," in *Environmental Ethics in Theory and Application*, eds. Louis Pojman, Paul Pojman, and Katie McShane (Boston, MA: Jones and Bartlett, 1994), pp. 102–5.

Northover, Alan, "Animal Ethics and Human Identity in J.M. Coetzee's *The Lives of Animals*," *Scrutiny 2: Issues in English Studies in Southern Africa* 14.2 (2009), pp. 28–39.

Onega, Susana, "The Trauma of Anthropocentrism and the Reconnection of Self and World in J.M. Coetzee's Dusklands," in Nadal, Marita and Monica Calvo (eds.) in *Trauma in Contemporary Literature: Narrative and Representation* (New York: Routledge, 2014), pp. 207–2.

Steffen, W., R.A. Sanderson, P.D. Tyson, et al. *Global Change and the Earth System*. Berlin: Springer-Verlag, 2004.

Yao, Vida, "Two Problems Posed by the Suffering of Animals," *The Journal of Speculative Philosophy* 33.2 (2019), pp. 324–39.

Chapter 10

Namina Forna's *The Gilded Ones*: An Afrocentric Vision of the Beloved Community

MOHAMED KAMARA

Namina Forna's[1] debut novel *The Gilded Ones* (2021) – the first in her Deathless trilogy – is a sprawling fantasy and apocalyptic tale with myriad characters representing various racial, ethnic, sexual, gender, and other identities. It is a story about Deka and other ostracized and persecuted girls coming together to confront patriarchy and its legacy of lies and oppression of women, children, and other so-called powerless members of society in the One Kingdom. Because they bleed gold instead of blood like most girls, Deka and girls like her are labeled as "*alaki*" (that is impure, unnatural, monstrous beings),[2] and subject to the Death Mandate, which requires that all *alaki* girls should be rounded up and executed. Rescued, regrouped, protected, and trained by older women known as matrons and *karmoko*s[3] led by the ageless White Hands, Deka and her comrades eventually constitute a formidable all-female army reminiscent of the 'Agojie,' the all-woman African fighting force that reached its apotheosis in the nineteenth-century Kingdom of Dahomey.[4] But

---

[1] Namina Forna, like her older compatriot, Aminatta Forna, left Sierra Leone at a very young age running for her life. While Aminatta left Sierra Leone by the mid-70s following the execution of her father, Mohamed Sorie Forna, Namina, in the middle of the Sierra Leone Civil War (1991–2002), was sent at age nine to the USA by her father, Sembu Forna, to live with her mother in Atlanta. Their experience of personal and national trauma has given both writers raw material for talking about individuals and the world. A point Aminatta Forna made in a 2015 interview with the Guardian: "I was propelled into writing by war" (Aminatta Forna, 2015).
[2] *Alaki* is a Sierra Leonean krio word denoting someone that is cursed and worthless.
[3] A title reserved for Islamic teachers who are traditionally men.
[4] Europeans referred to these warriors as Amazons, after the fighting women in Greek mythology. The Agojie, also known as the Mino, have been popularized in the *The Woman King* as well as in *Black Panther* (comics and movies) where they are known as the Dora Milaje.

the *alaki*, the all-female army in Forna's novel, are more than the Agojie, or the Amazons; they represent a new and resilient Sisterhood of teenage girls – with a new humanist vision and battle cry for the perennially oppressed – who realize they have the power to shape their present and future. But to do these, they need allies among men and nonhuman creatures. At the end, they succeed in defeating the emperor's elite forces (called "*jatu*") and their religious acolytes. However, because some *jatu* and high priests and elders unwilling to give up their privilege have fled in order to regroup and organize a resistance, Deka and the newly liberated Gilded Ones must prepare for a prolonged battle to reconstruct the kingdom they created and over which they presided several centuries back.

I propose to read Forna's novel as representing and promoting an Afrocentric vision of the Beloved Community. The Beloved Community as espoused by Martin Luther King, Jr. (like L.S. Senghor's Civilization of the Universal)[5] is not a melting pot where race, cultural, and personal differences are dissolved; it is rather a meeting place of dialogue and sharing, where giving and receiving have equal value. It is a place where hegemony of one over another is shunned, where love and mutual respect and empowerment determine the terms of engagement, and where interactions are informed by a clear acceptance of the complementarity and interdependence of all telluric forces (mineral, vegetal, animal, human) in empathic communion with one another. It is a vision of the perfect socio-political community that would emerge inevitably through the practice of cooperation, justice, and love.

I argue that Forna's vision of such a community is Afrocentric for two reasons. First, this novel about young girls coming of age in a male-dominated society offers a feminist vision that is more expansive than the first three waves of Western feminism[6] that mostly failed to include non-Western perspectives in the struggle for women's rights. Second, unlike the standard Western superhero narratives (in literature and pop culture), with their fascination for one person at the expense of other members of the community whose individual contributions are also if not equally important for the well-being of all. In the manner of *Black Panther*, *The Gilded Ones* promotes a community of heroines and heroes working together out of mutual respect and love

---

[5] The term 'Beloved Community' originated with American philosopher and theologian, Josiah Royce (1855–1916), a founder of the Fellowship of Reconciliation (of which Dr. King became a member). Royce's definition of a community is a collection of individuals in which all the members agree on and work toward the achievement of their goals for the good of all. In *The Problem of Christianity*, he states: "My life means nothing, either theoretically or practically, unless I am a member of a community" (357). Senghor borrowed the concept of the *Civilisation de l'Universel* from French Jesuit priest, palaeontologist, and philosopher, Pierre Teilhard de Chardin (1881–1955).

[6] For a full discussion of the four waves of feminism, see Martha Rampton's "Four Waves of Feminism," https://www.pacificu.edu/magazine/fourwavesfeminism.

toward a common goal. The thematic thrust of *The Gilded Ones* is grounded in the long history of Black intellectualism and activism. Accordingly, my engagement with Forna's novel draws from the poetics and praxis of the human as proposed by Martin Luther King, Jr. and Léopold Sédar Senghor, as well as from the Black humanist-feminist discourse of Sylvia Wynter and Alice Walker, among others.

In their intellectual and activist careers, both Léopold Sédar Senghor and the iconic American civil rights leader, Martin Luther King, Jr., were concerned with what Gaston Bachelard calls the "*tissu de relations* [network of relations]" (*Le Nouvel esprit scientifique*, 25). In other words, the human being in the universe, being and living in relation not only to other human persons, but to the rest of the universe. And more concretely, their realization that the human, as Immanuel Kant suggested in his *Groundwork for the Metaphysics of Morals*, was not a means to an end but the end itself of existence (229) became the basis of their humanist poetics and praxis, one that is more inclusive and morally universal than it is self-consciously (and aggressively) universalizing in its will to imposition. Unlike Enlightenment humanism, a major foundation of Western Judeo-Christian civilization, with its "blind spots and dramatic failures" (Stanton 2006, 1518), and which Aimé Césaire called "pseudo-humanism" (*Discourse on Colonialism*, 37) for preaching the sub-humanity of non-White-European races and peoples, the humanism preached by Senghor and King is more enduring because it is based on love and a deep understanding and acceptance of individual and group differences.

In "Ce que l'homme noir apporte" ("What the Blackman Contributes")[7], Senghor explains what he considers to be at the heart of the humanist problem:

> *Nous voilà au cœur du problème humaniste. Il s'agit de savoir 'quel est le but de l'homme'? Est-ce en lui seul qu'il doit trouver sa solution…? Ou l'Homme n'est-il vraiment homme que lorsqu'il se dépasse pour trouver son achèvement en dehors du moi, et même de l'Homme…?» Il s'agit bien… de 'concentrer le monde en l'homme' et de 'dilater l'homme au monde'.*

> [Here we are at the heart of the humanist problem. It is about knowing 'what is the goal of man'? Should he find in himself alone his solution…? Or is Man not really man until he transcends himself in order to find his fulfillment outside of the self, and even outside of Man…? It is ultimately a matter of condensing the world into man and opening man unto the world]. (27)

And as Hanes Walton notes, the same questions were key to King's ontology:

> Three questions that can be found at the center of all political thought, and to which King addressed himself, are the nature and functions of man, his

---

[7] This piece was originally published in 1939 as "L'Homme de couleur" ("Man of Color").

relation to the rest of the universe – which involves a consideration of the meaning of life as a whole – and, emerging from the interaction of these two, the problem of the relation of each man to his fellow men. (Walton *The Political Philosophy of Martin Luther King, Jr.*, 39–40)

It can be said that every society, every association of individuals, has been guided in its worldview and actions by a vision of a beloved community of sorts. This is so because every society has sought to build the ideal world for those it considers its legitimate members. A society's vision of the beloved community determines to a large extent the means and method it will employ to attain it. Thus, the more parochial the vision of the community, the more dubious and unidimensional the means used to achieve it could be. If one's vision of the beloved community includes only one's family, clan or tribe, race, sex, region, nation, disregarding other communities and their interests, one would employ any means necessary to secure that vision. It is therefore possible to imagine many so-called beloved communities (each imperfect because incomplete, exclusionary, discriminatory) seeking to achieve their dream by deferring or destroying the dreams of others, by making life, liberty and the pursuit of happiness of others difficult or impossible. However, there is only one Beloved Community (the one that is all inclusive, because based on love and mutual acceptance of our common humanity and destiny). It is the only community that will ensure that all its citizens' basic spiritual and material needs are provided for. In the preface to the *New International Economic Order*, Senghor provides an insight into this ideal community:

> *Le Nouvel Ordre économique doit atteindre deux objectifs, qui, pour nous, sont indissociablement liés: transformer le monde et changer la vie afin que l'homme, mieux nourri, mieux vêtu, mieux éduqué, plus fort et plus beau, soit plus homme*
>
> [The New International Economic Order must achieve two inextricably linked goals: to change the world and to transform life in such a way that the human being can be better fed, better clothed, better educated, stronger and more beautiful, indeed more human] (1980, vii–ix).

The same sentiments were expressed by King in his Nobel Peace Prize acceptance speech: "I have the audacity to believe that peoples everywhere can have three meals a day for their bodies, education and culture for their minds, and dignity, equality, and freedom for their spirits" (107).

Senghor described the Civilization of the Universal as the "*symbiose de toutes les civilisations différentes* [symbiosis of all the different civilizations]" ("Hommage à Pierre Teilhard de Chardin," 12)[8]. It is the acceptance of the interdependence of telluric forces and the relentless quest for universal peace

---

[8] Translation mine.

born out of a shared motivation for living in harmony with others. Senghor infused into this idea what he regarded as the virtues of black culture and civilization, namely active dialogue and exchange with others. Talking about the technological advances that make it possible for time to be compressed, to leave Tokyo on Sunday and arrive in Seattle on Saturday, King in his 1961 Lincoln University commencement address observed that "the world in which we live has become a single neighborhood... [t]hrough our scientific genius," but that "now through our moral and spiritual development we must make of it a brotherhood" ("The American Dream," 209). This brotherhood that spiritually undergirds the 'neighborhood' is the life force of the Beloved Community. The Beloved Community is the place where civilization (the instruments and technics of our living) and culture (the intangible moral and spiritual essence of our being) meet in harmony at a time when the "shift from a thing-oriented society to a person-oriented society" ("Beyond Vietnam," 157) would have been effectuated.

The One Kingdom

The One Kingdom (also known as Otera[9]) was founded by women known as the Gilded Ones several millennia back. These divine founding mothers were overthrown and imprisoned by their own sons, who have since coopted the name One Kingdom and, using the power inherited from their mothers, transformed it from a diverse and inclusive space to one that tolerates no diversity and that stigmatizes and punishes difference. God and religion provide the most effective legitimacy to the evil perpetrated by the patriarchal system. As the narrator observes, "who can argue with the holy books?" (50). Everyone, especially girls and women, are taught that women are inferior to men; that the only reason for their existence is to serve men and to be submissive to them, and that in fact they come from men. The obscurantist religious system in operation in the One Kingdom is guided by the text known as the Infinite Wisdoms, which is supposed to be the divine revelation of Oyomo, the god of the One Kingdom. The priests of Oyomo (and through them the reigning political elite) use the scriptures to oppress the people. Everyone in the kingdom is required to repeat every morning the verse "Blessings to he who waketh to witness the glory of the Infinite Father" (2), a quote from the Infinite Wisdoms. More specifically, every girl in the One Kingdom is expected to memorize specific verses from the religious text. One such verse – "Blessed are the meek and the subservient, the humble and true daughters of man, for

---

[9] *Otera* is also a Japanese word for temple, especially a Buddhist temple. The connotation of sacredness is not lost upon the reader. An empire, like a temple, can be perverted or used for the redemption of souls. As we shall see, the One Kingdom is a place where a corrupt vision and interpretation of religion holds tremendous sway, with religion used as an instrument of indoctrination and oppression, especially of women.

they are unsullied in the face of the Infinite Father" (4) – helps to promote their own devaluation. It is no surprise therefore that the current emperor, face-to-face with Deka just before his overthrow by the *alaki*, vows to never allow one of the "filthy bitches to sit on the throne again" (394).

To Be a Woman in the One Kingdom

Every system of oppression, guided as it were by the monologic vision of its purveyors, seeks to bend everyone to its will. In the One Kingdom, everyone is required to wear a mask, in one setting or another. Even the nobles at the emperor's court wear masks "to show their submission to the emperor the same way women wear masks so as not to offend the eyes of Oyomo" (268). The emperor is the only one who does not wear a mask, which differentiates him from his entourage just as the requirement of mask for all women all the time and everywhere differentiates them from men. Yet, in this system of general oppression, women in the One Kingdom are the principal targets of patriarchy's will to domination and control. Thanks to the socialization system that denigrates women across all segments of society, the One Kingdom has become a place where even "a shabby man" and "an old grandmother ... accompanied by two young boys – her male guardians, no doubt" feel empowered and obligated to haul insults at powerful women like Deka and her *alaki* sisters (216–17). All this makes the One Kingdom the very bastion of patriarchy.

According to Adrienne Rich:

> Patriarchy is the power of the fathers: a familial-social, ideological, political system in which men – by force, direct pressure, or through ritual, tradition, law, and language, customs, etiquette, education, and the division of labor, determine what part women shall or shall not play, and in which the female is everywhere subsumed, under the male ... The power of the fathers has been difficult to grasp because it permeates everything, even the language in which we try to describe it. It is diffuse and concrete; symbolic and literal; universal, and expressed with local variations which obscure its universality ... I have access only to so much of privilege or influence as the patriarchy is willing to accede to me, and only for so long as I will pay the price for male approval. (59)

The first thing the laws of the One Kingdom seek to do is to erase women, literally and figuratively.

This erasure starts with the Infinite Wisdoms which states that "only the impure, blaspheming, and unchaste woman remains revealed under the eyes of Oyomo" (3). The movement of women is restricted in public spaces: "In most villages, women can't leave their homes without a man to escort them" (6). Even in the capital of the empire, Hemaira, few women are seen on the streets. When they do go out, they must wear masks (73). In fact, the worth of a woman does not extend beyond her utility to a man. According to Elder Durkas, the high priest who performs the ritual cutting of girls to see if they are pure, woman was created on "the fourth day" of creation as "a helpmeet to lift man to his sacred potential, his divine glory. Woman is the Infinite Father's greatest gift to mankind. Solace for his darkest hour" (18). Deka's hometown, Irfut, is a remote outpost of the empire with a reputation for "pretty girls." Consequently, men come from far and wide for the women (5), just as potential buyers visit fairs in search of consumer and service commodities. From an early age, women carry the burden of their gender. They are not allowed to do anything only men are supposed to do: run, touch sharp objects, or exercise any talents they may have other than being an object to satisfy a man's desire.

> The Infinite Wisdoms forbid running, as they do most things that don't prepare girls for marriage and serving their families. Girls can't shout, drink, ride horses, go to school, learn a trade, learn to fight, move about without a male guardian – we can't do anything that doesn't somehow relate to having a husband and family and serving them. (136)

Between the ages of 15 and 16 years, girls must stay away from sharp objects. And if they injure themselves before they turn fifteen, they are cleansed in the temple, their families are ostracized, and they lose their marriage prospects (15). Women are also victims of exploitation, sexual and otherwise. This happens even in the sanctuary of the temple. The narrator notes that "Elder Durkas's temple maidens ... are not maidens anymore" (79). Ultimately, the happiness and righteousness of women are measured by the degree of their obedience to the laws of men presented as God and nature's law.

Interestingly, the empire pays homage to women and femininity. For example, the emperor's elite guard is called *jatu* (6), which is a woman's name in Sierra Leone. Also, arguably the most powerful and visible monument of the empire located in the capital city is of "Fatu the Relentless, mother of the first emperor and keeper of the waters around Hemaira ... a woman with tightly curled hair and a slender but sinewy build" who "gazes out into the water, her arms outstretched toward the horizon in warning" (74). This symbolic display of the power of women, specifically the power and value of the mother, reveals the hypocrisy of patriarchal power. How can one pay homage to the mother while disrespecting women in the way they are in the One Kingdom where the girls are "the Emperor's property" (92) and their mothers fare no better?

Difference, Exclusion, and Belonging in the One Kingdom

The system of power in the One Kingdom does not tolerate difference, yet it comprises paradoxically a society and government that are structured and operate on difference and differentiation. *The Gilded Ones* opens with the sentence: "Today is the Ritual of Purity" (1). This incipit becomes the driving force of the novel: the existential struggle for the soul of the community between the forces of exclusion and those of inclusion. As the name suggests, the ritual is that which determines whether 16-year-old girls have red blood (not gold) that will allow them to "officially belong ... in the village" of Irfut (2). This ritual takes place all over the empire and allows girls to become women, wives, and mothers. Failing the test leads to the ultimate exclusion from the community, gruesome death.[10]

Irfut, like elsewhere in the One Kingdom, is a place where difference is stigmatized and punished. Elder Durkas has as his primary mission the eradication of "impurity and abomination" (17). Deka's mother and father come from different parts of the empire; one is a northerner and the other a southerner. Their very union is considered by her father's family as an abomination. Deka's father was "disowned ... by his entire family" for marrying a dark-skinned "woman of unknown purity ... a foreigner" (3). An interracial child who inherited her mother's dark skin, Deka tells us: "I have been in Irfut my entire life, born and raised, and I'm still treated like a stranger – still stared and pointed at, still excluded" even if her face is the "spitten image" of her father who comes from the village (3–4). Ultimately, Deka suffers triple exclusion on the bases of her gender, her golden blood, and as an interracial child. Aware of her difference, she prays for her blood to be "pure" so she can be accepted and be safe. Even Deka's father prays for his daughter to pass the purity test: "Today, you'll show them you belong" (16).

The politics of exclusion, discrimination, and subsequent punishment manifests in other ways, such as in physical appearance, mainly in regards to beauty standards. If Deka is discriminated against because of her skin color, described by one woman "as dirty as her mother's" (12), a friend of hers, Elfriede, is singled out because of a "dull red birthmark covering the left side of her face" (5). And if Ionas, the son of one of the elders of Irfut, is considered a paragon of male beauty ("one of the handsomest boys in the village" because of his "blond hair and dimples" (8)), Deka is the opposite of feminine beauty. She remarks: "No matter what I wear, I'll never be as pretty as the other girls in the village, with their willowy figures, silken blond hair, and pink cheeks. My own frame is much more sturdy, my skin a deep brown" (10). Agda, "the prettiest girl in the village," has "pale skin and white-blond hair" (11).

---

[10] We see in the Ritual of Purity another example of the cooption of women's power, namely the Sande and Bondo initiation societies responsible in traditional West African societies for setting the parameters of gender and womanhood – a further manifestation of the potential patriarchal origins of these female secret societies.

Deka, White Hands, and the Gilded Ones: Generations of Indomitable Women

Deka eventually fails the purity test and must face the consequence of that failure. However, the arrival of the "delicate" (34) White Hands[11] into Deka's life (and the lives of other girls like her) changes everything for the teenager exploited by the elders and abandoned by her father, her boyfriend (Ionas), and her community. White Hands wears a war mask, something reserved for men, according to the narrator. "White Hands is the most beautiful woman I've ever seen ... Small of stature, she has short, tightly curled hair and glowing skin that gleams a smooth bluish-black, like the night sky at midsummer" (37). White Hands' black beauty is an epiphany for Deka. She gives Deka purpose in the darkest moment of her life, locked in a cell, where she is being dismembered multiple times and bled continuously for her gold-blood. White Hands tells her she can be and do better: "While you cower in misery, those elders sell your gold to the highest bidder so nobles can make pretty trinkets from it" (41). The older woman promises Deka she will find her kind and together they will find absolution.

White Hands is a powerful role model for Deka as she seems to be one who has endured much but has thrived, "becoming stronger for her pain." (38). Later on, when Deka discovers that her difference is more complex than she thought (she is protean, just like her pet, Ixa[12]), White Hands tell her: "you are not unnatural, or whatever other horrific supposition ... Neither is your pet." (294). Like her pet, Deka is the epitome of flexibility and adaptability. In a world that pushes conformity and the single story, these are qualities that will help Deka and the other girls (and women in general) survive and thrive in a male-dominated society. As it turns out, White Hands herself is one with tremendous abilities of adaptation. The Fatu in the "Fatu the Relentless" statue mentioned above is White Hands. She is the great-great grandmother of the current emperor.

White Hands rides in a carriage pulled by *equus*, creatures with "human chests sprouting from horselike lower bodies, and talons where hooves should be" (45).[13] She oversees the Warthu Bera and all the other military training grounds in the empire. Her history of traumatic experience in the hands of men has endowed her with a radar for the perennially oppressed and exploited:

---

[11] Deka gives her this name during their first encounter because of the white gloves the woman wears.

[12] Ixa, a shape-shifting creature Deka found in a lake as the girls prepared for battle, becomes Deka's "pet." It is described as "a horned creature that looks feline half the time but occasionally transforms into a gigantic monstrosity when the need arises" (285).

[13] These creatures, like Deka's pet, become significant allies in the women's struggle for gender and community liberation.

"I don't breed monsters for the emperor, I find them. Find the creatures this empire deems impure, undesirable, dangerous" (294). She has been there all along, protecting Deka (even carrying her in her womb at some point) and other *alaki*. She is the unbroken and strongest link between the current generation of girls (*alaki*) and all the women that came before, the Gilded Ones. The Gilded Ones (female warriors) are "Four ancient demons, they preyed upon humanity for centuries, destroying kingdom after kingdom until everyone finally banded together for protection, forming Otera, the One Kingdom" (51). But this is the official narrative, inculcated in gullible and unsuspecting citizens through ritual and indoctrination: "Every winter, villages enact plays chronicling the Gilded One's defeat" (51). Everyone participates in this distortion of history: "Elderly aunts wear masks carved in their images to frighten naughty children, and men burn straw figures in their likeness to scare evil away" (51). However, before they were imprisoned using their innate power (their celestial blood-gold turned into unbreakable bonds[14]), they made sure they left behind their seeds who then intermarried with "humans," a union that engendered the *alaki* who would become their liberators (238). These divine beings, "ageless – somehow old and young at the same time" (239), come from each of the four provinces of Otera: "Their features are distinct, as are the clothes they wear" (238). Their diversity is their uniting force and their enduring strength.

Warthu Bera: An Oasis of Freedom in the Stifling Desert of the One Kingdom

"Our whole lives, we have been taught to make ourselves smaller, weaker than men. That's what the Infinite Wisdoms teach – that being a girl means perpetual submission" (149). This was before the girls came to Warthu Bera, a world within a world. An experiment. A microcosm of a more expansive vision of humanity. The blueprint of a once-thriving beloved community.

The military training camp called Warthu Bera is located on "a series of isolated hills at the very outskirts of the city, just next to the wall" (105). Even though the statue of Emperor Gezo occupies a central spot in the campgrounds, and that the lookout towers are manned by empire male soldiers called *jatu* (105–6), the highly protected space is thoroughly female. The protection protocol is meant mostly to keep the outside out than to keep its occupants imprisoned. This universe governed by women is the most honored and elite training ground in the empire. It is first and foremost "the House of Women" (115),[15] under the full supervision and governance of an all-female team pretending to be the emperor's personal spies (97). The three women

---

[14] Unbreakable until Deka comes along, using her own blood to free them from centuries of imprisonment.

[15] *Warthu bera* is a Temne phrase which means young girl or woman.

teachers here, called *karmoko*s – Thandiwe, Calderis, and Huon – are under the leadership of White Hands. Warthu Bera is the place where the power of the woman is allowed to be freely displayed and nurtured, a fact immediately evident to the girls upon their arrival there. Deka tells us of one of the teachers (Karmoko Thandiwe): "her voice is so powerful. I've never heard a woman speak like that, never heard such authority coming from a female throat" (116). In this place, women can reach their full potential. Here, even "a cabbage farmer's daughter" (126) can become a fearless and respected warrior.

But Warthu Bera is more than a place where girls learn to be the most powerful fighting force in the empire. It offers in practical terms an alternative vision of womanhood that is in stark contrast to that imposed by the man-made laws of the One Kingdom. Upon arrival at Warthu Bera, the girls are cleaned and shaved bald, with their hair tossed into a furnace (111–12). According to the Infinite Wisdoms, "a woman's hair is her greatest pride, the source of her grace and beauty" (112). No surprise therefore that the girls are dismayed at the removal of the quintessential marker of their feminine identity. We see this in Deka's reaction to the ceremony: "As of this moment, I'm truly nothing more than a demon, my last claim to femininity stripped away" (112). Naturally, she is "grateful" to see her hair swiftly "regrown to its former length" (146). However, after their initial disappointment, most of the girls "started" hacking their hair off "every morning," with some of them keeping "their heads perfectly bald." (146). Deka herself would eventually get over the fetishism of hair ingrained in her by the Infinite Wisdoms. With this cleansing act, the girls are born anew.

Unlike in the world outside where girls are primed to be "terrified" of their natural abilities (140), at Warthu Bera they are encouraged to embrace them. For example, whereas outside they are taught that "[l]ight and graceful are the footsteps of the pure woman" (134), at Warthu Bera, they are free to run (134). Indeed, the simple act of running becomes the most powerful symbol and exercise of their new-found freedom and discovery of their hitherto stifled natural talents. "I've never felt this happy before. Never felt this free" (135), Deka says. "You can't slow down for them ... You have to make them keep up with you" (148), she tells the other girls who seem to be slowing down deliberately so as not to outrun the boy recruits with whom they are running up a hill. It is here, at this place and moment of self-discovery, that the girls finally accept their so-called "demonhood" and vow to use it to liberate themselves. "'Demon. I am a demon,' each girl declares, bleeding herself to display her golden blood. The blood we have so long been told is cursed. The blood that binds us to each other" (151). After this proclamation of self, the girls "don't hold back" when they run. Eventually, some of the boys become "frightened" of the girls' power (159).

Warthu Bera is the site par excellence of unity in difference, a place where stereotypes, complexes, and prejudices are destroyed. One of the first signs of the new dispensation and the emerging beloved community Deka notices is that the girls come together right away: "To my surprise, they haven't separated themselves by province, the way visitors to Irfut so often do ... Instead, they all lean closer" (126). For Deka, personally, Warthu Bera offers her the opportunity to come face-to-face with her miseducation and to be eventually reeducated and liberated from her irrational biases. Two incidents at the Warthu Bera illustrate her growth. The first involves the homosexuality of two of her *alaki* sisters: "We all know Adwapa is forever sleeping in Mehrut's bed. It shocked me at first, the fact that two women would have such inclinations, but affection is affection. If there's one thing I have learned these past few months, it's that you must treasure it wherever you can find it" (331). The second involves the question of virginity. As the boys and girls get to know each other,[16] they discover new things about one another. For example, Keita, shunning the toxic hypermasculinity so often characteristic of patriarchal societies, admits in front of everyone that he is a virgin, noting that not all men go around chasing women just for the sake of it when they do not love them. Acknowledging this revolution in male-female interaction and the role their training school has played in it, Deka remarks: "I could have never even thought such a thing before, growing up in Irfut, but being in the Warthu Bera has changed me. The Infinite Wisdoms no longer hold as much sway over me as they used to" (333).

Warthu Bera is the place where the girls will be prepared for the battle of restoration of self and community, with men and women working together as equal partners, the one complementing the other. Warthu Bera is where the girls realize they must first come together as women, unifying their strength. This female solidarity – grounded in a common experience and history of selective degradation by society's laws – becomes a precondition for global cooperation in the struggle for the rebuilding of the Beloved Community. Here they learn that, beyond their personal, social, regional, and ethnic differences, they are all human and that their shared humanity supersedes all their specific and individual identities. The ability of White Hands to keep the secret of her race as well as the legacy of the Gilded Ones is crucial to the eventual success of their plan for the overthrow of the emperor and the concomitant reinstatement of the Gilded Ones and the beloved community they built and governed. The creation of the Warthu Bera thanks to White Hands' "cunning" and "meticulous" (384) work, as well as the training of the girls are the first two stages in the struggle for the reinstatement of benevolent power in Otera. After their initial victory over the emperor's forces, White Hands leads Deka to this next stage, which involves the liberation of the Gilded Ones: "Once you wake the goddesses, they will make Otera what it once was: a land of freedom, a land where men and women ruled equally, where women weren't

---

[16] This in itself is an iconoclastic act since such conversations tend not to be allowed outside the walls of the Warthu Bera.

abused, beaten, raped. Where they weren't imprisoned in their homes, told that they were sinful and unholy" (376).

Feminism and *The Gilded Ones*

According to Molara Ogundipe-Leslie, feminism is "the recognition of a woman as a human being – her humanity being guaranteed; a recognition that she is not a tool for anybody and that she did not come into the world to work and serve and be an appendage. Her humanity is just as important, as valuable, as that of a man" ("African Literature, Feminism, and Social Change," 316). For feminism (and women) to succeed, women must have a clear understanding of systems of power that, through laws and practices, make them less human than men. Carole Boyce-Davies underscores this point when she notes that "[f]eminism questions and seeks to transform what it is to be a woman in society, to understand how the categories woman and the feminine are defined, structured and produced" (*Black Women, Writing and Identity*, 20). One of the ways patriarchy succeeds in maintaining power is through a pedagogy of the oppressed whereby women not only fail to see the source of their oppression, but also participate in it. For example, we see how the emperor seeks to use the *alaki* to destroy another female army, the "deathshrieks", by presenting the latter as monsters bent on destroying the One Kingdom. Ultimately, female solidarity wins for the *alaki* realize that deathshrieks[17] are their sisters. The existence of Warthu Bera as an oasis of women's freedom and the exercise of that freedom is arguably the single most convincing evidence of the novel's feminist bent. We see in this space the effort to eradicate the male-controlled One Kingdom's objectification and instrumentalization of women that Ogundipe-Leslie decries in her definition of feminism.

In *In Search of our Mothers' Gardens*, Alice Walker uses the neologism "womanism" as an alternative to feminism, which she considers to be too limiting. She provides a few definitions of the word womanism. Of interest to us here is a segment of Walker's second definition of the term:

> Committed to survival and wholeness of entire people, male and female. Not a separatist, except periodically, for health. Traditionally a universalist, as in: "Mama, why are we brown, pink, and yellow, and our cousins are white, beige and black?" Answer. "Well, you know the colored race is just like a flower garden, with every color flower represented." (2)

According to Patricia Hill Collins, the mother's answer to the child's question "both criticizes colorism within African American communities and broadens the notion of humanity to make all people people of color ... womanism thus

---

[17] Deathshrieks are transmogrifications of *alaki* rescued from the Death Mandate.

furnishes a vision where the women and men of different colors coexist like flowers in a garden yet retain their cultural distinctiveness and integrity" (11). Collins cites William Van Deburg who locates Walker's vision of womanhood within the discourse of "another major political tradition within African American politics, namely, a pluralist version of black empowerment" (11). This pluralist vision sees society not as a vortex assimilating surrounding entities into its insatiable cavity, but rather as an expansive and versatile space of constant negotiation of interests aimed at creating an equitable access to and distribution of resources in a symbiotic relationship.

Forna's approach to feminism in *The Gilded Ones* can also be located within another intellectual and activist Afrocentric tradition, namely that of Négritude.[18] *The Gilded Ones* is reminiscent of Senghor and Césaire's engagement with blackness via Négritude.

First, we see in Césaire's neologism "Négritude" a reappropriation and inversion of the pejorative term *nègre* ("nigger"). As Bernard E. Harcourt notes, "Négritude is, then, for Césaire, an idea of a retrieved identity, of a heritage. What Césaire created, what he offered us, is a revolutionary reappropriation of one's self from the clutches of slavery, oppression, and domination" ("Aimé Césaire" 2016). Likewise, Forna creates characters willing to reappropriate, invert, and instrumentalize the terms "demons" and "*alaki*" as resistance and counter-discourse to a dominant, domineering, limiting, and oppressive masculinist discourse.

Second, Négritude (at least as envisioned and promoted by Senghor) was a necessary transit point on the road to an inevitable planetary humanist discourse later expressed in his idea of the Civilisation de l'Universel (Civilization of the Universal). The primary goal of Senghor and the other bards of Négritude was to give back to Africans and Blacks everywhere the dignity and humanity denied them for centuries through reductionist Western theories and praxis of identity. Even as he preached the uniqueness of blackness, Senghor was quick to note that Négritude was not a value judgment, but rather an expression of black cultural specificity and difference: "*Il y a différence, qui n'est pas infériorité ni antagonisme*" ("There is difference that constitutes neither inferiority nor antagonism," "Le problème culturel en A.O.F.," 13). Négritude was a specific brand of humanist discourse that sought to mobilize immediately identical elements, apprise them of their human rights, encourage their solidarity, while reminding them of the potential for their improvement if

---

[18] Négritude's founding is credited mostly to Senghor, Césaire, and Léon Damas. However, others like the Nardal sisters (Jeanne, Paulette, and Andrée) played a major role in the inception and early years of the movement. In *Ce que je crois*, Senghor defines Négritude as "*l'ensemble des valeurs de la civilisation noire*" ("The sum total of the cultural values of the black world," 136). As for Césaire, "*La Négritude a été une révolte contre ... le réductionnisme européen*" (["Négritude has been a revolt against European reductionism"] 'Discours sur la Négritude' 84).

they operate in a symbiotic relationship with other telluric forces. Similarly, the kind of feminism Forna advances in her novel is one that starts with the raising of oppressed women to a position of self-love and self-empowerment. Once this has been achieved, as we see in the training of the *alaki* at Warthu Bera, the girls can then reach outward, joining forces with other oppressed groups for the total liberation of their community.

From Feminism to Humanism or How to Build the Beloved Community

Forna's novel is undoubtedly a feminist novel, where feminism means a belief in the fundamental equality among the sexes, even amidst their manifest differences, a belief that must be accompanied by the willingness to fight for the empowerment of women and the reclaiming of their natural and individual rights wherever and whenever these rights may have been diminished or eliminated. As a feminist manifesto, *The Gilded Ones* reaffirms the centrality of women in the community. However, it will be a disservice to Fornah's capacious vision in *The Gilded Ones* to limit the novel's thrust to its feminist ethos. The novel's feminism refuses to operate in and on a binary. While she recognizes such forms of classification as gendering and sexualization (what Sylvia Wynter labels in *Black Metamorphosis* as the "femalization of the woman," quoted in Tanya Haynes, 93), Forna engages them only as symptoms of a bigger problem: the human problem. "The Western invention of the human, Man," Wynter proposes in her theory of the human,

> necessitates the production of "Others" ... the lower classes as the lack of the normal class, that is the *middle class*; all other cultures as the lack of the normal culture, that is *Western culture*; the nonheterosexual as the lack of *heterosexuality*, represented as a biologically selected mode of erotic preference; women as the lack of the normal sex, *the male*. ("1492: A New World View," 42; italics original)

If we focus only on feminism and gender, Wynter argues, we risk mistaking the "map for the territory" ("On How We Mistook the Map for the Territory"), mistaking the symptom for the disease.

How does the vision of the Beloved Community or the Civilization of the Universal specifically manifest in Namina Forna's *The Gilded Ones*? If the male-controlled One Kingdom is the space of artificial differentiation and constraints, the Beloved Community is its antithesis. This community has no laws forbidding individual expression, only encouragement to honor and respect others. While we see in the One Kingdom the instrumentalization of others to selfish ends, in the Beloved Community, the individual's potential is acknowledged and enhanced for their own and the greater community's good. No one is a pawn in anybody's game, because it is not a game; it is rather a battle for the survival of the collective. As a space of inclusion, cooperation, and expansion, the Warthu Bera offers a glimpse into the Beloved Community.

Here, boys and girls unlearn old rules of engagement that pit one sex against another, or more generally, one identity against another. One of the first things the teenagers learn is that they will be working together as they prepare for the impending war of liberation. Each boy partners with a girl, the boy recruits serving as the *alaki*'s "*uruni*," their "brothers in arms" (86). The commander of the boys asks them to "[e]xtend [their hands to the girls] in the spirit of fellowship" (90), expressing his hope that they "will form lasting and deep partnerships" with each other (86).

The relationship between Deka and Keita is the kind of relationship upon which the Beloved Community is built. The two teenagers shed old habits, adopt new ones, and surmount their traumatic experiences. Keita is a 16-year-old *jatu* who has been a soldier since he was eight. He relinquished his title as Lord of Gar Fatu to be a recruit, after witnessing the massacre of his family supposedly by deathshrieks.[19] Deka first encounters the boy soldier when she and other *alaki* are brought to Jor Hall, the seat of imperial power in the capital, Hemaira. Keita is one of a hundred boys to be paired with the hundred *alaki* being trained for the imminent campaign against the deathshrieks. While the girls were being demeaned by other boys, Keita steps up to defend them. He becomes the first male to say publicly that as soldiers, the *alaki* also have rights (81). Having been betrayed by men in her prior life, her father and her boyfriend, not to mention the priests of Oyomo, Deka is pleasantly surprised by Keita's intervention even as she remains wary of the young aristocrat: "Keita will be no different when the time comes. No matter what he does now, he will show his true colors soon enough. They all do" (83). Nonetheless, Keita's action "blossoms like a distant hope" in the young girl (81). It will take months of working together before Deka finally accepts and trusts Keita. Deka moves from being what Werewere Liking calls a "*misovire*" (a woman who cannot find a man worthy of her admiration) to being a friend, ally, and lover of Keita. As a male, the onus is upon Keita to earn Deka's trust. Recognizing Deka's power, Keita offers his loyalty to Deka: "No man has ever offered me his hand before, as if we were equals, but that's exactly what Keita's doing" (168).

Speaking specifically about Alice Walker's womanism, Patricia Hill Collins notes that "[as] an ethical system, womanism ... is not a closed fixed system of ideas but one that continually evolves through its rejection of all forms of oppression and commitment to social justice" ("What's in a Name?" 1996, 11). Likewise, what we have at the end of *The Gilded Ones*, even with the defeat of the emperor's army, is not yet the Beloved Community as envisioned and elaborated by Senghor and King. It is rather a prelude to it. To be sure, the beloved community is not a well-circumscribed space that you come to at the end of one battle. After Selma and the passing of the Voting Rights Act in

---

[19] Keita learns later that the emperor was behind the death of his family.

1965, Martin Luther King, Jr. cautioned against complacency that may come after momentous victories: "the persistence of racism in depth and the dawning awareness that Negro demands will necessitate structural changes in society have generated a new phase of white resistance in North and South". (*Where Do We Go from Here*, 12). The beloved community, like the womanist and humanist ethic upon which it is founded, is work in progress. At the end of *The Gilded Ones*, the foundation for the new community has been laid with the convergence of men, women, and nonhuman entities and their interests. And because it is a work in progress, there is need for constant vigilance. As *The Gilded Ones* and the two other novel's in Forna's Deathless trilogy (*The Merciless Ones [2022] and The Eternal Ones [2024]*), reveal, there are still powerful empire forces intolerant of a change in the dystopian status quo. The victorious allies only have a chance to succeed against these forces by remaining steadfast and united. When, after the defeat of Emperor Gezo, one of the boy soldiers asks Deka "[w]hat happens now?" Deka responds: "I don't know ... but I expect we will move forward together" (411).

Criticizing colonial oppression, Bernard Dadié proposes an alternative vision in his autobiographical novel, *Climbé*: "For the races, by their very differences, make only a single bouquet, whose pleasant fragrance will fill the universe when every individual has found his place in the community" (91). Like any true fantastic and apocalyptic novel, *The Gilded Ones* carries, embedded deep in its narrative structure, characters, setting, and themes, an indomitable DNA of resilience as well as hope for a community such as Dadié describes. An allegory of and for our time, Forna's novel is a hymn to diversity and inclusiveness that addresses some of the most vexing personal and communitarian concerns of the day. Moreover, it suggests a way forward out of the marasmus and vicious cycle of hate, ignorance, hubris, and violence so characteristic of human history.

Works Cited

Bachelard, Gaston, *Le Nouvel esprit scientifique* (Paris: Librairie Félix Alcan, 1937).

Boyce-Davies, Carole, *Black Women, Writing and Identity: Migrations of the Subject* (New York: Routledge, 1994).

Césaire, Aimé, *Discourse on Colonialism*, trans. Joan Pinkham (New York and London: Monthly Review Press, 1972).

Césaire, Aimé, "Discours sur la Négritude," in *Discours sur le Colonialisme suivi de Discours sur la Négritude* (Paris: Présence Africaine, 2011 [1955]).

Chardin, Pierre Teilhard de, *Building the Earth and the Psychological Conditions of Human Unification* (New York: Avon Books, 1969).

Chardin, Pierre Teilhard de, *The Human Phenomenon*, trans. Sarah Appleton-Webe (Brighton: Sussex Academic Press, 1999).

Collins, Patricia Hill, "What's in a Name? Womanism, Black Feminism, and Beyond," *The Black Scholar* 26.1 (1996), pp. 9–17.

Dadié, Bernard Binlin, *Climbié* (London: Heinemann Educational – African Writers Series, 1971; original French 1956).

Forna, Aminatta, "Aminatta Forna: Don't judge a book by its author," *The Guardian*, 13 February 2015, http://www.theguardian.com/books/2015/feb/13/aminattafornadontjudge-bookby-cover [accessed 11 May 2024].

Forna, Namina, *The Gilded Ones* (New York: Delacorte Press, 2021).

Forna, Namina, *The Merciless Ones* (New York: Delacorte Press, 2022).

Harcourt, Bernard E, "Aimé Césaire: Poetic Knowledge, Vitality, Négritude, and Revolution" (2016), https://blogs.law.columbia.edu/nietzsche1313/aime-cesaire-poetic-knowledge-vitality-negritude-and-revolution [accessed 25 May 2024].

Haynes, Tonya, "Sylvia Wynter's Theory of the Human and the Crisis School of Caribbean Heteromasculinity Studies," *Small Axe: A Caribbean Journal of Criticism* 20.1 (49) (2016), pp. 92–112.

Kant, Immanuel, *Groundwork for the Metaphysics of Morals*, trans. Arnulf Zweig; Thomas E Hill, Jr. and Arnulf Zweig, eds. (Oxford: Oxford University Press, 2002).

King, Martin Luther, Jr., "Beyond Vietnam," in Clayborne Carson and Kris Shepard (eds.), *A Call to Conscience: The Landmark Speeches of Dr. Martin Luther King, Jr.* (New York: Warner Books, 2001).

King, Martin Luther, Jr., "The American Dream," in James Melvin Washington (ed.), *A Testament of Hope: The Essential Writings of Martin Luther King, Jr.* (San Francisco, CA: Harper & Row, 1986).

King, Martin Luther, Jr., *Where Do We Go from Here: Chaos or Community?* (Boston: Beacon Press, 1967).

Liking, Werewere, "A la rencontre de… Werewere Liking," interview by Bernard Magnier. *Notre Librairie* 79 (1985), 17–21.

Ogundipe-Leslie, Molara, "African Literature, Feminism, and Social Change," interview by Irène Assiba d'Almeida, *Matatu* 23–4 (2001), 307–22.

Rich, Adrienne, *Of Woman Born: Motherhood as Experience and Institution* (New York: W.W. Norton, 1976).

Royce, Josiah, *The Problem of Christianity* (Washington, DC: Catholic University of America Press, 2001 [1913]).

Senghor, Léopold Sédar, "Ce que l'homme noir apporte," in *Liberté 1 : Négritude et humanisme* (Paris: Éditions du Seuil, 1964).

Senghor, Léopold Sédar, "De la Négritude," in *Ce que je crois: Négritude, francité et civilisation de l'universel* (Paris: Grasset & Fasquelle, 1988).

Senghor, Léopold Sédar, "Hommage à Pierre Teilhard de Chardin," in *Liberté 5: Le dialogue des cultures* (Paris: Éditions du Seuil, 1993).

Senghor, Léopold Sédar, "La Révolution de 1889," in *The Collected Poetry*, trans. Melvin Dixon (Charlottesville: University of Virginia Press, 1991).

Senghor, Léopold Sédar, "Le problème culturel en A.O.F.," in *Liberté 1: Négritude et humanisme* (Paris: Éditions du Seuil, 1964).

Senghor, Léopold Sédar, "Negritude: A Humanism of the Twentieth Century," in Gaurav Desai and Supriya Nair (eds.), *Postcolonialisms: An Anthology of Cultural Theory and Criticism* (New Brunswick: Rutgers University Press, 2005).

Senghor, Léopold Sédar, "Préface" in Hans Köchler (ed.), *The New International Economic Order: Philosophical and Socio-Cultural Implications* (Guildford: Guildford Educational Press, 1980).

Stanton, Domna C., "The Humanities in Human Rights: Critique, Language, Politics," *PMLA* 121.5 (2006), 1518–25.

Walker, Alice, *In Search of our Mothers' Gardens: Womanist Prose* (Boston: Houghton Mifflin, 1983).

Walton, Hanes, Jr., *The Political Philosophy of Martin Luther King, Jr.* (Westport: Greenwood, 1971).

The Woman King. Directed by Gina Prince-Bythewood, Sony Pictures, 2022.

Wynter, Sylvia, "1492: A New World View," in Vera Hyatt and Rex Nettleford (eds.), *Race, Discourse, and the Origin of the Americas: A New World View* (Washington and London: Smithsonian Institution Press, 1995), pp. 5–57.

Wynter, Sylvia, *Black Metamorphosis*. Unpublished

Wynter, Sylvia, "On How We Mistook the Map for the Territory, and Reimprisoned Ourselves in Our Unbearable Wrongness of Being, of Desêtre: Black Studies Toward the Human Project," in Lewis R. Gordon and Jane Anna Gordon (eds.), *Not Only the Master's Tools: African American Studies in Theory and Practice* (New York: Routledge, 2006).

Wynter, Sylvia. 2006, "Proud Flesh Inter/Views: Sylvia Wynter Interview by Greg Thomas," *Proud Flesh: New Afrikan Journal of Culture, Politics & Consciousness* (2006), pp. 1–35. https://monoskop.org/images/6/65/Proud_Flesh_InterViews_Sylvia_Wynter_2006.pdf.

Chapter 11

Smartphone Literature in Today's Sierra Leone: Assessing Claims of Continuity with Traditional Fireside Folktales

STEPHEN NEY

In the chapter Patrick Muana penned for *Knowledge Is More Than Mere Words*, the 2008 critical introduction to Sierra Leonean literature that in many ways anticipates the present volume, he asserted that

> Research encounters must not be determined by an alarmist inclination that the folklore performances being recorded are dying out. Tradition should be seen as thriving but evolvable. ... As indicated in the historical survey of folklore collection in Sierra Leone, Sierra Leonean folklore emerges in various genres and among various population groups. Its performance and its appropriations are therefore worth studying. (306–7)

This chapter explores two recent collections of Anglophone Sierra Leonean poems and short stories that perfectly illustrate Muana's point. As he argued, folklore traditions are (1) thriving already; yet still (2) capable of evolution; and (3) their performance and appropriations are definitely worth studying. If successful, this chapter will be evidence of all three parts of this claim.

The texts discussed in this chapter are not the oral texts Muana had in mind. They are, rather, the kinds of texts that Abioseh Porter had in mind when he wrote the chapter that immediately follows Muana's – "Non-conventional literary media: New poetic voices on the internet." It is a chapter on the "new beginnings" that the internet made possible in the years following the 1991–2002 war: [responding to] "the lack of access to traditional publishing houses and the presence of a new, internet-savvy audience ..., some Sierra Leoneans have been using the internet as a major forum to highlight their creativity" (315). The reader will not be surprised that there is now much to add to the story that Porter began telling.

The poems and stories that I discuss here were written and shared in a WhatsApp group called the Sierra Leonean Writers' Forum (SLWF or SWF) that is the successor of the Leonenet online discussion group – the very forum that Porter saw as a new beginning for highlighting literary creativity. *Contemporary Fireside Poems: An Anthology* (2016, henceforth *Poems*) and *Contemporary*

Fireside Stories: An Anthology (2017, henceforth *Stories*) were both collected and edited by Dr Fatou Taqi and Dr Philip Foday Yamba Thulla, then published by the Sierra Leonean Writers Series. Twenty-five Sierra Leonean authors contributed to the first collection, between one and twelve poems each. Fourteen Sierra Leonean authors contributed to the second collection, each a story or two. Several of the authors are newcomers on the scene, but others, including Oumar Farouk Sesay, Mallam O. (Osman Alimamy Sankoh), Sheikh Umarr Kamarah, and Gbanabom Hallowell, would be well known to any scholar of contemporary Sierra Leonean literature.

Apart from title and background colour, the covers of the paperback books are identical. They both feature a large reproduction of an evidently hand-drawn cartoon of a dozen people, old and young, dressed in traditional and modern attire. They sit and stand alertly around a cluster of three mobile phones that lie on the ground, in the centre of the cartoon, and that we can tell (because of the little wi-fi icons above each one) are linked to a larger network. The three mobile phones are clearly occupying the place formerly taken up by a wood fire. Three of the people hold large books in their hands, but the majority – including those who look younger – hold in their hands their own networked devices, so that their attention is presumably divided between their handheld phones and the communal phones that have taken the place of the fire. In the background of the scene is a video projection of a traditional pot cooking on a wood fire – the kind of fire that the three central mobile phones presumably

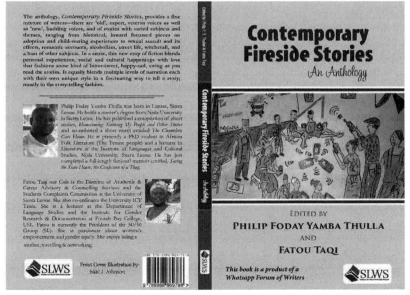

Figure 1. Contemporary Fireside Poems: An Anthology (2016), edited by Fatou Taqi and Philip Foday Yamba Thulla. Reproduced by permission of the Sierra Leonean Writers Series

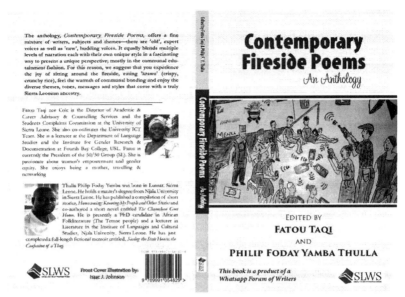

Figure 2. Contemporary Fireside Stories: An Anthology (2017), edited by Fatou Taqi and Philip Foday Yamba Thulla. Reproduced by permission of the Sierra Leonean Writers Series.

replaced. This chapter will have much to say about the relationship between the old and the new centrepieces.

The cartoon I have described adds some depth to the pair of words, "Contemporary" and "Fireside", that appear in both collections' titles and implicitly make a claim about continuity that I argue is both true and fertile for thinking not only about the anthologies themselves but also about contemporary literature more broadly. My argument will occupy the bulk of this chapter, but first I would like to say that the claim is also confrontational. It confronts what Muana called the "alarmist inclination that the folklore performances being recorded are dying out" by insisting that the traditional verbal arts are in several ways continuous in both form and function with what phones are used for today. In that sense, the traditional arts are not dying out at all. Also, less directly but inescapably, my argument confronts the view that the wonders of mobile and digital technologies insert Sierra Leonean and other African users into a narrative from elsewhere, a narrative that only began to make mention of them once colonialism had brought them into the world system. As I read them, these collections provide a refutation to that view because they consist of literature that was born on social media and that nevertheless stand in continuity with preliterate and precolonial traditions. The refuted view reflects colonialist and technological-determinist assumptions.

I think this continuity claim is made unambiguously by the books' covers, but the editors' preface adds support. Taqi and Thulla propose that "a social media-sourced anthology" could "be a futuristic alternative to the 'fireside gathering'". Responding to the view that communal fireside gatherings and their stories, songs, education, and entertainment are dying out, and that the internet deserves much blame, the editors suggest that "the communal medium [has been] substituted by affordances that have closely paralleled the ancient fireside gathering" (*Stories*, iii). The editors' claim corresponds of course to the claim I have discerned in the volumes' covers and it is this claim that I argue is true and fertile. My argument gives attention in sequence to two implications of this claim for continuity: first, that there is no reason for us to accord to technology a central place in our understanding of literary texts dependent on social media; and second, that there is more to be gained by looking at the social situation than at the technological medium of such texts. Although my argument will refer to many of the individual texts in these volumes, I do not want to assume that my readers are already acquainted with the stories and poems. For that reason, I will focus my attention on the technological, social, and historical questions implicitly raised by the covers and prefaces of the volumes.

Not Much is New about New Media

In media studies, determinism is the position that particular media have essential qualities that imply how the media should be used and what can be done with them. It is associated with Walter Ong (*Orality and Literacy*) and Elizabeth Eisenstein (*The Printing Press as an Agent of Change*), who explained in different ways how the arrival of print changes a society and its ways of thinking. According to determinism, a technology has a power of its own to make possible something new. So we might say that smartphones are killing folklore because this now-dominant technology forces us to communicate and even to think in a new way that is somehow incompatible with folklore.

Against determinist positions, Jay David Bolter's and Richard Grusin's influential 1999 monograph, *Remediation*, implied that *new media* is in many ways a misnomer, for new media are not helpfully understood to surpass and supersede old media. Rather, new media respond to the old by borrowing from and competing with them: "In the remediation of one form by another, there is always a relationship of homage and rivalry" (Bolter, "Remediation and the Language of New Media", 26). Bolter and Grusin use the binary of transparency and hypermediacy to describe two opposing representational strategies used by artists to respond using newer media to older media forms. Transparency pursues immediacy, where the viewer forgets the medium altogether, imagining that she is really *there,* where "there" might be around a village campfire. Hypermediacy, in contrast, encourages viewers to give attention to the media interposed between themselves and what is mediated. A prime example for Bolter and Grusin is the visually hyperactive CNN website of the late 1990s, "arranging text, graphics, and video in multiple panes and windows and joining them with numerous hyperlinks" (*Remediation,* 9); this website made it impossible for a viewer to lose themselves in a single news story, because all the stories shared simultaneously on the page were constantly interrupting each other.

Yet though immediacy and hypermediacy are opposite strategies, Bolter and Grusin find them, paradoxically, to be constantly coinciding and often collaborating. They point out that television news broadcasts, including those of CNN, are borrowing and thus remediating "the windowed and multimediated look of the computer screen" and "are increasingly willing to use digital technology in the service of hypermediacy without giving up their claim to be live" (189). Remediation shows why the binarism of innovation vs. stagnation can be unhelpful, providing a more nuanced way of charting the effects of technological developments on cultural forms. The covers and editorial introductions of *Poems* and *Stories* invite us to understand the collections as remediations, not repetitions, of older forms. The video projection of a traditional pot cooking over a wood fire (with an icon for signal strength in the upper left corner of the screen and a MENU button in the lower left) provides hypermediacy since we are made aware that we are not *really* seeing a traditional village scene. The blurb on the back of *Poems* invites us to "experience the joy of sitting around the fireside, eating 'krawo' (crispy, crunchy rice)" but of course we know this is make-believe, and even as we read the blurb, we are reminded of how far we are away from that fireside. In contrast to the covers and editorializing of the two collections, their prevailing strategy is not hypermediacy but transparency: the stories and poems are intended to carry us imaginatively away from our homes and our jobs, our books and our smartphones, into a new fictional reality. Very rarely in the collections is there anything to remind us we are in the digital age.

An example is Jedidah Adlyn Olayinka Johnson's short story, "Letter to my Beloved" which, apart from a brief and dramatic coda, consists of a single long letter that talks about letters and about itself as a letter: "Egertina, I am writing you this letter though I do not know where you are and I am almost certain you will never read it" (*Stories*, 71). The narrator, Momoh, says he has been watching the lives of the Kardashians on television before sitting down to write the long letter, so we know the story is not set before the age of smartphones. The story might have seemed more realistic, in fact, if Momoh had written a long email or a very long WhatsApp message. But like the other texts in these collections, the story, though we know it was written and first disseminated via a smartphone, cares very little about digital technology. The new technology is so transparent that readers can easily forget about it.

Scholars of technology use the word "skeuomorphism" to describe the inefficiency when a new technology mimics an older technology in such a way that adds nothing: the shutter-clicking sound of a smartphone camera, the LCD minute and hour hands on the face of a digital wristwatch, the fake wood-grain on the plastic panel on a car-door. These reminders of an old technology make it easier for those comfortable with the old to embrace a new technology; but in doing so, their detractors say, they encumber or inhibit the benefits of the new, and they reveal stagnation despite the appearance of dynamism. Is Momoh's handwritten letter and are the digital firesides of the collections' covers skeuomorphisms? Do they add nothing but nostalgia and the badge of a precolonial African authenticity? In other words, is it merely a gimmick that the texts seem to be asking for special attention and to be read differently because they use new media in a way that evokes the old?

Teju Cole, in his 2017 article, "Do African Digital Natives Wear Glass Skirts?" addresses exactly this allegation, and answers that, yes, sometimes evoking the older cultural forms (grass skirts evoked by certain contemporary clothing, or talking drums evoked by certain contemporary African music) inhibits us from "freely inhabiting all the complications that we are in" (40). Cole's point is that it is too easy and too restrictive to demand that authenticity be grounded in traditional forms. African digital natives do *not* need to wear glass skirts, or any kind of skirts for that matter. But what the *Contemporary Fireside* collections reveal is that grounding a contemporary cultural expression in traditional forms is not necessarily gratuitous and essentialist at all. Here it is an invitation to find unexpected continuities even when new, digital technologies seem to constitute a rupture. These continuities are generative, not stagnant.

Take, for example, two pieces in *Poems*. Kemurl Mustapha Abdul Fofanah writes in "The Writer's Coming Home" without any irony about the African homeland and the lover he is returning to, after a long time abroad during which he developed as a cosmopolitan and a writer: "The writer's sailing home to his own soil, to meet his beloved" (14). Samuella Julia Conteh's poem "The Writer Never Left" is obviously an ironic retort to Fofanah's poem, imagining the perspective of the lover left behind. Conteh mimics Fofanah by referring to the same exotic destinations that the writer saw – "the Asian deserts," "the Australasia depths" (6) – but claims that he only ever visited them in his imagination. She mimics him as well by replicating the highly repetitive structure of his stanzas, concluding each one with "though he never left home, / He was never home with his beloved" (6) effectively accusing him of neglecting and betraying the one he claimed most to love.

Like "Letter to my Beloved," these poems make the digital medium transparent, giving no clues that they were written and shared via WhatsApp. However, if we look carefully, we can see that they provide good reason to deny that the collections' reference to fireside folktales is a nostalgic skeuomorphism. The editorial introduction I mentioned earlier suggested that these texts were composed in a manner that recalled the interactive "communal medium" of the fireside; editor Fatou Taqi told me in an interview that this process involved iterative adjustments made in response to comments like "I prefer it this way ... No, no..." This was effectively an informal process of editorial review. And if this was the process by which the texts came into being, we need not be surprised that traces of the process remain, as for example in the way Conteh responds critically to Fofanah. Certainly, the ease and the intensity of a literary debate like Conteh's and Fofanah's are much greater with digital than with print media. Thus, this pair of poems adds weight to the continuity claim implied by the books' titles and covers, and invites us to look for more ways in which digital forms reactivate possibilities that are easily neglected by those who adopt the myth of the autonomous and virtuosic literary artist, a myth that has often been associated with books and with Western literature, and that has imagined a great divide between oral and literate cultures.

It was when the British anthropologist Ruth Finnegan was studying the storytelling of the Limba people in northern Sierra Leone in the 1960s that she developed her claim, now generally accepted, that "there is no good reason to deny the title of literature to African forms just because they happen to be oral" (*The Oral and Beyond*, 95). Before Finnegan's influential publications in the 1960s and 1970s, "oral literature" was generally regarded as a contradiction in terms; but she showed that "we can consider Limba stories as possessing much the same characteristics as our own literature" (*Limba Stories*, 63). She analysed the performative elements and the audience involvement in Limba storytelling as well as the specific circumstances in which the stories were performed. She found the messages of the stories to be complex, impossible to reduce to a moral imperative, for "there is, after all, no reason to assume that the Limba, any more than we ourselves, see life as a simple matter" (ibid.). In later years, as her thinking developed, Finnegan came to generalize her conclusions and to argue convincingly that "the once-accepted information technologies of orality and literacy respectively have not, after all, been proved to bring definitive consequences for human society and experience nor to give support to a technologically based great divide between the oral and the literate" (*Literacy and Orality*, 14).

I invoke Finnegan here to strengthen my case that there is nothing gratuitous about how the *Contemporary Fireside* collections ask to be read as continuous with traditional literary traditions. Because of their interactivity, multimodality, and linguistic and social sophistication, the texts Finnegan looked at deserve to be seen as a current flowing through contemporary literary production rather than as dead and done. The *Contemporary Fireside* collections refuse to allow us either to view technology as providing altogether new possibilities for literary form and content or as attempting to hide stagnation; technology rather activates latent potentials or recovers forgotten achievements. The assumption of technological determinism fails to generate insight into these texts, but I will now show that attention to social contexts is much more illuminating.[1] In this way, I will continue to follow in the footsteps of social scientists like Finnegan, talking about contemporary texts in some of the same ways that social scientists have talked about oral texts.

The World Through the Text

In giving so much attention to the cover and the editorial comments of *Stories* and *Poems*, I may have implied that Bolter's and Grusin's concept of hypermediacy is more useful for studying these texts than their concept of immediacy. But in this section, I would like to change directions and imagine these texts as transparent windows into the world in which they were composed, shared, and revised – all on the smartphones, of course, of the members of the Sierra Leone Writers' Forum (SWF or SLWF) WhatsApp group. This world is not the fictional world of the texts, for example the Kenema where Momoh first set eyes on Egertina, two decades or more ago. Social scientists (as opposed to formalist literary scholars) read stories and poems with this same eye for contexts of production and reception. Philip F.Y. Thulla, one of the collections' editors, described for me in a WhatsApp message the immediate context of production and reception:

> The idea to record the literary conversations of SWF writers was first lighthearted[ly] proposed and later agreed upon. [...] Just as the fireside was a podium for indigenous African peoples to enjoy the warmth and the simple pleasures of a good Palmwine and great storytelling and riddling sessions, SWF served much the same space, in the sense that it was a domicile for both local and diasporan Sierra Leonean writers; budding and professional writers, who wrote spontaneous anecdotes, witty statements and the like. In a sense, these writers did free writing, without worries about rhetorical concerns or conventions and mechanics.

Thulla seems to be saying that the poems and short stories are not fixed and standalone art objects, but elements of a dynamic social system.

One of the immediate implications of this approach is that there is very little value in critiquing the texts' lack of polish. It is true that several of the short stories give the impression of being unfinished. James Bernard Taylor's "Falling Leaves", for instance, creates vivid characters and a realistic family conflict set in Freetown's Congo Market, but closes too soon, before it has cashed in on its own investment, seemingly forgetting about the questions

---

[1] My perspective here echoes Ann Overburgh's claims ("Technological Innovation"), to which I am indebted, on how technological innovation has affected storytelling in contemporary Kenya.

it raised: How does Mello's rags to riches story matter to the principal story line of Adeline and Fatu's animosity? What happens to that animosity, which takes centre-stage in the first fifth of the story but then recedes to antecedent action? Why is the story even called "Falling Leaves"? The story provides no satisfaction to the asker of these questions. Similarly, Joan Adama Kainessie's "Submission" seems not to realize its own potential for insight. It begins with a striking portrayal of an abusive marriage. But after a third of the story, when the abused wife dies, all wrongs are forgiven and everything goes swimmingly for the family, almost as though the opening tension provided no lesson to learn, no reflection to deepen.

A formalist reader would be tempted to call these stories "unsuccessful"; a reader with colonialist inclinations might go further and call them "primitive", as so many of Amos Tutuola's contemporaneous Western readers did.[2] But this fails to appreciate a crucial part of their value. Even a reader with rigid and ethnocentric notions of formal excellence should be able to recognize in them what an important early critic saw in Tutuola's novels: an "imaginative recreation of African culture" (King "Introduction", 2). I would like to propose that the fireside texts are windows into society and, in particular, into the SLWF – that is, into the part of society that has given them birth. Their being unpolished does not impede our looking through them to discern how SLWF members (likely as prone as the rest of us to skim WhatsApp messages and even abandon them when they get too long) may have provoked them and responded to them. This SLWF community is at the same time the community of reception and the community of composition, since the SLWF is a "communal medium" much in the same way as are Finnegan's Limba stories, and the sharing of each text in the WhatsApp group was a kind of lively performance, inseparable from the conversations that preceded and followed it.[3] Approaching these published texts as elements of interactive, communal performances reveals much that would otherwise be obscured. So if, as I have argued, they have an unfinished feel, this is an asset in the sense that it invites further contributions from the community, thus illustrating how the text fits the rhetorical situation that gave it birth. "I prefer it this way ... No, no..." There is a form of call-and-response interactivity beneath the surface of these texts.

---

[2] For example, Selden Rodman in the *NYT Book Review* called Tutuola "a true primitive" (15).

[3] Muana, in the article discussed above, credits Finnegan's 1967 monograph, *Limba Stories and Story-telling*, with redirecting "the focus of this scholarship [on folklore] to the immanent features of performance, individual creativity, and therefore the changing nature of texts of folklore as they emerged from performances" (301). So here again I am proposing to study contemporary texts in ways similar to how Finnegan studied folklore.

The texts reveal thoughts in progress about issues that mattered to members of the SLWF. Several of the most prominent issues are the abuse and the empowerment of women, topics which were at the centre not only of SLWF members' attention during the 2010s: in Sierra Leone this was a time of burgeoning government, NGO, and academic attention to gender inequality. Consider a series of snippets from some of the dozens of poems that highlight these issues:

"Scream 'til someone listens; / Speak 'til someone does you right; / See that you are made human too" – from "Woman, Reinvent Thyself!" by Samuella Julia Conteh (11)

"Neglected and battered, she stood alone" – from "Tainted Petal" by J.E.M. Kainwo (67)

"she begged for mercy and forgiveness / But the demons seemed to rage the more in his head" – from "Ruthless Pleasure" by James Bernard Taylor (151)

"with watery eyes, it salivates and wags, / and then jumps to snatch" – from "The Dog and its Bone" by Celia Thompson (166)

"What do I do with you now / in your battered, bloody body?" – from "Remember Her; Hannah" by Celia Thompson (162), commemorating a young woman murdered by a rapist

"womanhood will fight on / For a change" – from "A Cry of Hannah" by Princess Mildred Ndelei Kailey (62), commemorating that same young woman

Similar concerns about gender-based violence and women's empowerment preoccupy several of the prose pieces, such as Fatou Taqi's "A Complex Situation" and Celia Thompson's "My Brother's Confession" which are both built on a demonstration of the destruction that stem from one young man's sexual aggression and profligacy. In comparison with the impression Porter gives of the texts produced in the Leonenet forum, the *Contemporary Fireside* collections demonstrate a reduced concern with the nation and political events, and an increased concern with individual relationships.

Some of these relationships, of course, are with other members of the SLWF. Gbanabom Hallowell's poems make this particularly clear, and the two poems on pages 27 and 28 of *Poems* directly name four fellow poets: Thulla, Thompson, Oumar Farouk Sesay and Mallam O. (Osman Sankoh).

At moments like these the text is revealed as an interactive performance rather than a polished and fixed art object. No wonder that of the 124 poems at least eight (including two discussed above) directly discuss the writing of poetry. Hallowell's "Ever since" refers to the announcement that poems shared on the forum could be published, and confesses a "little fear" that it "No longer sounds / Like the poem / My father read to me / Before my birth" (38). At such moments of poetic reflexivity, the usefulness of social scientific approaches like Finnegan's is particularly clear. The poems are a window into a social world.

An Invitation to Hypermediation

In the discussion above, I have tried to show the benefits of accepting the invitation of the two *Contemporary Fireside* collections to read them effectively as fireside literary conversations in a new guise. Now I would like to propose how collections like these, by exploiting some of the affordances of digital media, could make this same invitation even more compelling. My invitation would be for the texts in such collections to give more attention to, and exploit more of the possibilities implicit in their own media, thereby adopting some of the strategies Bolter and Grusin call hypermediation. For instance, the poem referring to the murder of Hannah Bokari ("A Cry of Hannah", *Poems*, 62) could hyperlink to a newspaper's website. A story about a decades-long epistolary relationship ("Letter to My Beloved", *Stories*, 70) could allow its style and its formatting on the page to reflect the media through which the lovers communicated. Some of the commentary that took place on SLWF *about* the stories and poems could be published *with* the poems. Once we see how embedded the texts themselves are in the conversations and relationships hosted on the forum, we realize that the distinction between text and paratext is a very faint line. And the same goes for the canonical distinction between the genres of short story and poem. Even though the two collections define themselves according to this distinction, it turns out to be somewhat artificial, since both groups of texts came about in the same way, around the "fireside", through the same contemporary-yet-traditional literary conversations in the same social world.

What I have not discussed at all is that the form in which the *Contemporary Fireside* texts have come to me is paperback. Their covers and their editorials make no mention of this, focusing instead on the traditional oral antecedent and the contemporary digital medium. That these collections are now books rather than digital files interposes between the reader and the traditional folktale a new layer of (re)mediation and invites another layer of analysis. It complicates the task of demonstrating continuity between oral and digital forms; further analysis might even lead to the conclusion that these continuities are dismantled by the return to print. The reader of these collections will have a harder time appreciating the editors' claims that "the communal medium [has been] substituted by affordances that have closely paralleled the ancient fireside gathering" (*Stories*, 3), because those "affordances" are obscured by the form of the book into which the digital texts were converted. This goes beyond the problem of stagnation that Teju Cole's discussion of a skeuomorphism is meant to reveal: here a new technology not only mimics an old technology but becomes imprisoned inside it.

To put it succinctly, the print format of the collections prevents them from fully embracing the invitation, implied in their covers, to exploit the untapped potential of digital media. On the one hand, it is worth considering whether in fact the medium of the book is, at this point in history, more of a hindrance than a help to literary expression and exploration. On the other hand, digital technologies continue to invite Sierra Leonean writers to explore the thriving, evolving literary traditions to which the two collections testify.

Works Cited

Bolter, Jay David, 'Remediation and the Language of New Media', *Northern Lights* 1.5 (2007), pp. 25–37.

Bolter, Jay David and Richard Grusin, *Remediation: Understanding New Media* (Cambridge, MA: MIT Press, 1999).

Cole, Teju, 'Do African Digital Natives Wear Glass Skirts?' *Journal of the African Literature Association* 11.1 (2017), pp. 38–44.

Eisenstein, Elizabeth, *The Printing Press as an Agent of Change: Communications and Cultural Transformations in Early-Modern Europe* vols. 1&2 (Cambridge: Cambridge University Press, 1979).

Finnegan, Ruth, *Limba Stories and Story-telling* (London, Oxford University Press, 1967).

—— *Literacy and Orality: Technological Determinists Large and Small* (Old Bletchley: Callender Press, 2017 [1988]).

—— *The Oral and Beyond: Doing Things with Words in Africa* (Chicago, IL: University of Chicago Press, 2007).

King, Bruce, 'Introduction', in *Nigerian Literature* Bruce King (ed.) (Lagos: University of Lagos Press, 1971), pp. 2–11.

Muana, Patrick, 'Folklore Studies in Sierra Leone: Trends, Issues, and New Directions', in *Knowledge Is More Than Mere Words: A Critical Introduction to Sierra Leonean Literature*, (eds.) Eustace Palmer and Abioseh Michael Porter (Trenton, NJ: Africa World Press, 2008), pp. 297–314.

Ong, Walter, *Orality and Literacy: The Technologizing of the Word* (London: Methuen, 1982).

Overbergh, Ann, 'Technological Innovation and the Diversification of Audio-visual Storytelling Circuits in Kenya', *Journal of African Cultural Studies* 26.2 (2014), pp. 206–19.

Porter, Abioseh, 'Non-Conventional Literary Media: New Poetic Voices on the Internet', in *Knowledge Is More Than Mere Words: A Critical Introduction to Sierra Leonean Literature* (eds.) Eustace Palmer and Abioseh Michael Porter (Trenton, NJ: Africa World Press, 2008), pp. 315–38.

Rodman, Selden. 'Tutuola's World; The Palm-Wine Drinkard', *The New York Times Book Review*, 20 September 1953. Retrieved 25 March 2023 from https://www.nytimes.com/1953/09/20/archives/tutuolasworldthepalmwinedrinkard-byamostutuola130ppnew.html.

Taqi, Fatou. Personal Interview. Conducted by Stephen Ney, 17 January 2020.

Taqi, Fatou and Philip Foday Yamba Thulla (eds.), *Contemporary Fireside Poems: An Anthology* (Warima: Sierra Leonean Writers Series, 2016).

——— *Contemporary Fireside Stories: An Anthology* (Freetown, Sierra Leonean Writers Series, 2017).

Thulla, Philip Foday Yamba. WhatsApp message received by Stephen Ney, 11 June 2020.

Chapter 12

The Intersection of Life and History in Eldred Jones' *The Freetown Bond: A Life under Two Flags*

SAMUEL KAMARA

Over the last two or so decades, Sierra Leone has witnessed the publication of different life narratives such as autobiographies, memoirs, autoethnographies, testimonios, among others. Most of these life-writing acts,[1] often written by prominent Sierra Leoneans,[2] have not received much academic attention. While the field of life writing seems to be festering in Sierra Leone from a lack of critical attention paid to it, it is flourishing in North America, Britain, and Australia with publications, conferences, workshops, and academic curricular. This chapter envisages a reversal of this trend of the dearth of critical essays on life writing in Sierra Leone by situating the significance of Eldred Jones' *The Freetown Bond: A Life under Two Flags* (2012) within the context of Sierra Leonean life narratives.

In this chapter, I argue that the publication of *The Freetown Bond* ushered a generic invention of life writing in Sierra Leone that intersects life and history. To make such a claim begs the question of whether every life-writing act (memoir, autobiography, letter, diary, testimonio, etc.) does not place the self within historical, cultural and political temporalities. So, what is inventive

---

[1] The word act is derived from the concept of speech act which stipulates that the performativity of language in life writing underscores the truth value of the work.
[2] Including: Francis Steven George, *What Life Has Taught Me: A Political Career of Dr. Siaka P Stevens and National Building: A Republication of the Autobiography* (Scott Valley: CreateSpace, 2014); Ahmed Tejan Kabbah, *Coming Back from the Brink in Sierra Leone - A Memoir of Ahmed Tejan Kabbah* (Accra: EPP Book Services, 2010); Osman Sankoh, *Hybrid Eyes: A Reflection of an African in Europe* (Freetown: Sierra Leonean Writers Series, 2013); Sama Banya, *Looking Back: My Life and Times* (Freetown: Sierra Leonean Writers Series, 2015); Andrew Keili, *Ponder My Thoughts* (Freetown: Sierra Leonean Writers Series, 2015); Eustace Palmer, *My Epic Journey: The Making of a Cosmopolitan* (Freetown: Sierra Leonean Writers Series, 2023).

about *The Freetown Bond*? Jones' autobiography, I would contend, belongs to a genre of life-writing acts that Jaume Aurell refers to as "intellectual autobiography" (247), "academic life writing", or "historical autobiography" (2015, 245). Aurell's research focused on the study of 450 autobiographies by historians in North America, Britain, and Australia and concluded that by the beginning of the twenty-first century, a new form of autobiography emerged that "challenged established conventions and resisted generic classification" (245). These forms are exclusively interventional in the sense that they re-established the subgenre of historiography which was considered marginal until the 1970s. Furthermore, most of these autobiographies were written by historians, born between the 1930s and 1940s, who had "witnessed the linguistic, narrative and cultural turns" and were reacting against "modernism and poststructuralist theory" of selfhood (247).[3] As noted by Aurell, these generic inventions "provide ways to track academics' contemporary struggles with the purpose and definition of subjectivity and with other theories that centrally define the humanities during the 1990s and into the twenty first century" (247). Jeremy Popkin, whose research places the birth of these historians between 1920s and 1930s, further states that they "had been conscious of living through an age of great historical upheavals – the era of Nazism and communism, of World War II and the Holocaust" (694). That is, because these scholars' lives were touched by these events, they were compelled to bear witness to them.

The attempt to merge autobiographical and historical 'truths' is a key feature of academic autobiographies. Most life-writing scholars/historians, such as Sheila Fitzpatrick, Ann Moyal, Jenifer Wallach, Jaume Aurell and Rocio Davis, agree that in attempting to recollect the past our personal experiences can impinge and be impinged upon by collective cultural experiences. Although Fitzpatrick distinguishes between subjective autobiographical 'truths' and objective historical 'truths', there are multiple ways in which one's individual and collective pasts can merge and fuse to recall 'truths' whose affective associations compel a reality that is uncommon in collective memory. For intellectual autobiographies, the "personal experience is inseparable from ... intellectual activities" (Aurell and Davis 2019, 505). And I would add that this is especially true in cases where those intellectual activities have socio-political, cultural, and economic implications. It is for such reasons that Wallach admonishes that these "individual [life narratives] should not be read in isolation, but along with secondary scholarship about the time period in question" (449). In other words, despite the fact that these narratives adopt unconventional ways of remembering the past, they are able to pass as historical documents.

---

[3] It must be noted that the poststructuralist conceptualization of the self as decentred, layered, multiple and incomprehensible clashes with life writing's notion of selfhood as knowable and comprehensible, even if complex.

While one cannot categorically call Eldred Jones a historian in the disciplinary sense of the word, he is certainly participating in the historiographic project of understanding the past by contextualizing his public/private life within the context of the socio-political and cultural history of Sierra Leone. The outcome of Jones' effort is the production of an academic autobiography that resists generic categorization; one that is a mixture of the genres of autobiography and memoir.[4] The generic confusion of Jones' narrative is reflected in the different book reviews published about his text so far. In the cover jacket of the 2012 James Currey edition, Martin Banham, Emeritus Professor of Drama and Theatre Studies at University of Leeds, refers to *The Freetown Bond* as a memoir. Mauricia John refers to it as an autobiography and a memoir (2013, 407). Arthur Edgar Smith calls it a memoir (2013, 140). In my previous engagement with Jones' text, I referred to it as a memoir and autobiography (Kamara 2013, 1). The reason for this confusion resides in the fact that in the first five chapters of Jones' narrative, he adopts almost a linear narrative structure from his birth/boyhood at Leah Street to his early manhood as a lecturer at Fourah Bay College (FBC). Such a narrative structure runs similar to that of an autobiography. However, in Chapters 6 through 10, he uses the narrative structure of a memoir – that is, selecting incidents which are sutured into a narrative whole. The seeming absence of what Philippe Lejeune refers to as the autobiographical pact further complicates generic categorization of Jones' text.[5] This categorization problem can be easily solved in the reader's mind when one accepts the fact that it is possible for Jones to work within the conventions of both a memoir and an autobiography. Such generic hybridity affords him the opportunity to summarize his larger-than-life personality and distinguished academic career into a 174-page life narrative. But, as an academic, Jones is also pushing the boundaries of generic limitations to weave the story of a life that has socio-political and historical implications. Furthermore, in trying to articulate an intellectual perspective of the past, Jones has sacrificed the perspective of the narrated 'I', which is very common in traditional autobiographies, to tell his story only with the narrating 'I'. Doing away with the narrated 'I' affords Jones the opportunity to re-view and comment on Sierra Leone's history as an adult and as an academic.

Born in 1925, Jones' birth puts him at par with those academics that Popkin and Aurell refer to in their researches. He also knew and experienced some of the evils of Nazism, Communism, the Second World War, and the Holocaust, as an academic and as an individual. In fact, at age 14, Jones almost got enlisted

---

[4] While an autobiography records an author's life from birth to the moment of writing, a memoir records selected incidents of an author's life and sutures them into a narrative whole.

[5] The autobiographical pact certifies that the narrating 'I' in the text represents the voice of the author whose name usually appears on the titular cover of the text.

into the Royal Air Force to fight on Britain's side of the Second World War. However, he later volunteered for service "as an Air Raid Precaution Warden and duly received an ARP arm band, a steel helmet, a black-out torch, and was given training in First Aid" (31). Two of his school mates, though, were enlisted and flown to the war. Nevertheless, the historical upheavals that motivated Jones to bear witness to them have to do with the trauma of colonialism, post-independence political and economic malaise, and the eleven-year Civil War that tore Sierra Leone apart from 1991 to 2002. As an academic and a public figure, Jones is compelled to give an account of his stewardship and present a scholar's perspective of a past characterized by political ineptitude, flagrant corruption, economic mismanagement, and educational decline.

The bifurcation of Jones' authorial purpose is encapsulated in the title of his autobiography: his bonding to Freetown and the dual political dispensation of his life – colonial and postcolonial. By casting himself both as a colonial and postcolonial subject, Jones is rhetorically and ethically positioning himself as a credible historian and storyteller. Indeed, he witnessed the transfer of power from colonialism to independence in 1961 and lived long enough to see Sierra Leone gradually dwindle into a failed state in the 1990s through political chicanery. As an octogenarian, Jones had not only witnessed the history of colonialism, missionary intervention and the establishment of churches and Western education, independence, the 1967 military coup, the political rivalry between the All People's Congress (APC) and the Sierra Leone People's Party (SLPP), the ascension to power and misrule of Siaka Stevens, the execution of Mohamed Sorie Fornah and fourteen others, the 1977 student riot at FBC, the plummeting of FBC from glory, the Civil War of the 1990s, and the feeble post-civil-war recovery effort, but he also played an active role in trying to forestall, reverse, or prevent some of these political ills from happening. A typical example is Jones' letter to then Governor-General Sir Banja Tejan-Sie upon the arrest of Mohamed Bash-Taqui, John Kerefa-Smart, Raymond Sarif Easmon, and Mohamed Sorie Fornah on charges of treason:

> What needs to be done, in my opinion, is that forces now likely to move on a collision course should somehow be brought together. We have a constitution over which you preside, and under this there is room for dissent. If by some means you could bring the two sides together and get a measure of agreement to work within the terms of the constitution to effect their differing aims, you would have done Sierra Leone a worthy service ... what I think should not be allowed to happen is that people should languish in prison without trial or justification (as many did in Ghana and other places) and a feeling should thus be encouraged that justice is not available by constitutional means. (153)

This reasonable advice to settle political differences within the framework of the Sierra Leonean constitution was not adhered to. Jones never "received a reply to this letter" (154). Sierra Leonean historians such as Joe A.D. Alie had written about the aforementioned execution before (see Alie 2015, 93–6), but it is through Jones' reproduction of his letter to Sir Banja Tejan-Sie that his personal experience with this incident intersects with national history. Other examples include his push for the adoption of a Proportional Representation system in the 2002 election, his service as Chairman of the National Policy Advisory Committee during the presidency of Ahmed Tejan Kabbah, his fight to maintain the Fourah Bay College bookshop against students' hankering for their book allowances to be handed to them, and his support "for public education as a means to a sound democracy [which] manifested in papers, seminars [and] personal letters to authorities on a wide variety of subjects" (154). In one of his articles published in *The Sierra Leone Daily Mail* in the early 1960s, Jones had called on "citizens to submit ideas on how to build Sierra Leone after independence" and further "proposed that in order to build up [its] industrial strength [the country] should add value to [its] iron ore by investing in a steel mill, so as to export processed products rather than crude ore" (150). Unfortunately, this brilliant idea of an iron ore smelting foundry was never countenanced by those in authority.

In spite of this regretful image of a post-independence nation bereft of ideas to govern itself and intolerant of good ones, one cannot miss the self-reflexivity of Jones as a patriot and a nationalist. As someone whose education and experience qualified him to lecture at any tier 'A' university in the West, his refusal to pursue such prestigious jobs in order to serve his country certainly demonstrates his love for Sierra Leone. As narrated by Jones:

> Almost everywhere I went, I received flattering offers to take on more permanent appointments in America where in the 1960s Africa was beginning to take on a new interesting and sometimes troubled association with America. My standard response was a polite 'no' in view of my commitment to Fourah Bay College. I always returned to my country with its numerous opportunities for service and its sometimes debilitating frustrations. (79)

As stated earlier, part of the title of Jones' autobiography, *The Freetown Bond*, underscores this point. Such a bonding to Sierra Leone and Africa, generally, afforded Jones the opportunity not only to serve his country in diverse ways – political, academic, religious and social – but to also found and edit the *African Literature Today* journal for thirty-three years, essentially making him a doyen of African literary criticism. Jones' published book, *Othello's Countrymen: The African in English Renaissance Drama*, became a seminal text in postcolonial studies, and his scholastic contribution to both African history and African literature earned him the enviable position of ranking as the first African professor of English south of the Sahara. But this huge academic success completely belies colonial education projects in Africa. Most African historians (see Palmer 2022; Whitehead 2005) agree that colonial education in Africa was limited in content and intended to produce a subservient cadre of African staff under their colonial masters. Palmer brilliantly sums this up when he states that:

> Imperialism was meant to benefit the Europeans, not Africans, and the education of Africans would not have been conducive to the continuation of the colonial grip on African territories. Even when the colonialists began to show an interest in African education it was largely because they needed a cadre of Africans who would man the lowest levels of the administration and thereby help advance the colonial effort. (236)

The veracity of Palmer's statement is clearly reflected in the way the Sierra Leone Government Scholarship Committee[6] handled Jones' application for the Colonial Office backing, in 1950, to do postgraduate studies at Corpus Christi College, at Oxford. After his first application was rejected, Jones had secured a loan from Lloyd's Bank in England to fund his education and was only asking for an endorsement from the Colonial Office in Sierra Leone. In evaluating Jones' application, the Committee raised the question of "whether a candidate should be sponsored by the Committee to pursue what in this case was considered a 'fancy' degree" (47). The final argument for Jones' rejection, however, is summed up below:

> The Committee gained the impression that Mr. Jones's desire to obtain an Honors Degree was to qualify for a lectureship at Fourah Bay College. Members were very favorably impressed by the keenness and personality of the candidate but felt themselves unable to recommend that his candidature be sponsored as it was not thought that a student should start off with a debt of £750/00, which might tend to weigh on his mind and [have] a deterrent effect on his studies and his work after completion of the course. (48)

Inherent in such a flawed logic and colonial hypocrisy regarding the civilizing mission of colonialism is the insidious stereotypical packaging of the black man's mind as weak and incapable of enduring financial stress. Jones' loan was not only interest-free, he was also supposed to start paying it after completing his studies. How such an arrangement would impact a students' academic or work performance is difficult to understand. All the same, Jones was able go to Oxford, and not only completed his studies with flying colors, but also repaid his loan in record time – three years instead of ten.

While the so-called civilizing mission of colonialism is only possible through education, an enlightened colonial subject is clearly a threat to colonial

---

[6] The Sierra Leone Government by the 1950s was essentially colonial, with a Governor General and his administrative cadre of white staff.

establishment. Education makes it possible for the reasonable and reasoning mind to see the hypocrisy, exploitative tendencies, and ideological contradictions of colonialism. This is what is revealed in the story of Mr. M.O.J.T. Sackey at the celebration of Empire Day in Sierra Leone in 1938:

> For many years Mr. M.O.J.T. Sackey who led the Holy Trinity School procession was the star of the show. Everybody waited for him to appear in the arena [where] he did not just march but danced his way around the field with the most exaggerated steps and body movements, thrilling the spectators to the point of near ecstasy. One year, however, the crowd wild with anticipation on seeing the Holy Trinity banner, were shocked to see Mr. Sackey almost indifferent to the beat of the band, in a desultory stroll. The groans of disappointment were heartfelt. Empire Day was almost ruined for many. Why did Mr. Sackey lose his enthusiasm for the Empire Day march past? Had he become aware of the irony of the victims of the Empire celebrating to the glory of their exploiters? Was he expressing doubts latent but unexpressed among his compatriots? ... [F]uture events were to bring [these doubts] out in his compatriots more openly but with far less acrimony than in other British colonies. (21)

The relationship between the dissatisfaction with colonialism resulting from enlightenment, on the one hand, and the clamor for independence and eventual overthrow of colonialism, on the other hand, cannot be missed here. And it comes as no surprise when twenty-three years after Mr. Sackey's public display of his disappointment with colonial rule, Sierra Leone gained its independence from the British colonial masters.

Quite apart from Jones' self-reflection as a patriot, he has also delineated his distinguished academic career in his life narrative. Jones' career success transcends Sierra Leone to include other African countries like Nigeria, Ghana, Kenya, Senegal, and countries such as the United States of America, Canada, and China. As Jones himself testifies, "[he] gave occasional lectures on Shakespeare and his contemporaries, as well as on African literature, to several universities in and around the [D]istrict of Columbia" (88). Funding from the United Negro College Fund gave Jones "the opportunity to give lectures on African literature and history to [N]egro colleagues and universities throughout the southern states at a time when interest in Africa coincided with the struggle of the blacks for emancipation from racial discrimination" (88). It is scholarly engagements like these that gave Jones world recognition as a consummate scholar and earned him four honorary doctorates: "D. Litt., Williams College, Mass., 1985; D. Litt., University of Sierra Leone, 1989; D. Phil, University of Umea, Sweden, 1996; D. Litt., University of Birmingham, UK, 2005" (167). In addition to these honorary recognitions, Jones also bagged a lot of awards such as Fellow of the Royal Society of Arts (FRSA) in 1972 and the Silver Medal awarded by the Republic of South Africa in 1974. He was decorated with the Premier Order of the Republic of Sierra Leone in 1980. He received the Distinguished Africanist Award of the African Studies Association, UK, in 2001, and he was granted Honorary Fellow of Corpus Christi College, Oxford in 2002. In 1979, Jones was invited to chair the Noma Award for Publishing in Africa.

Although Jones' accomplishment of an international academic stature can be accredited to his hard work, he has woven a narrative in which he also retraces his greatness to his parents. Jones' reference to his family history underscores the autobiographical 'truth' that self-reflexivity is always in tangential relationship with other lives. Thus, the historical importance of one life will continue to shape, and be shaped by, other lives. And in the nexus of human relationships, various histories overlap and reinforce each other, further highlighting a complex and multiple intersection of lives and histories. According to Jones, his mother, Ethline Marie Jones, was a "Maroon descendant. The Maroons were Jamaican slaves who had rebelled against British rule and [had] been transported to Nova Scotia in Canada, where they joined the slaves who had escaped from the southern states during the American War of Independence against the British" (2). Jones' mother was a strong woman with an indomitable spirit which she inherited from her mother, Emily John – a successful businesswoman and a matriarch who presided over her "clan at No. 8 Liverpool Street ... and the Lakes, Awoonor-Williamses, and Tregson-Roberts ... [at] Waterloo Street" (4). An example of Jones' mother's strength of character can be seen at the time when she was giving birth to Jones' younger sister. We are told that she was heavily pregnant and had just finished acting at their Pleasant Sunday Afternoon Gatherings (PSAG) when she "walked half-a-mile to Dr. Isaac Pratt's Nursing Home at Sackville Street and delivered her daughter within hours" (6). Ethline Jones also took after her mothers' mercantile spirit and operated a shop on Kissy Street for several years. The role of Ethline Marie Jones in the life of Eldred Jones cannot be overlooked. Both share streaks of character that suggest familial histories of hard work.

Jones' father, Eldred P.W. Jones, equally had a successful life. He worked as a customs officer for thirty-five years. Before that, he had worked as a surveyor. After his retirement from customs, he took up a job as an accountant with the Syrian firm of M.K. Bahsali. Through sheer hard work, he built the family's two houses at Leah Street and owned a farm at Kingtom where Ethline, Jones' mother, planted corn and groundnuts to supplement the family's income. Mr. E.P.W. Jones was also active in the Holy Trinity Church where he served as organist for several years.

He was also the organist at the Anglican Parish Church, St. Matthews, when he worked as customs officer in Bonthe (southern Sierra Leone) where one of Jones' brothers, Toot, sang soprano in the choir. The acme of Jones' father's professional success is recorded in the first edition of Graham Greene's book, *Journey Without Maps*, where Greene writes about meeting a customs officer in Bonthe called Jones who treated him kindly, contrary to his expectations. Although Eldred Durosimi Jones as an English professor had never seen the original of that text, his comments reveal how proud he was to learn about his "father's encounter with one of the most illustrious English authors of the twentieth century" (161). E.P.W. Jones lived to be eighty-seven before he passed away. What is particularly important in Jones' reference of his father's longevity and coincidental meeting with Graham Greene is the historical parallel it creates with his own life and history. Both of the Joneses – father and son – lived up to eighty and the son's literary destiny, more or less, was foreshadowed by that chance meeting between the father and Graham Greene. However, the greatness of these parents continued to manifest in the lives of their children and grandchildren. We are told that Jones' elder brother, Doc, inherited his father's musical talent and excelled at playing the harmonium. Although he died at a young age in 1919, Toot was regarded as E.P.W. Jones' most brilliant son. Toot's precocity is illustrated by the fact that he was ready for Grammar School at the age of ten. But it was actually Jones' sister's son, Kenneth, who showed the streak of brilliance running in the Jones family. We are told that:

> At two, Kenneth declaimed the first few lines of Mark Antony's "Friends, Romans, countrymen lend me your ears" while Rachel, his sister, some eighteen months older who knew many more lines, smiled indulgently as he excused himself "and I am only two". He sailed through school and university, went into banking and at thirty nine [became] J.P. Morgan Chase & Co. vice president and oil futures trader ... he achieved center spread in the *Washington Post* of 21 March 2003, in the middle of an oil crisis [after he struck a deal] at the perfect moment. (24)

Kenneth's career success, certainly, parallels that of his uncle, and they both typify a greatness derived from their parents and grandparents. In addition to Jones' academic fulfilment is the portrayal of himself as a dutiful husband and his wife, Marjorie Jones, as a loving, devoted, and supportive wife. Quite apart from the fact that Marjorie Jones is equally well accomplished academically and also received a lot of meritorious awards, it is her role as a loving wife to her husband, especially when Jones became blind, that makes her character outstanding. Her unwavering devotion to Jones is exemplified by the fact that she accompanied him in all of his national and international travels, co-edited and co-authored Jones' scholarly works when he became blind, and she sacrificed her own academic pursuits to enhance her husband's. We are told that for over fifty years, "she took a deliberate decision when she abandoned Law, trained as a Dress Designer at Oxford Polytechnic, and devoted herself to supporting the work of her husband as an international scholar" (167).

Thus, Jones' academic success should largely be accredited to the loving support of Marjorie Jones. Their union was exemplary and certainly full of love and happiness, even without biological children of their own. Jones equally adores Marjorie. He refers to her fondly in this narrative, especially when she performs her wifely duties of decorating their beautiful home at Leicester village in Freetown or when she entertains their guests. This is how Jones describes their marriage:

> We got married on 23 June 1952 and had a short honeymoon in Geneva as guest of our Fourah Bay College friend, Solomon Pratt and his wife, Victoria. We settled down to studying and house-keeping in a newly refurbished flat in Kingston Road in north Oxford.

> It was a happy year ... Our friends came to tea and a couple of them celebrated their 21st birthday with Marjorie baking a cake for the occasion. My visits to the college became rarer and, in my new state of happy domesticity, I even forgot to turn up for the annual college photograph in 1953. (57)

The bond of love between the Joneses stood the test of times. As mentioned above, Marjorie stood by her husband in thick and thin. The Joneses were blessed with two adopted daughters: the late Esse, and Mimi. Other girls who came under their parental tutelage included Elisabeth, Zainab, and Jeannette Eno.

The culmination of Jones' effort to do something for Sierra Leone that would benefit posterity is certainly realized in his retirement project – Knowledge Aid Sierra Leone (KASL). This organization represents a vision of the fourth industrial revolution – technology in education – that Sierra Leone must latch onto for technological development, global networking with other citizens of the world, and international career opportunities. As noted by Jones, the Internet is "the path to the acquisition of new knowledge through the vast network of computers which make up the world information highway" (157). In pursuit of this belief, Jones, through the support of international donations and funds from the Sierra Leone government, set up the first teaching center at Government Secondary Technical School, Congo Cross in 2008. The purpose of this cyber center was to enable "trained personnel, preferably teachers, [to] be in a position to access the vast stores of knowledge and information for the benefit of their pupils and equally important to make our own input into the fund of world knowledge" (157). This project positions Jones as someone whose vision for Sierra Leone transcends national boundaries. Although now deceased, the Joneses will always be remembered in Sierra Leone as an exemplary couple, consummate scholars, nationalists, and champions of education.

Jones' *The Freetown Bond: A Life under Two Flags* has set the pace for intellectual autobiographies in Sierra Leone. His narrative skill of weaving his personal experiences to collective memory is quite admirable. Jones has represented the historical past of Sierra Leone with equanimity and devoid of judgment and acrimony. As an octogenarian and a public servant, his stewardship report is blameless. His individual effort in trying to harness a derailed postcolonial nation through academic and artistic means was doomed to suffer setbacks in the hands of arrogant and corrupt politicians. Nevertheless, Jones' academic and career success will always stand the test of time, and he will go down in history as one of the Sierra Leoneans whose scholarly accomplishments put Sierra Leone on the map of great minds.

Works Cited

Alie, Joe A.D., *Sierra Leone Since Independence: History of a Postcolonial State* (Freetown: Sierra Leonean Writers Series, 2015).

Aurell, Jaume, "Making History by Contextualizing Oneself: Autobiography as Historiographical Intervention," *History and Theory* 54 (2015), pp. 244–68.

Aurell, Jaume and Rocio G. Davis, "History and Autobiography: The Logics of a Convergence," *Life Writing* 16.4 (2019), pp. 503–11.

Fitzpatrick, Sheila, "Writing History/Writing about Yourself: What's the Difference?" in *Clio's Lives: Biographies and Autobiographies of Historians*, Doug Munro and John G. Reid (eds.) (Canberra: ANU Press (2021), pp. 17–37.

John, Mauricia, "*Freetown Bond: A Life under Two Flags*," Review, *African Identities* 11.4 (2013), pp. 407–8.

Jones, Eldred Durosimi, *Othello's Countrymen: The African in English Renaissance Drama* (London: Oxford University Press, 1965).

Jones, Eldred Durosimi, *The Freetown Bond: A Life under Two Flags* (Woodbridge and Rochester, NY: James Currey, 2012).

Kamara, Samuel, "*The Freetown Bond: A Life under Two Flags*," Review, *Research in Sierra Leone Studies (RISLS): Weave* 1:1(2013), pp. 1–3.

Lejeune, Philippe, "On Autobiography," *Theory and History of Literature* 52 (1989), pp. 3–29.

Moyal, Ann, "The Female Gaze: Australian Women's Autobiographies," in *Clio's Lives: Biographies and Autobiographies of Historians*, Doug Munro and John G. Reid (eds.) (Canberra, ANU Press, (2017), pp. 65–78.

Palmer, Eustace, "Education in Africa," in *Africa: An Introduction*, Eustace Palmer (New York: Routledge, 2022), pp. 229–45.

Popkin, Jeremy D., "History, Historians and Autobiography Revisited," *a/b: Autobiography Studies* 32.3 (2017), pp. 693–8.

Smith, Arthur E.E., "Eldred Durosimi Jones. 2012. *The Freetown Bond: A Life under Two Flags*," Review, *African Studies Quarterly* 14.1&2 (2013), pp. 140–1.

Wallach, Jenifer J., "Building a Bridge of Words: The Literary Autobiography as Historical Source Material," *Biography* 29:3 (2006), pp. 446–61.

Whitehead, Clive, "The Historiography of British Imperial Education Policy, Part II: Africa and the Rest of the Colonial Empire," *History of Education* 34.4 (2005), pp. 441–54.

Chapter 13

Relatability, Spaces, Symbols and Legends: Fiction as a Mirror Image for Social Transformation in Abdulai Walon-Jalloh's "Dharmendra Died"

GIBRILLA KARGBO

Titles of short stories can be very attractive, if not captivating. Abdulai Walon-Jalloh's "Dharmendra Died" is one such title. It warrants attention in order to showcase the richness and depth of one who writes with passion and addresses those issues that are both familiar and creatively interesting. In this chapter, I propose to do two things. First, I evaluate Walon-Jalloh's short story in the context of the author's background, while also examining the roles of setting and characterization in elucidating meaning. I explore plot as an intricately woven network in the lives of the characters whose names are very familiar to the Sierra Leonean reader. This question of familiarity, both in terms of names of character and setting, and its contribution to meaning is also addressed. I do so through an exegesis of the didactic import of the work and its implications for national unity, reconciliation, and social cohesion. I further examine key themes addressed and implied in the story, in tandem with the mindset and creative thinking of the writer as far as it relates to the title of the story. Other aspects of style, including the writer's use of dialogue and language to conjure atmosphere, are also examined. Second, this chapter engages the writer's use of legend, symbols, and space to convey meaning. From these analyses, I argue that Sierra Leonean writing has come of age, and that short-story writing, like that of Walon-Jalloh's, showcases the literary potential of the Sierra Leonean writer even as fiction becomes a mirror image for social transformation.

Walon-Jalloh's "Dharmendra Died" is a masterfully written short story. The characters, setting and themes should be familiar to all those who grew up in the East End community of Freetown. One of the key themes discussed in the story is that of poverty. This theme and its implications for the development of character and plot are clearly discernible and, with artistic dexterity, the author makes them relatable without the stigma of destitution and humiliation.

Walon-Jalloh refrains from depicting poverty as a curse because even while experiencing it, he emphasizes that life can still go on – and with relative peace and joy. Using the twenty-four-hour cycle to tell his story of innocence and triumph, Walon-Jalloh succeeds in presenting a story that pushes the reader to introspection and reflection, especially on the question of what it means to grow up from very humble beginnings. The narration captures and holds the reader's attention as it takes them from one end of the Upgun Market to the other and through familiar landscapes and themes in the course of a day. The implication of this depiction of character and landscape lends credence to the adage that "who feels it knows it."

The key themes explored by the author are family and cultural ties, childhood relationships and friendships, communal living, the hustle and bustle of market life, and the social interactions of characters. Wurie's symbiotic relationship with his father is integral to his life. There is clear evidence of reciprocal respect and love between Wurie and his parents that emphasizes family and cultural ties. He is raised without a sense of entitlement and given responsibilities to earn whatever support is provided by the parents. He goes on errands on behalf of his parents, he accompanies the father to sell bread and butter, he does chores and is expected to be accountable in that regard.

The relationship between Jeneba and her single mother, Yeli, also receives significant attention in the story. Yeli is a strong woman who, despite her difficult circumstances, manages to give her family a decent life. She even treats herself occasionally with a stylish dress similar to Wurie's mother's dress. Yeli plays tough and cheerful to give hope to her daughter, Jeneba, even if it means preventing the family from knowing the depth of her financial struggles to make ends meet. And she, like Wurie's mother, is celebrated by the author for her dedication to her family with or without the presence of the father or a male figure.

The plot takes us physically from the room of the panbody shelter (a shelter made of sticks and zinc) to the market stall to the tailor shop to the lorry park and back, all within the context of the Upgun Market community. Using the journey motif to highlight the physical and psychological journeys of the characters, Walon-Jalloh takes us to the Racecourse Cemetery, Bombay Market, Dove Cot Market, the nearby streams (Gutters 1, 2, and 3), Ross Road Police playing field, and Starco cinema. In this technique of plot construction, the author invites reader participation and witnessing, as he takes us to the different places and introduces his characters one after the other with remarkable precision. One gets the impression that in this juxtaposition of character and landscape, and through the "miniature picaresque" tradition of character movement and mobility, the characters' influences on each other overlap and are reciprocated.

"Dharmendra Died" presents us a gallery of characters. We first encounter Nene, Wurie, and Baben. Other characters are then mentioned via their common names, including an "anxious trader," an "assertive businessman," a "fishmonger," etc. We also meet Yero, the meat carrier, introduced in an air of toughness, strength, and stamina that reflect the demands of his job, as he shuttles among the market stalls to distribute meat. On account of his movement from one place to the other, he seems to know so many things including the latest films in town. Other characters, like Wurie, seem to depend on him for the latest trends in popular media and culture. In fact, it is thanks to his conversation with Wurie at the marketplace that the title of the short story emanated. Mention is also made of the "council market keeper" afterwards with an indirect reference to "stall owners" and "drivers." There is also a reference to market authorities – local council officials, self-appointed tribal authorities, and youth leaders. Jeneba and her mother, Yeli, are then introduced, followed by the tailor, Yerime. The provincial supplier who provides palm oil to Yeli on credit, Jibao, is then mentioned. The next set of characters to be introduced are Kalilu, Tejan, and Idrissa, friends of Wurie and Jeneba. In presenting each character or sets of characters in turn, the author allows for reader engagement with them on a personal level. The introduction of characters is panoramic and illustrates a process of engagement that engenders familiarity, relatability, and memory of characters and their actions.

The question of relatability, especially in the presentation of the adult world – men and women – should warrant one's attention in the 24-hour narrative. It is the women (Nene and Yeli) that are presented in a positive light, thus reflecting an attempt by the writer to speak to the subject of women's contribution in the family space even though it is predominantly a man's world. The women are presented as more influential in the family space, especially with the upbringing of the children. Conversely, Wurie's father is the absent father figure whose passive role as bread winner of his family is noticeable. In fact, Jeneba's unnamed father is presented in a more derogatory manner as the absentee father who has taken a younger wife and abandoned his wife and daughter. One of the hallmarks of Walon-Jalloh's story is the prominence given to the mother figure as a symbol of love and resilience in the home and family.

The pace of the narrative is breath-taking as the author tells a story whose plot is woven around the lives of Wurie and Jeneba, young and innocent and having a relationship that has not been contaminated or corrupted by the vagaries of life. The story is told from the points of view of Wurie and Jeneba, both of whom are still under the positive influence of their mothers, Nene and Yeli, respectively, which sets obvious limits to their romance. There are shifts of scenes in the development of the story. One such shift is Wurie's movements from one end of the sprawling Upgun Market to the other; a trajectory replicated by Jeneba. Running errands for their mothers facilitates their meetings. Wurie goes to Jeneba's mother with a bundle containing a dress whose replica should be sewn for Jeneba's mother by Yerime, the neighborhood tailor. Wurie sees this as an opportunity to meet Jeneba, who is also eager to see him. The tailor shop is the location for their meeting. The narrative gestures to a synchrony of movements that are timed and well-choreographed to reflect the wishes of their parents, their adherence to the norms and values of the community such as respect for other members of the community, who in turn play their parts in raising them to be decent citizens in society.

The writer is very much interested in all those related or connected to Wurie and Jeneba: their parents, community elders, tradesmen, and friends. Unlike Jeneba's Nene, whose name is later revealed as Yeli, the traditional titles of Mother (Nene) and Father (Baben) are used for Wurie's parents, reflecting the deference shown to parents within the Fula ethnic group to which the writer belongs. The opening of the story not only indicates the author's concerns with family relationships, but it is also instructive in engaging gender relations in the society: "Nene asked him, 'what are you doing in bed?'" This does not amuse the father, who would wish his only surviving son to rest more when the latter is home during the holidays. Here, sleep is a structural device delineating gendered perspectives within the family unit with implications for childhood nurture, social boundaries, and images of masculinity. The mother and father view sleep from two different perspectives, which highlights the contrasting relationships between father and son, and mother and son. This social tension also plays out in a larger way in the society; the market and tailor shop become two spaces where these symbolic and stereotypical roles clash and overlap. In the case of Jeneba, she has to contend with an absentee father that leaves the mother, Yeli, to fend for the family of four from the petty palm-oil trading she does.

The relationship between Wurie and Jeneba is given special treatment. They look forward to every opportunity to see each other at the market stalls, Yerime's tailor shop, and Wurie's panbody residence. Wurie and Jeneba's relationship should be understood within the context of their family, social, and cultural ties as they are shown as an integral part of their community. Their rendezvous seems to be the usual routine as they would choose where to eat their meals and what other activities to embark on together. In all of their activities, their parents are not left out. In their community, nothing is too small to be shared. The collective morning meal is revelatory as all the parents, one after the other, would bring out the dishes and urge their children on in the context of a very healthy competition regarding whose child would outdo the other in eating the food provided. Indeed, it takes a village to raise a child. Wurie and Jeneba's good upbringing is reflected in the respect they show not just for their parents, but for every other adult in the community.

The marketplace, where much of the story's action unfolds, helps portray the rich complexity of the community Wurie and Jeneba call home. We are given a taste of the hustle and bustle of market life where the noise of the market can be deafening and at times very irritating. In the movement of Wurie, Jeneba and their friends, we see the other side of market life with angry and anxious traders and impatient customers who at times are engaged in boisterous exchanges that can be unpalatable to the sensibilities of certain people. Despite the market environment being distasteful and filthy sometimes, it is clear that Wurie loves his community and for him living in the marketplace can be very exciting and even rewarding. He seems to look forward to every waking day as he takes in what the marketplace can offer him, including with regards to his relationship with Jeneba.

This situation about the movie presents a mirror to the Sierra Leone society regarding the obsession of the country's youths with Indian movies similar to their fanaticism around the English Premier League. The response to the death of Dharmendra in the Bollywood movie *Rajput* is shared by Wurie, Jeneba, and their friends. Even the market women discuss the situation with all seriousness. Arguably, Bollywood movies offer them an escape from the harsh realities of the life they live in the Upgun Market community.

In a very subtle manner, the writer brings up an issue regarding the average Sierra Leonean's fascination with all things foreign at the expense of local artistic and creative production. The power of such a mindset to shape social relationships is stunning. It reveals the psychology of the ordinary Sierra Leonean in doting on things foreign as being superior to things local. "Dharmendra Died" suggests the need for a change of mindset as deliberate effort is made to improve on and appreciate locally produced social and cultural forms of entertainment. From a conceptual framework, Walon-Jalloh in his short story reminds us of the postcolonial malaise of privileging the foreign over the indigenous, and points out by implication, the capacity of this preference to undermine social unity and undercut the development of local talent and industry.

With reference to the specific question of national unity, the relationship between Yeli and Jibao appears as an attempt by the writer to discuss the subject of national unity, tolerance, and social cohesion. Jibao, the palm-oil supplier, is from the southeast (also the source of the palm oil), and Yeli, the retailer who gets her palm oil on loan from Jibao is more likely from northern Sierra Leone. Yeli lives and does her business in the Western Area where her business is patronized by people from different backgrounds. In the fellowship of the children and the support received by and from all the parents especially when they come together for their collective morning meal, it is clear the writer is addressing the subject of a united front regardless of the ethnic/ethnolinguistic or regional backgrounds of individuals.

Another aspect of the story worth drawing attention to is the use of dialogues and its impact on the story line and characterization. The author makes effective use of dialogues to establish the relationship between and among the story's diverse characters. The bond between children and parents is evident in the dialogues. The relationship between Nene and Wurie is a case in point. The depth of their friendship is evident in each conversation they have. For example, Nene asks Wurie "What have you been doing?" with the latter replying, "I washed the plates, spoons, pots and arranged the bed," and Nene noting delightfully that "[o]ne day, your wife will have to bless me for having you as her husband."

The conversations between Yero and Wurie at the market is another example of the effective use of dialogue in the Walon-Jalloh's story. When Yero and Wurie sit at their usual spot to discuss the happenings around town, it is easy to know who, between the two, holds sway over the other. In his conversation with Wurie, Yero remarks "Hm...hm, people are going to kill themselves today," to draw attention to the movie to be featured that afternoon. He further notes that "Dharmendra has done it again", thus warranting a question from Wurie about the name of the movie. To that Yero replies "*Rajput*", with the additional information that "Dharmendra will die in this movie". Wurie's response to this piece of information reveals his inability to distinguish between fiction and realism as revealed in his statement "you know that will never happen. Dharmendra does not die in movies." This pushes Yero to remind Wurie that "it's a movie." Wurie's young mind cannot fathom the reality of evil triumphing over good since for him Dharmendra is a symbol of good that must always triumph over evil.

The marketplace is central to the plot and our appreciation of "Dharmendra Died." First, this is where we meet Yero, the meat carrier, who serves as a kind of mentor to Wurie who eagerly awaits news of goings-on around town from him. Of particular interest here is their conversation around the death of Dharmendra in the Bollywood movie *Rajput*. The death of Dharmendra, one of the beloved characters in Bollywood, instigates passionate conversations around the issue of good, especially regarding the expectation by many that good always triumph over evil. Wurie and his friends have a feeling that the Director has not done a good job in allowing their action hero, the symbol of good, to die, a death that they intend to protest by their posture as fans of Dharmendra when watching the movie later in the day. Accordingly, the opposition should be felt by the fans of Amitabh Bachan, another hero and presumed rival of Dharmendra in Indian movies.

The author's use of space is indicative of the power of images and symbols to convey meaning, and it warrants critical investigation and analysis. Space in the story is gendered. Wurie's presence in the market (where he is sent by his mother) puts him in a space that is usually reserved for women. In this case, then, one would argue that gendered boundaries are being crossed and are being blurred. By extension, the market can be seen as a space where social norms are depicted, making the tensions here palpable, as seen in the restlessness, rudeness, anxiety, anger, and revulsion in the interactions between hawkers and clients. In a sense, the tensions within the family play out in a larger way in the market space, an externalization and amplification of the social norms and their manifestations in human relationships. Accordingly, the market can be seen as a space where social anxieties are externalized, deepened, and concretized. In this regard, the market is emphasized not only as a gendered space, but one where economic transactions and social interactions reveal the underlying anxieties, fears, impoliteness, and tensions in the relationships amongst the people as a whole.

The tailor shop in Walon-Jalloh's story becomes a space-symbol exploited by the author to make specific statements about society. One could argue that the dress is used to show the need for a new garment for society. The craft of tailoring a new dress symbolizes the power of art to transform society. The new dress could be seen as a metonymic reflection of the new norms and values that would replace or at the least engage erstwhile social tensions. The tailor becomes the transformer and the art of tailoring, the mechanism of transformation. The creativity of the tailor is the transformative capacity of the society. This is the power of art or craft, through the creative process, to foster national unity and collective endeavors by bringing together diverse sectors of society, dressing them in a new vision for the future.

Wurie's reaction to the supposed death of Dharmendra in the movie *Rajput*, helps reveal Walon-Jalloh's message about the power of fiction to transform society by holding it up as a mirror to it. The tailor, like the movie star, especially a protagonist like Dharmendra, is tasked with destroying evil and restoring moral rightness to society. The dress like the movie is a text to both recognize the social malaise but also the transformative power of legends and fiction through the exploration of symbolic spaces like the market and the tailor shop. Fiction, like other crafts, is an instrument of reform, intended to uphold certain social and moral values. That is why society should never lose its legends and mythology, which become guiding principles to life. enabling transformation and restitution of values. Dharmendra is a metaphor of the legends in life necessary to destroy evil and establish moral order in the universe.

"Dharmendra Died" is a well-written and instructive short story. As its dénouement reveals, the responsibility for social transformation ultimately lies with the community. Fiction like craft provides a mirror to see the ills and negative consequences of certain norms and values but should initiate agency and urgency for change. The significance of myths and legends lies not in their actions on screen or on stage in the theater, but rather in the ability of society to transpose their actions to real-life situations.

Work Cited

Walon-Jalloh, A., "Dharmendra Died" (Freetown: Sierra Leonean Writers Series, 2018).

INDEX

Abraham, Arthur 20
African Ethics 134, 138
Afrocentric Vision 8, 154
Afrocentrism 154
American Dream 157
Animal rights 134, 138
Anthony, Raymond Farid 20
Anthropocene 134
Anthropocentrism 135–138, 142, 144, 147
Anthropomorphism 145–146, 150
Aristotle 43
Autobiography 10, 27, 188
   Academic 184, 186, 191
   Intellectual 186
   Historical 186
   Novel 169
Autoethnographies 9, 184

Bachelard, Gaston 155
Ballanta Academy 25
Bangura, Saidu 5, 59
Beah, Ishmael 1, 25
Beloved Community 154, 156, 164, 167–168
Black Poor 15
Blood Diamond 20
Blood diamonds 113
Blyden, Edward Wilmot 22
Bodily disfigurement 102
Bollywood 201
British Council 25
British Standard English 51, 55

Cardew, Governor 22
Caruth, Cathy 77, 78
Casely-Hayford, Gladys 1, 19, 27
Castle, Gregory 62
Césaire, Aimé 155
Cheney-Coker, Syl, *Stone Child & Other Poems* 1, 78–79, 84–85, 88–89
Child soldiers 111
Civilization of the Universal 154, 166
Clarkson, Governor 18
Coetzee, J.M., *Disgrace* 19, 133, 135, 137, 140–141, 151
Cole, Ernest 6–8, 65–66, 68, 71, 85, 102
Collins, Patricia Hill 165
Collocation 51–52
Colonialism 190–191
Craps, Stef 103
Cultural diversity 37
   Heritage 38
   Landscape 38

Transformations 38
Culling 144
Cyrulnik, Boris 6, 103

Da Cintra, Pedro 15, 16
Deep Ecology 135
De Souza George, Raymond 22–23
Digital literature 174
Diop, Oumar Chérif 5–6, 91
Dustmann, Christian 7, 121
Dystopia 2, 39

Easmon, Sarif 19, 24
Ebola pandemic 28, 101
Eco-criticism 101
Eco-sustainability 135
Ethics of reciprocity 134
Enlightened humanism 155
Esoteric fraternity, Esoteric Societies 36
Exclusion 160

Falui Poetry Society 24–26, 33
Feminism 166–167
Feminist vision 8, 54
Finnegan, Ruth 9, 178, 180
Fireside Folktales 8, 174
Folklore Tradition 172
Forna, Aminatta 59–60
   Ancestor Stones 59–60, 62, 64–65, 67–68, 105
   The Memory of Love 59–60, 62–63, 68–69, 70–72, 105, 109, 112, 115
   The Window Seat 1, 133–134, 139, 141, 151
Forna, Namina, 2
   The Gilded Ones 153, 162, 164, 167–169
Foucault, Michel 91, 92
Fourah Bay College 23, 28, 187, 194
Freetong Players 25
French, Toni 23
Freud, Sigmund 78
Frost, Robert 43, 44
Fyle, Cecil Magbaily 21

Galgut, Elisa 136, 138
Garden of Eden 65
Gender roles 73
George, Crispin 1
Granville Town 16
Greene, Graham 20, 192
Gibran, Khalil 32
Gola Forest 95–97, 99

INDEX

Gullah 18

Hallowell, Gbanabom 27, 33, 173, 181
Healing 102
   Communal 110
   Embodied 113
   Spiritual 104, 114
Historical Amnesia 40, 71
   Hybridity 1, 3
   Treatise 10
   Trajectory 2
Hollist, Pede 1, 4, 25
Holy Communion 86
Homophones 52
Human-animal coexistence 138
Human-animal relations 7, 133–135, 137, 139, 143, 150
Human-animal relationships 7, 133, 138, 147
Humanist discourse 167
Hunter, Yema Lucilda 1, 20
Hypermasculinity 164
Hypermediacy 176
Hypermediation 182

Ideology of Creation 147
Idioms 51
Idiomaticity 2, 50–51
Idiom Dictionaries 51
Immediacy 179
Indigenous Languages 50–51
Intelligibility 4
Interspecies relations 133, 136
Intertextuality 98
Isale Eko 33, 35, 36, 40, 46–48

Jalloh, Gudush 141, 144, 146
James, Frederic Borbor 23
Jarrett-Macauley, Delia, *Moses, Citizen & Me* 92, 96, 99, 107, 110–111, 115, 117
Johnson, Lemuel 1
Jones, Eldred 29, 50
   The Freetown Bond: A Life Under Two Flags 1, 19, 50, 185–187, 189, 193–194

Kabba, Yusuf 7, 103, 106, 113
Kamara, Elizabeth L.A. 5, 7, 120
Kamara, M'Bha, *When Mosquitoes Come Marching In* 1, 8
Kamara, Mohamed 7–8, 153
Kamara, Samuel 9–10, 185
Kamarah, Sheikh Umarr 25, 28–29, 73
Kant, Immanuel 155

Kargbo, Gibrilla 10, 196, 201
King Jr, Martin Luther 155, 156, 169
Kopnina, Helen 135, 141
Koroma, Ahmed, *The Moon Rises Over Isale Eko* 4, 32–33, 37, 40, 44
Koso-Thomas, Kosonike 4, 27, 33, 125
Kundera, Milan 134, 147

Language
   Acquisition 55
   Addition 53
   Deletion 53
   Substitution 53
   Variety 56
Lefebvre, Henri 6, 97
Leopold, Aldo 135
Life-writing 9, 185
Lingua Franca 52

Maddy, Yulisa Amadu 1, 19, 23
Madonna Figure 81, 85
Male Chauvinism 68
Mande languages 18
Maroons 192
Marquez, Gabriel 24, 30
Memory
   Embodied 104
   Traumatic 124
Migration 38–39, 121–123
Muana, Patrick 9, 172

Nabulya, Eva 135, 136
Naess, Anne 135
National literature 4, 11
Negritude 166
Ney, Stephen 7, 9
Ng'umbi 61, 67
Nicol, Abioseh 24, 27
Nostalgia 24, 32, 34–35, 38

Odokoko River 34, 38
Orature 3, 15, 23
Ogundipe-Leslie, Molara 66–67, 73, 165
Osundare, Niyi 40

Pabel, Annemarie 62
Patriarchy 153, 157, 159
Patriarchal Hegemony 67
Palmer, Eustace 1, 2, 5, 10, 63, 77
Pen International 26
Performance poetry 25
Porter, Abioseh 1, 2, 9, 10
Post-conflict Sierra Leone 62
Postindependent era 60
Post-traumatic healing 6

INDEX

Polygamy 61, 66, 68, 72
Polygyny 67
Province of Freedom 15

Revolutionary United Front 25, 80,86, 94, 125
Richards, I.A. 41
Richard, Paul 20
RUF Rebels 108

Sankoh, Foday 125
Sankoh, Osman A. 173, 181
Senghor, Léopold Sédar 154, 156
Sesay, Mohamed Gibril 3, 10, 28
Sesay, Oumar Farouk
    Landscape of Memories 4, 120–130
    The Moon Rises Over Isale Eko 4, 7, 32–49
Shakespeare, William 23, 47, 96
Sharpe, Granville 16
Sheriff, Mohamed 28–29, 36
Social degradation 2, 120–121
Sierra Leone Broadcasting Service 22
    Civil War 7, 120, 130, 143, 152
    Collection 22
    Colony 16
    Company 16
    Dramatists 22, 23
    English 55
    Fiction Writers 9
    Forum 26
    Films 26
    Languages 29
    Literature 1, 2, 9–10, 15, 17, 23, 30
    Music 25
    Writers 29, 56, 102, 201
    Writers Series 26, 33
    Writing 1–2
Skeuomorphism 176–177, 183
Smartphone literature 172
Smeathman, Henry 15–16
Social degradation 119, 129
    Disintegration 39
Spatial theory 6
Sterilization 144
Strasser, Valentine 80
Stratton, Florence 62
Subaltern 59

Tacugama Chimpanzee Sanctuary 147, 149
Tadjo, Véronique, *In the Company of Men* 104–105, 107–108
Tarawalie, Sheka 27
Taqi, Fatou 4, 27
Technological determinism 9, 174, 178
The Whiteman's Grave 15
Thulla, Yamba, *Contemporary Fireside Poems: An Anthology*, *Contemporary Fireside Stories, An Anthology* 9, 27
Toponym 4
Transformative resilience 6
Traumatic experience 78, 161
    Impact 79
    Memories 124
    Pedagogy 99
    Psychology 79, 80
    Representations 78–80
    Resilience 6
    Survivors 102–103
    Theory 77–79, 103
Turay, Momodu 4, 50
Truth & Reconciliation Commission 6, 91–92

Uraizee, Joya 5–7, 101

Violence
    History 122
    Physical 64
    Psychological 64
    Sexual 69, 73

Walker, Alice 165, 168
Walon-Jalloh, Abdulai 10
    Dharmendra Died 196–197, 200–202
    Panbody Blues 2
Walton, Hanes 155
Weiss, Yoram 7, 121
Wellesley-Cole, Robert 19, 27
West African Examinations Council 56
Western feminism 154
Western Judeo-Christian Civilization 155
WhatsApp group 27, 172, 176, 179–180
    Literature 9, 177
Womanism 165, 168
Women's empowerment 181
Wynter, Sylvia 155

Xenophobia 122

Yao, Vida 136

Zeitgeist 2

Printed in the United States
by Baker & Taylor Publisher Services